A WEST COUNTRY VILLAGE
ASHWORTHY

DARTINGTON HALL
STUDIES IN RURAL SOCIOLOGY

RURAL DEPOPULATION IN ENGLAND AND
WALES, 1851–1951
by JOHN SAVILLE

THE COUNTRY CRAFTSMAN: A Study of some Rural
Crafts and the Rural Industries Organization in England
by W. M. WILLIAMS

A WEST COUNTRY VILLAGE: ASHWORTHY: Family,
Kinship and Land
by W. M. WILLIAMS

A WEST COUNTRY VILLAGE
ASHWORTHY

Family, Kinship and Land

by
W. M. WILLIAMS
Senior Lecturer in Geography, University of Keele

LONDON
ROUTLEDGE & KEGAN PAUL

First published 1963
by Routledge & Kegan Paul Limited
Broadway House 68–74 Carter Lane
London, E.C.4

Printed in Great Britain
by Cox & Wyman Limited
London, Fakenham and Reading

To 'Nipper'
and the people of Ashworthy

CONTENTS

TABLES

FIGURES

xi

INTRODUCTION

'ASHWORTHY' is a pseudonym for a small rural community in the West Country. Sociologists working in Britain have learnt the somewhat painful lesson that their studies bring unwelcome and often 'sensational' publicity from certain national newspapers, which offends the many people who have helped them. For this reason, the identity of Ashworthy and of its people has been very carefully disguised. All the personal and place names used in this study are fictitious. All the dates, ages of individuals, sizes of farms and many other factual details have been systematically altered. Ashworthy is not a parish, although it is so described below, and the boundaries shown on the maps are not parish boundaries. All the maps and the statistical data refer to an area which is not an administrative unit. These changes have, however, been made in a way which retains the validity of the material for analytical purposes.

Ashworthy was chosen for study during a pilot survey made in the summer of 1957: the field work was carried out in the summer of 1958. The aim of the pilot survey was to find a community which would form a suitable base for the study of the effects of rural depopulation on family and kinship. It was therefore necessary to seek a community which had experienced a declining population for a relatively long period, at least a century: the community had to be large enough to make a study worthwhile and yet small enough to be intensively studied as a complete whole. A population of between five hundred and seven hundred inhabitants was taken to be a suitable size. An adequate collection of documents covering the recent history of the community—Parish Registers, Tithe Awards, etc.—was a prerequisite for study. It was also desirable that the community should be as free as possible from extraneous influences, such as those which might come from the presence of a large town or factory near by, or from an annual invasion of tourists. Remoteness was not in itself considered to be absolutely necessary, but it was essential that the community should be *rural*, that is, based on an agricultural economy.

Four communities were chosen which appeared at a distance to fit these requirements very closely. The first was rejected because, in fact, it did not: the second was suitable but seemed, on intuitive grounds, 'unpromising': the third was Ashworthy. The field work in the following year showed it to be an admirable choice; its people were remarkably kind, hospitable and helpful. It is not, however, in any sense a *typical* rural community; such a vague entity does not exist. This study is of one small area with its own special features: the generality of the conclusions which have been reached can only be tested by similar studies elsewhere.

The initial aim of the research was, then, to examine the effects of rural depopulation as a process on the structure of family and kinship within one small rural area. General studies had been made of rural depopulation, notably John Saville's *Rural Depopulation in England and Wales 1851–1951*,[1] but almost nothing was known of its social effects in detail. In this respect the study was intended to break new ground. However, as the field work progressed, new and clearly important problems emerged which, while related to the original theme of the investigation, made it necessary to re-examine the basic orientation and underlying assumptions of the study and this led in turn to a complete re-appraisal of existing rural community studies in Britain.

Before I went to Ashworthy my view of English rural social structure was based partly on the experience gained in studying Gosforth, a parish in Cumberland[2] and in making a survey of rural craftsmen on a regional scale,[3] and partly on the small number of published studies of rural communities in Great Britain and Western Europe. Both my own and these other studies portray rural society as conservative, traditional, resistant to outside pressures and above all slow to change. It is in

[1] Dartington Hall Studies in Rural Sociology (London 1957).

[2] *The Sociology of An English Village: Gosforth* (London 1956).

[3] *The Country Craftsman*, Dartington Hall Studies in Rural Sociology (London 1958).

short a stable social system. In Wales, for example, it is said that in the rural way of life:

> 'Much of what is distinctive is an inheritance from the pastoral and tribal past. . . . Viewed from without, the old social life displays a remarkable tenacity, and, in spite of the spread of machine-made goods, recreation and entertainment are still almost entirely home produced.'[1]

In a more recent study of four Welsh rural communities we are told that (in a Montgomeryshire parish)

> 'Even though the district is less isolated today than it was a generation or two ago—the railway came here in 1868—much of the peasant way of life has been retained'; while in the Llŷn peninsula the 'survival of ancient loyalties may serve as a token to express the unbroken unity of the area from very early times on to the present day. . . .'[2]

In the same way, C. M. Arensberg's classic study of County Clare stresses the conservatism of rural Eire:

> 'When I first came to Luogh I knew only that in this remote little community of small farmers I should find something of the old tradition still alive.'
> 'We have followed the countryman a long way . . . He is part of an intricate social system which patterns his life along definite channels, which brings him rewards, gives him incentives, and deals its own punishments. The traditional patterns of old custom have a place in this system; folklore surrounds it as in the dichotomy between men's and women's work. But tradition is not all its secret; it is a living structure with a balance and a growth of its own.'[3]

In the western Isles of Scotland:

> 'The significance of Island life—not so much for the past, which cannot be changed, as for the future which can—lies in the intensity of its communal traditions, extinguished elsewhere.'
> 'Comprehension of this break-up of community brings out the

[1] Alwyn D. Rees, *Life in a Welsh Countryside* (Cardiff 1960), pp. 162 and 168.

[2] Elwyn Davies and Alwyn D. Rees (Eds.), *Welsh Rural Communities* (Cardiff 1960), pp. 176 and 187. Glan-llyn, the Montgomeryshire parish, was studied by Trefor M. Owen, and Aberdaron in the Llŷn peninsula by T. Jones Hughes.

[3] *The Irish Countryman* (London 1937), pp.22 and 69-70.

value of the enduring elements of communal life still recorded, remembered and surviving in the "Outermost" Hebrides, at the core of "the North and West".'[1]

The same point of view can be seen in studies of rural communities in England and in continental Western Europe:

'*Closed* This type of society is by far the most common in the area (i.e. in the west of England). There appears to be no disharmony within the society, but harmony is maintained by mechanisms which exclude external influences. Such societies present a compact impenetrable front behind which life is carried on in well-defined grooves. The mechanisms whereby it is effected vary, however, from locality to locality.'[2]

'It would be misleading to say that rural England has undergone no social change at all, but it is nevertheless true that over a long period of years change has been slow, and has failed to alter the essential social structure. . . . In other words, speaking generally, we may say that rural society has been characterized by a low degree of social change whilst modern urban society has undergone a high degree of social change.'[3]

'Side by side with, and perhaps in part due to, the oneness of the village form, there has grown up amongst village people a sense of belonging to the village and to each other as a community. This has taken many centuries to develop and has grown out of the dependence of village inhabitants on the village for the various services necessary and/or desirable in their season. The sense of community has persisted in spite of present-day forces, the majority of which are antagonistic to its creation or preservation.'[4]

'Hence Château-Gérard is still very really Gallia Belgica et Romana, is even yet a village under the crusading monks while it is being drawn more and more into the money market of Seraing steel.'

'The long continuity of Château-Gérard's culture is undoubtedly pushing it ahead, while the possibilities inherent in ancient

[1] Arthur Geddes, *The Isle of Lewis and Harris* (Edinburgh 1955), pp. 14 and 22.

[2] G. Duncan Mitchell, 'Depopulation and Rural Social Structure', *Sociological Review*, Vol. XLII (1950), p. 81.

[3] G. Duncan Mitchell, 'The Relevance of Group Dynamics to Rural Planning Problems', *Sociological Review*, Vol. XLIII (1951), p. 5.

[4] H. E. Bracey, *English Rural Life* (London 1959), p. 24.

Introduction

Walloon metallurgy can be thought of as projecting into the
beyond and constituting a pull from the future.'[1]

These short extracts reveal a common orientation; their
authors may be well aware that social and economic change
does take place in the countryside, but they regard it as modify-
ing a way of life which is tenaciously stable. Many (if not all)
of them appear to accept a view of country life as fighting a
stubborn rearguard action against antagonistic external forces,
perhaps urban in origin. This dichotomy, first elaborated by
Ferdinand Tönnies,[2] is still found in studies which are explicitly
concerned with social, economic and technological change in
rural areas. There is a strange reluctance to abandon the notion
of the unchanging, traditional countryside:

'There are still people who believe that the farmer—perhaps it
would be better to say the peasant—should continue to live his
quiet life on his farm in his village community, as little touched
as possible by the outside "urban" world. He should try to
maintain the old social structure and organization of his neighbourhood and his village. In this way the traditional values of
rural life and rural culture in general, as opposed to the urban
culture, would be kept alive, and preserved for posterity. The
number of those who take this point of view is diminishing, but
it would be wrong to underestimate their influence in some
countries.'[3]

'Le progrés rapide et incessant vient de pénétrer la vie des
campagnes françaises qu'il est en voie de transformer radicalement.
Certes, l'apparente stabilité des sociétés paysannes traditionelles
n'interdisait pas toute innovation; ... mais il s'agissait toujours
d'un progrès lent; ces transformations suivaient la méthode
empirique, faite d'essais et d'erreurs, d'échecs et de réussites. ...
Les différents aspects du conflit entre les exigences d'un progrès
technique continu et des structures datant d'un époque de rela-

[1] H. H. Turney-High, *Château-Gérard. The Life and Times of a Walloon
Village* (Columbia, South Carolina 1953), pp. 279 and 281.

[2] In *Gemeinschaft und Gesellschaft* (Second Edition, Berlin 1912). This
book was first published in 1887.

[3] E. W. Hofstee, 'Rural Social Organization'. Presidential address to
the Second Congress of the European Society for Rural Sociology, in
Changing Patterns of Rural Organization (Oslo 1961), p. 18.

tive stabilité représentent un champ d'études nombreuses et variées pour toutes les sciences sociales.'[1]

Indeed, in some Mediterranean countries the traditional peasant way of life is often attributed with virtues that are important to the well-being of the nation, and agricultural reform is designed deliberately to foster and preserve them.[2]
Seen from this point of view, an examination of the effects of rural depopulation on the life of Ashworthy would be in terms of the decline of a traditional social system. However, during the field work and in the period of analysis which followed, it became more and more evident that Ashworthy was not a stable community of the kind I had expected. Moreover, a re-examination of my own field material on Gosforth and the published studies by Rees, Arensberg and others suggested that rural life is characterized by conditions of 'dynamic equilibrium', i.e. that while the social structure *as a whole* appears relatively unchanged and unchanging in the absence of external stimuli, within it constant and irregular changes are in fact taking place. Country life, as exemplified by Ashworthy, is subject to piecemeal changes, is constantly in a state of internal adjustment between one part and another. This is a much less neat and tidy concept than the orthodox 'Gemeinschaft' view of rural social structure.

Once this general approach had been formulated and the evidence roughly assembled, the central problem was seen to be the maintenance of equilibrium. In other words, how is continuity of social life achieved within such an "unstable" framework? This led in turn to considering the nature of this framework, which was seen to be ecological. The social and economic life of Ashworthy has always been based on the land, which families have farmed for centuries. Family farming has persisted from one generation to another, so that a balance has been maintained between people and land—but in conditions

[1] H. Mendras, *Les Paysans et la Modernisation de l'Agriculture* (Paris 1958), p. 7.

[2] See, for example, the various publications of *Servicio de Concentracion Parcelaria, Instituto de Estudios Agro-Sociales* and *Instituto Nacional de Colonizacion* (for Spain) and of SVIMEZ (for Italy).

where individual families die out, split up, move from one farm to another: where people leave the parish and others enter; where the ownership and occupation of land has changed constantly; where farms are split up, amalgamated, or alter their shape.

This view of Ashworthy as a dynamic ecological system has two important consequences. First, it makes it virtually impossible to use the results of the very considerable study of urban social life, characterized by the analysis of rapid change, since—in Britain at least—it pays little or no regard to the environment.[1] Secondly, it has very largely determined the form of this study and in particular the emphasis which has been given to the land, its occupation, use and ownership. Sociological studies of rural areas in this country and elsewhere have paid far too little attention to analysing in detail the *spatial* relationships of social and economic change. The first Part of this study documents these relationships in the context of family farming; the second Part is largely devoted to the original aim of the research, i.e. the effects of demographic change on the structure of family and kinship within one small community. In accordance with the general orientation outlined above, rural depopulation is regarded as one of the processes of change within an ecological system. It is merely one aspect of the dynamics of rural life.

This concern with the spatial and environmental aspects of the social structure of Ashworthy has also led to re-appraising existing 'community studies' from another point of view. The notion of a rural community as a social isolate has become progressively abandoned in recent years as the importance of relationships with 'the outside world' has been realized.[2] However, the geography of these relationships has been very largely

[1] With some rare exceptions, for example, Terence Morris, *The Criminal Area* (London 1958). For ecological studies of urban societies in general, see George A. Theodorson (Ed.), *Studies in Human Ecology* (Evanston, Ill. 1961), where their status within the general field of social science is fully discussed.

[2] This is clearly demonstrated in the various contributions to *Changing Patterns of Rural Organisation*, which gives a conspectus of recent trends in West European rural sociology. See, for example, the paper by Dr. H. Morgen on West Germany, pp. 83–92.

neglected in spite of its significance to the notion of a community and its 'social field'. In this study a preliminary analysis has been made of some aspects of this problem, which shows that it is often extremely difficult to separate the social and economic life of Ashworthy from that of the parishes which surround it.

This brief outline of the general approach to the study of a small, remote rural area in the south-west of England is in part intended to give some idea of the broad purpose of this book. It is 'a sample study', which can be compared with others in order to provide the data necessary for generalizations about rural social and economic life in our own country. Large-scale investigations based on statistical material or general surveys, however valuable they may be, raise countless questions that cannot be answered by further studies of a similar kind, but only by detailed inquiries grounded in intensive field work. Thus the analysis of continuity of family farming which is given in the first Part of this study differs markedly from the generally accepted view; the detailed description of population change in Chapter Five conflicts with many of the general statements that have been made about rural depopulation in England and Wales and also gives a new perspective to studies of rural family and kinship structure. Finally, this is an essay in social geography, concerned with country life as an enduring relationship between society and the physical environment: the importance which is given in the following pages to family farming comes from the simple fact that it is a manifestation of this relationship.

There are no well-tried and established techniques for studying a rural area from this point of view. The evidence is in part demographic, in part sociological and in part geographical, considered within a historical continuum. Since rural sociology in Britain lags so disgracefully behind almost every other civilized country, and since social geography is one of the newest branches of a relatively young academic discipline in this country, this study attempts to present both a new view of rural life and a new way of investigating it.

The techniques of investigation and the methods of analysis which have been used are largely derived from geography and rural sociology, or rather the social anthropology of rural communities. The time available for field work was limited, but this limitation was overcome by the use of documentary evidence. The data collected during the field work were deliberately confined to material which could only be elicited by interview and 'participant observation'. Perhaps because of the striking success of social anthropological studies of primitive communities and its influence on rural community studies in this country, far too little attention has been paid to documentary sources of information. A great deal of field work time has been spent in asking questions about size of farms, ages of individuals, place of birth, etc. In this study such information was collected from Registers of Local Electors, Rating Valuation Books, Tithe Awards, Parish Registers, School Attendance Registers, Census Schedules and the like, which are available after the field work is complete. In addition, other sources—for example Wills, Letters of Administration and farm deeds were used: they provided data of a kind which is extremely difficult to collect in the field and which threw light on many aspects of family and kinship. We live, after all, in a literate society.

One of the most pleasant aspects of writing an account of a rural community is the acknowledgement of the help and kindness of other people. The farmers and villagers of Ashworthy have been unfailingly helpful, courteous and friendly, both during the actual field work and in the protracted correspondence which has followed it. They always took considerable time and trouble to provide answers to my interminable questions. Since I have disguised the identity of Ashworthy and its people, I cannot, unfortunately, thank individuals by their full names, but I am particularly grateful to Kenneth and Marian G., Bill and Joyce W., John and Lily W., William and Betty S., John and Florence A., Lucy A., Alec B., Richard F. and Richard P. for their assistance and advice. Above all I am indebted to 'Nipper' S. for his interest and unflagging co-operation.

Many people outside Ashworthy have provided advice and information, particularly Mr. C. T. Smith, Miss J. Sinar, Mr. E. W. Martin, Mr. A. O. Elmhirst, Professor Harald Uhlig, Mr. H. W. B. Luxton and Mrs. M. G. Bawden. I am mos grateful to the officers of the Principal Probate Registry at

Somerset House, the District Probate Registry for the South West, the Public Record Office and the General Register Office. Sheila J. Boyle, who patiently and efficiently drew all the maps and most of the diagrams and Geoffrey Barber, who drew Figs. 9, 14 and 17 with such skill, are also thanked for their assistance.

Finally I should like to record my debt to the Trustees of Dartington Hall, who have most generously supported this study. No research worker could wish for greater understanding, helpfulness and co-operation.

PART ONE

CHAPTER ONE

ASHWORTHY

On one of the main roads of the West Country there is a signpost that marks the way to Kimberford, a small market town which attracts few visitors. Three miles along this side road, a further road—little more than a lane—branches off; there is no signpost to say where it leads. For a mile or so the high banks and hedges on either side shut out much of the light, then the road widens slightly and, after four miles of sharp corners and several cross-roads and forks, arrives at the village of Ashworthy. The newcomer, travelling this way for the first time, sees little of the landscape and can easily lose his route without a good map. Everywhere high banks obscure the view: cows, sheep or a combine-harvester appear suddenly around a corner: the surface of the road is thickly strewn with pot-holes. It is almost as if Man and Nature have joined forces to discourage strangers from visiting the locality.

Ashworthy is a civil parish in Kimberford Rural District. It covers an area of nearly fourteen square miles and is the home of some five hundred and twenty countryfolk. Seen from one of the few good vantage points it appears no different from the surrounding parishes. The surface of the land is sharply dissected by deep, steep-sided valleys: between them, hills and ridges of irregular shape extend as far as the eye can see. The fields, each one enclosed by a substantial hedge, vary in size and shape to no apparent pattern: copses and small plantations add to the complexity of the landscape. The farms and cottages, lying often at the end of a long twisting lane, seem isolated and lonely. The village itself cannot be seen from a distance, even though it occupies the top of one of the larger ridges.

Centuries of careful farming and continuous occupation of the land have ameliorated the harshness of the natural environment. The climate is wet, with strong winds, and the soils are

3

cold and heavy. The district is generally recognized as being poor and difficult to farm. Many of the local place-names reflect the difficult natural conditions—Heath Farm, Bogland, Little Comfort, Starve All and No Great Things. Other place-names recall the distant past. Ashworthy has a long history. Like so many other villages it was founded in the Saxon period, following the invasion during the second half of the seventh century: many of the hamlets and farmsteads are recorded in the Domesday Book. Medieval stone crosses stand at several of the cross-roads.

Evidence of a long social and economic development can be seen everywhere. The small fields with their great hedges originate in the colonization of Saxon times. The font and some small parts of the Church tower are Norman; much of it is fourteenth and fifteenth century in date, built of local stone. Coats of arms of families who are recorded as holding land in the parish between four and five hundred years ago can be found in the Church and in a few farm buildings. Nearly all of the farmsteads are, however, much more recent. Many of them, of the ancient 'long house' type, with thick cob walls and a thatched roof, were built in the latter part of the seventeenth century. It was clearly a time of prosperity in Ashworthy, since three of the five large stone-built farmhouses of the lesser gentry or richer yeomen were erected during this period.

As one progresses nearer to the present the evidence becomes more abundant. The nineteenth century was a period of many changes. Years of plenty and enterprise are reflected in the building of new farmsteads, square, solid and somewhat forbidding in appearance. They replaced the traditional long houses, particularly in the years 1840–60. In contrast, the many ruined or half-derelict buildings which are common both in the village and the surrounding countryside point to the decline in population which began in the middle of the century and continued steadily until its end.

These clues to the past are of much more than sentimental or antiquarian interest: they are (or should be) a constant reminder to the field worker of the importance of a historical perspective. Ashworthy's way of life and social structure were not made overnight. This seems obvious enough and needs to be stated only because far too many social scientists are content to pay lip-service to historical processes or to ignore them altogether.

Ashworthy has few visitors. It is difficult to reach and its landscape is unspectacular: there are no large towns near-by and practically none of the amenities which attract the tourist or holiday-maker. The village is not picturesque. There are a few fine thatched cottages, but the majority of the houses are austere buildings of dark stone with grey slate roofs. The centre of the village is dominated by a large chapel of an uncompromising Nonconformist type. Seen for the first time on a wet day the place appears bleak and unwelcoming. Normally, however, it is friendly and busy, since it provides a number of important services for the locality. There are two 'general stores', a butcher's shop and a bakery which sends four delivery vans far into the surrounding countryside. It has a small inn, a post office, a draper's shop and two garages, while among the village craftsmen are a shoe repairer, a smith, two tailors, four carpenters and a wheelwright-builder. Transport is provided by a haulage contractor who specializes in the carrying of farm stock and by a man who runs a bus and taxi service. There is a Church with a resident parson and a Methodist Chapel with a resident Minister.[1] The village school, with its staff of two—both of whom live in the village—takes about fifty children up to the age of eleven: older children travel by bus to schools at Longbridge, a small market town nine miles away.

The village is also a centre in many other ways. The people of the parish have to come there to collect their newspapers or periodicals and to change their books at the County Library van which visits once a fortnight. It has the only telephone kiosk in the parish. More important, the large Village Hall is the focus of many social activities. Ashworthy has a flourishing Men's Social Club, a Youth Club, Women's Institute, Boy Scout troop, a branch of the British Legion, a Village Band, a Football Team and Supporters' Club. There is a branch of the W.E.A., a Conservative Association and a Liberal Association. All these, together with the Parish Council and other local

[1] For a fuller discussion of religious life, see pp. 7–9 and 184–91 below.

bodies, meet in the Village Hall and use its room for dances, whist drives, 'social evenings' and the like.

These village services provide for many of the every-day needs of Ashbury folk: they make up to a considerable extent for the remoteness of the parish, which is isolated by its bad roads and the lack of a public transport service rather than by distance from the nearest towns. Kimberford, a small market town, lies only five miles from the village. It is an important market for the farmers of Ashworthy, many of whom own cars. Since there is no bus service, the majority of people go there only to see a doctor, dentist or solicitor, or for some other 'special' reason. There are many families in Ashworthy who do not visit Kimberford from one year to another. Longbridge, farther away, is much more popular because a bus runs there from the village three times a week.[1] This small town fulfils most of the needs for which there is no provision in Ashworthy. In the words of one villager: 'It's not much of a place, but I go there to see the doctor and to the bank. I get my hair cut there and the wife goes to the shops. It's got dentists and solicitors and auctioneers and people like that. . . . And, of course, there's the cinemas—but I haven't been there since before the war.'

Longbridge and Kimberford are, therefore, important to Ashworthy for certain essential services and this importance is only one aspect of the parish's relations with the outside world. The parish is part of the larger society and a complex pattern of social and economic ties joins it to other parishes near-by, to the county, and farther afield. Nevertheless, Ashworthy is sufficiently cut off to make personal relations between its people crucial in everyday life. It is a 'face-to-face' community, where 'everyone knows everyone else'. People work with others they have grown up with, they buy their food in shops owned by men and women who have a detailed knowledge of their personal and family history, and they spend their evenings in much the same company. The simple fact of living in a close-knit community dominates social relations.

Its influence can be seen, for example, in the ideas and behaviour of people towards social status. For reasons we shall examine later, class distinction is very poorly developed in

[1] Once on Wednesdays and twice on Saturdays.

Ashworthy. The elaborate class structure and the complex means of establishing and raising individual status which are so striking a feature of the social life of Gosforth in Cumberland[1] are almost completely absent from this West Country village. Some people have higher prestige than others but there are no social groups that are or can be identified as belonging to a particular social class. This does not mean that the men and women of Ashworthy are unaware of or deny the existence of class distinction. For many years people have come to live in the parish who have been accustomed all their lives to communities where status considerations are of very real importance. In addition to overcoming the considerable handicap of being 'a stranger' they are faced with a way of life where the 'normal' criteria of social class have little meaning. As a result, 'fitting in' —to use the local term—is a difficult and often painful process: many do not succeed and play no part at all in the social life of the parish. Those that do 'fit in' are successful because they accept the Ashworthy way of looking at things and of judging people. It is, then, only in respect of 'strangers' and 'outsiders' that the countryfolk feel class distinction to be important. The idea that someone you have known all your life, been to school with, and who has, perhaps, married a girl who is your first cousin, should be in a superior social position merely because he has a better job, or more money or lives in a bigger house, is foolish and irrelevant to the people of Ashworthy.

In the same way, the religious life of the parish takes place within a framework of close-knit personal relations. The people are either Church of England or Methodist, in roughly equal proportions. The Church is, of course, long established and was for centuries the only religion of the people. The parish as a territorial unit owes its existence to the Church and there are still ways in which it affects the lives of everyone, for example in the payment of tithes. Methodism first came to the parish early in the last century. On October the ninth, 1815 a small

---

[1] *The Sociology of An English Village: Gosforth*. Chs. *V* and *VI*. Far too little attention has been paid to the operation of a social class system in 'face to face' communities, where a knowledge of personal characteristics and of detailed individual histories influences status judgements and attitudes.

group broke away from the established Methodist Church with the formation of a Society of the Bible Christian Connexion at Lake Farm in Shebbear, Devon.[1] The 'B.C.'s'—as they came to be known—sent missions into the surrounding country and their chapels grew up over a wide area of the West Country with remarkable speed. A local man was largely responsible for the mission to Ashworthy, when a small number of converts was made. These numbers grew slowly but steadily so that by 1907, when the Bible Christians became joined into the United Methodist Church, they accounted for nearly half the population of the parish.

The early Bible Christians lived austere lives and their outlook and behaviour conflicted at many points with those of their Anglican neighbours. These conflicts must have assumed particular importance in such a close-knit community, where individual families were linked with many others by kinship ties, so that brothers and sisters, and even man and wife, might belong to different churches. Soon, therefore, two opposed forces were at work within the parish: the religious, which demanded of a person that he think and behave differently in certain important ways from those people who belonged to another church; and the social, which brought men and women together through bonds of kinship, neighbourliness and membership of the same group. Out of this opposition there grew up a *modus vivendi*, still subject to sharp stresses from time to time. 'We have,' said one man, 'got to live with each other and we manage to get along.'

On the one hand, the Methodists still live according to many of the precepts of their nineteenth-century predecessors. Only a tiny minority ever enter the bar of the village inn. A small number of others come on most evenings to the door of the bar, knock and withdraw down the corridor where they wait out of sight for the landlord to bring them cigarettes, matches or packets of biscuits. Most people consider this to be reasonable and proper, although it is the cause of irreverent comment

[1] For a comprehensive history of the Bible Christians see F. W. Bourne, *The Bible Christians: Their Origin and History 1815–1900* (London 1905). I am deeply indebted to the late George Friend for the benefit of his advice and great knowledge of this subject.

from time to time by the 'regulars'. Sabbatarianism makes Sunday a very quiet day in the parish, in contrast to the bustle of weekdays, and is strong enough to extend to the 'regulars' at the inn. They come six days a week: on Sunday nights the bar is often empty. The Men's Social Club is closed on Sundays, although several unsuccessful attempts have been made to have it open. Some people do not take Sunday newspapers: a minority listen only to religious programmes on the radio. Some disapprove of a wide range of activities, such as dancing and whist drives.

On the other hand, Methodists attend the fêtes and garden parties held in the Rectory garden, and the Anglicans go to the Methodist 'Sales of Work' and 'Social Evenings'. Joint services are held from time to time. No distinctions are made at christenings, weddings and funerals. Marriages between Methodists and Anglicans have taken place for many years and it is quite common for the husband to go to Church and his wife to Chapel. On special occasions, such as the Anglican Patronal Festival and the Methodist Anniversary Service, it is usual in these circumstances for the whole family to attend.

Religion does, then, play an important part in every-day life. It is pervasive enough to make it relatively easy for a stranger to discover quite quickly (without asking) whether people are 'church' or 'chapel'. Everyone in the parish knows the religious affiliation of everyone else and expects them to behave accordingly, so that whether a Methodist goes for a drink in the village inn is not merely a matter of individual conscience but also the concern of the community at large. In Ashworthy, as in all 'face-to-face' communities, 'what people will say' and what they think and do when a person behaves in an unexpected way is a very potent social force. It is no accident that most of the officials of the Football Team and its Supporters' Club are Anglican, nor that the officers of the Liberal Club are nearly all Methodists while those of the Conservative Association are Anglican. In Ashworthy this is regarded as part of the natural order of things.

Religion is, of course, only one part of the social structure of

9

Ashworthy. Kinship, which is one of the central themes of this study, is another. The economy is a third. Ashworthy is an agricultural parish: the way of life of its people is based fundamentally on the land and on the crops and animals this land supports. Farming provides a home and livelihood for forty-seven per cent of the population and a further thirty-four per cent is composed of farm workers and of craftsmen or tradesmen who give services to the farmers. From this point of view the present prosperity and future prospects of farmers and villagers alike depend on the land. The social life of the parish is adapted to fit the needs of the annual cycle of farm activity, although—as we shall see later—sharp distinctions can be drawn between farmers and villagers.

Ashworthy is, therefore, largely self-sufficent in its economic and social life, with characteristics that can only be explained and understood by examining closely the detail of its way of living. This kind of investigation is now well-established: in particular, social anthropologists have developed techniques for the study of relatively small homogeneous groups occupying a limited territory. Their methods work very well among primitive peoples living in remote corners of Africa or on Pacific islands, where it is reasonable to isolate a tribe or community from outside influences, but the few anthropologists who have worked in larger and more complex societies have found it increasingly necessary to relate the social structure of the local group they are studying to that of the larger society of which it is part.[1] New techniques are needed and, since the anthropological study of Western societies is still in its infancy,[2] it is natural enough that the well-tried methods of 'community study' still occupy a central place. Considerations of this kind clearly underlie the choice of location in the studies which have been

[1] See, in particular R. Frankenberg, *Village on the Border* (London 1957) and R. T. Smith, *The Negro Family in British Guiana* (London 1956).

[2] This is particularly the case in Britain, where anthropologists and sociologists alike have virtually ignored the British countryside. The methods developed by sociologists for the study of large urban areas are seldom useful in rural areas.

made: Ireland[1], Upland Wales[2], Cumberland[3] and the Outer Hebrides[4] are typical. They are all places remote from our great centres of population, where some local characteristics and individuality still survive.

Ashworthy is of the same kind, and was chosen partly for the same reason. In a field of research where so little is known, advances in the collection of information and the development of a methodology must be modest. This study is an attempt to examine some aspects of the social structure of the parish and to show how they are necessarily related to other parishes in the area. It will be argued that—in spite of its large measure of self-sufficiency—Ashworthy must be regarded as a part of a larger whole and that its social structure is intelligible only when seen in this light. It is true that the handful of parishes considered here are themselves related in turn to still greater groupings and also that changes on a national scale affect the lives of people in Ashworthy. For the purposes of this inquiry these larger aspects must form part of the background against which the countryfolk organize their lives.

[1] See, for example, the classic *Family and Community in Ireland* by C. M. Arensberg and S. T. Kimball (Harvard 1948) and R. H. Buchanan, 'Rural Change in an Irish Townland' *The Advancement of Science* No. 56 (March 1958), pp. 291–300.

[2] See Alwyn D. Rees, *Life in a Welsh Countryside* (Cardiff 1951) and Frankenberg, op. cit.

[3] *The Sociology of An English Village: Gosforth* (London 1956).

[4] For example, T. M. Owen, 'The Communion Season and Presbyterianism in a Hebridean Community'. *Gwerin*, Vol. 1, No. 2, pp. 53–66.

CHAPTER TWO

THE LAND

THE way of life of Ashworthy is based on the land. It follows therefore that natural conditions—the climate, relief, soils, etc.—are of direct and continuous importance in their influence on the lives of the country people. Nature has not been kind to the parish. The surface of the land is broken up into small irregular ridges and winding narrow valleys. Sharp changes of slope are very common. Geologically, the area is composed of slatey shales and hard sandstones, from which are derived cold, heavy soils, deficient in lime and phosphates. The shales give rise to a thick clay subsoil, lying often within a few inches of the surface and producing very difficult drainage conditions. The climate is relatively unfavourable. The rainfall exceeds forty inches a year (more than twice that of much of south-eastern England) and its seasonal distribution makes corn harvesting and hay-making difficult and very uncertain. Winds are strong, often just before the harvest, while the combination of a high rainfall and cold, 'late' soils makes for a relatively short grazing season. The quality of the land varies abruptly from place to place, even within a single small field. Rushes, rank grasses and sedge are common. Flat valley-bottom land is very limited and often subject to flooding.

In a general way, the landscape and the type of farming are a close reflection of these geographical conditions. The irregularity of the terrain makes for small fields: the enclosing banks and hedges often separate wet and dry land and together with their ditches are a necessary part of the drainage system, as well as a shelter for stock against driving rain. The climate, particularly the absence of a hot, dry summer, discourages arable farming and encourages an emphasis on livestock husbandry. The poverty of the soils militates against large farms, while the steep slopes and broken relief are unsuited to the use of certain kinds of farm machinery. Variations in slope, exposure and soil quality results in marked differences between individual farms.

Taken as a whole, the agricultural pattern is largely what one might expect in the circumstances which have been described. Most of the farm land is under grass. The pastures are generally *Agrostis*, some invaded by rushes and sedges. Where drainage conditions are reasonably good there is permanent grass, accounting for well over half the total farm land; in places where drainage is more difficult short leys are the rule, since the pasture deteriorates rapidly, and a further fifth to a quarter of the land is under temporary grass. In contrast, cereals account for roughly one-ninth of the total area, oats being by far the most popular crop because of the damp climate. Some wheat is grown. There are small areas under fodder roots and the remainder is taken up by rough grazing, much of it common land. The latter is poor, intractable land, which has resisted cultivation for centuries. It is mostly *Molinia* moor with many rushes and cannot be used in wet seasons. Cattle are the mainstay of the economy, with sheep of subsidiary—but still considerable— importance.

Farm practice has, through generations of experience, been adapted to suit the natural environment, but there are, of course, other factors which influence the type of agriculture. Tradition, the character and outlook of the individual farmer, his capital resources, government policy and a number of external economic pressures bring about changes from time to time. Between 1935 and 1955, for example, many farmers turned to the production of liquid milk for sale, in an area long associated with store rearing and some fattening. Since 1955 a number of men have changed back to cattle rearing, in response to a favourable demand for beef and to changes in the regulations governing the production of milk.

Natural and man-made influences combine, therefore, to give a wide variety in farm types and practice. These variations are fully recognized by the people of Ashworthy, who attach great importance to them. There are a number of ways of classifying the farms of the parish, most of them used by the country people in different contexts from time to time. Farms can be 'good' or 'bad'; they are sometimes divided into 'easy-worked', 'ordinary' and 'hard-working'. In terms of economic activity they fall into the three main groups of (1) dairy farms (2) livestock rearing farms (3) mixed farms. There are many sub-groups. Some of the dairy farms rear small numbers of store or fat cattle, others sheep or pigs: some concentrate entirely on milk production. Most of the livestock rearing farms specialize in cattle, but a few have substantial flocks of sheep. There are holdings on which cereals are important and many on which hay is the only crop. The mixed farms, in particular, exhibit considerable differences from one to another. Farms can be classified by size, by degree of mechanization—which ranges in the parish from the 'horse only' farm to those which are highly mechanized—and by the use or absence of hired labour. They can even be divided on the basis of the type of farmer as seen by the local people: there are 'real' farmers, old-established farmers, 'good young' farmers, 'dog and stick farmers'[1] and 'Up Country Johnnies'.[2] There are also farms which have a reputation for making money and others which are 'heavy on the pocket'.

These distinctions are important and will be referred to again. Some idea of the differences on which they are based may be indicated briefly here by describing three specimen farms:

Southcott

A holding of 116 acres, of which 20 acres are rough grazing and the remainder under grass. The farm is on poor land, with very heavy soils: parts are waterlogged, even after a long dry spell. Some fields are thickly dotted with rushes. The best land carries poor *Agrostis* pasture, the worst is wet *Molinia* moor suitable only for grazing under very favourable conditions. The pasture must be ploughed regularly to maintain a moderate quality of grazing. The present occupier came in 1949 and began with a dairy herd; in 1956 he changed over to beef production—'I

---

[1] This term is used in Ashworthy to describe in a derogatory way men who do little work or who think of themselves as 'gentlemen farmers'.

[2] These are people who have come to the parish from some distance away, usually well outside the South-west.

found out the land wasn't suited to a good dairy herd. I learned gradually that beef is much the best way for me'. No sheep are kept.

The farmhouse is a fine, late seventeeth century 'long house' and the outbuilding accommodation is adequate since there were formerly two farmsteads on the site. It stands about half a mile from the nearest road, joined to it by a winding track with a very poor surface, some of it under water even in summertime. The farmstead has electricity and a mains water supply.

The labour in this holding is provided by the occupier and his wife, helped by 'a boy half a day a week'. A contractor is employed for manuring, hay baling and many other major tasks.

This farm is locally recognized to be 'poor land', 'a very hard-working farm—on clay' and 'not one to get rich on'.

Hall Farm

A holding of 315 acres, which is very large by local standards. Most of the land is as good as the best elsewhere in the parish: much of it is reasonably flat or has gentle slopes which help to promote good natural drainage. Over 200 acres are under permanent grass and a further 35 acres under leys where the quality of the land is rather poor. Fifty acres of grain crops are grown, with wheat and oats in roughly equal proportions. Small quantities of swedes and kale are grown for fodder. It is a livestock rearing farm, with a pedigree herd of beef cattle: no milk is sold. A stock of a hundred breeding ewes is kept, so that sheep are an important addition to the main source of income.

The farmhouse is a good example of a late seventeenth century dwelling of the prosperous yeomanry. It has good outbuildings. A well-kept macadamed road runs to the farmhouse and the hedges and banks are carefully maintained. There is electricity and a mains water supply.

Labour on the holding consists of the farmer, his wife, a labourer who lives in a cottage across the courtyard from the farmhouse, and a boy who 'lives in'. Until recently there were three boys employed on the farm. The farm is highly mechanized: the owner borrows a neighbour's potato digger and hires a combine harvester, but is otherwise self-sufficient in machinery.

This farm is accepted by everyone as being one of the best in the parish: it is 'easy worked', on 'real good land' and its owner is 'a proper farmer'.

Stableford

A holding of 57 acres, situated on the gentle, southern-facing slope of a ridge. Apart from two small fields on the lower ground, which are badly drained and infested with rushes, the land is of good quality for the area. About 40 acres are under pasture, and ten under cereals. The present owner bought the farm in 1957: he described himself as 'a dairy farmer, pure and simple', but he provides agistment for 20 sheep belonging to a near-by farmer. The economy of this holding was summed up by the farmer in the words 'I live on the milk cheque'.

The farmhouse is almost identical with Southcott in architecture and date, but is in a poor state of repair. The roof leaks badly. Outbuilding accommodation is adequate but has been neglected. The farm roads are good. There is no electricity or mains water.

When visited in 1958, the farmer worked his holding alone: his wife had a young baby. He employs a contractor for hay-baling and corn harvesting and borrows machinery from other farmers.

This farm is ranked locally with Hall Farm in the quality of its land and is said to be 'a handy size'. The owner is an 'Up Country Johnny'.

These three examples are intended to give some idea of the individual farm economy and of some of the differences which exist between farms. A farm is, of course, a tract of land, sub-divided into individual fields and, in Ashworthy, occupied by a family. The family is, then, the unit of land-holding and in order to understand how the social and economic life of farmers is organized it is essential to examine the way in which the land is divided up among them and how this division has come about. In other words, in an area of family farming like Ashworthy, the system of land-holding is the institutionalized, lasting expression of the relationship between society and its geographical environment. If the land-holding system is rigid and unchanging it will provide a stable framework for the maintenance of

social and economic relations between individuals and groups :
if, on the other hand, the units which make up the total pattern
of land-holding change frequently in size and shape, are split
up or amalgamated, then such changes will be directly reflected
in the social and economic structure. In the next section of the
chapter the land-holding system of Ashworthy is described and
it will be shown that its outstanding characteristic is piecemeal
and frequent change.

LAND-HOLDING

There are three elements in any system of land-holding—(a)
the field pattern, i.e. the way the land is divided into units of
different size and shape, demarcated by banks, hedges, fences,
boundary stones or by other methods, (b) the occupation of
land, i.e. its use by individuals or groups and (c) the ownership
of land. These elements are, of course, closely interrelated, but
for the purposes of this study they will first be considered
separately.

The field system

Until quite recently it was believed that a great part of the
West Country lay outside the area of the open-field system
which formerly covered so much of lowland England.[1] The
South-west was held to be an area of early enclosure and its
general pattern of small irregular-shaped fields was compared
with much of Wales and parts of northern England where open-
field farming was unknown. During the last ten years, however,
detailed studies by agricultural historians, notably W. G.
Hoskins,[2] have shown that open-fields did exist to the west of
Gray's boundary, which ran through Dorset and Somerset.[3] It
is now clear that the West Country was a marginal area, where

---

[1] See, for example, G. S. and C. S. Orwin, *The Open Fields* (Oxford 1945)
and D. Jerrold, *An Introduction to the History of England from the Earliest
Times to 1204.* (London 1949.)

[2] In such works as *The Making of the English Landscape* (London 1955)
and (with H. P. R. Finberg) *Devon Studies* (London 1952).

[3] See H. L. Gray, *English Field Systems* (Cambridge, Mass., 1915)
frontispiece and *passim.*

the isolated farm with its enclosed fields existed side by side with open-field villages and hamlets. In very general terms, the latter were associated with better land, where arable cultivation could be developed without great difficulty. There is still, however, a great deal of work to be done before the detailed distribution of field systems in the region is fully known.

Research is also needed into types of field systems. Terms such as open-field and infield-outfield are little more than collective descriptions covering wide variations in pattern and agricultural practice. Here too, studies made in the last few years have shown that the classical open-field arrangement is only one of a number of distinctive systems.[1] For example, in some areas, where arable land was restricted, there appears to have been an economy based on one or more small arable fields in strips together with roughly rectangular fields under pasture or meadow. Small in scale, it was normally associated with a group of farms or hamlet. The relationship of this system to the orthodox open-field and infield-outfield is not yet clear and, in Britain at least, its existence has scarcely been noticed. Very little is known of its distribution, but it may be characteristic of such marginal areas as the South-west.[2]

With this general background in mind, we may now turn to Ashworthy. The earliest detailed record of the field system of the parish is the tithe map of 1841. It shows the greater part of the land divided into enclosed fields, mostly small, with a pattern that can be associated at once with the traditional view of the South-west as a region outside the limit of the open-field country. There seems no reason to doubt that it is a landscape created many centuries ago. There are also, however, some

[1] Unfortunately, most of these studies have been made by Continental scholars: this country is perhaps ten years behind them and shows little sign of catching up. For representative works see P. Flatrès, *Géographie Rurale de quatre contrées celtiques: Irlande, Galles, Cornwall et Man* (Rennes 1957) and the journal *Zeitschrift für Agrargeschichte und Agrarsoziologie*.

[2] This is very tentative, in a field of study largely untouched by British historical geographers and agricultural historians. For studies of local examples in Britain see H. Uhlig, 'Langstreifenfluren in Nordenengland, Wales und Schottland' *Deutscher Geographentag Würzburg* 29 July–5 August 1957 and his papers on the Highlands of Scotland in *Erdkunde*, Band XIII (1959). (See Bibliography.)

small parts of the parish with a different pattern (see Fig. 1):
they are the areas lying around the four hamlets. Each one is
the same. Near to the farms there are long, very narrow fields
arranged in line and around them a scattering of small, more or
less rectangular fields in compact groups, the whole partially
surrounded by tracts of common land and moor. They clearly
belong to a different tradition from the remainder of the parish
and it seems likely that they are in fact survivals of the 'transi-
tional' field system described earlier. Originally, the long
narrow fields would have been the arable land of the settlement, divided into strips and cultivated continuously. Later
amalgamation and enclosure have changed the character and
functions of the strips but have left unmistakable traces of their
existence in the landscape.

The third element in the landscape of Ashworthy in 1841—
the unenclosed common land—accounted for forty per cent of
the total area. It was badly-drained moorland, used by the
farmers for grazing according to an elaborate system of common rights. During the last hundred years tracts of common
have been enclosed and improved from time to time, particularly between 1890 and 1905, so that today it amounts to
about nine per cent of the land of the parish. This enclosure
represents the only significant change in the field pattern since
1841: apart from minor amalgamations, the remainder of
Ashworthy is exactly as it was a century ago. The reason for
this is not hard to find: the great banks and hedges which
border the fields are difficult and expensive to remove. A farmer
would need a powerful stimulus to undertake such a task. Thus,
although the long narrow fields around the hamlet of Southmoor End are unsuited to modern machinery and inefficient
by present standards, they remain almost as they were in 1841
(see Fig. 1).

The occupation of land

The individual fields which together make up the landscape are
grouped into holdings occupied by one or more people. The
groups may be of adjoining fields, giving a compact holding, or
of fragmented blocks of one or more fields some distance apart
from each other. On the common land, occupation is not

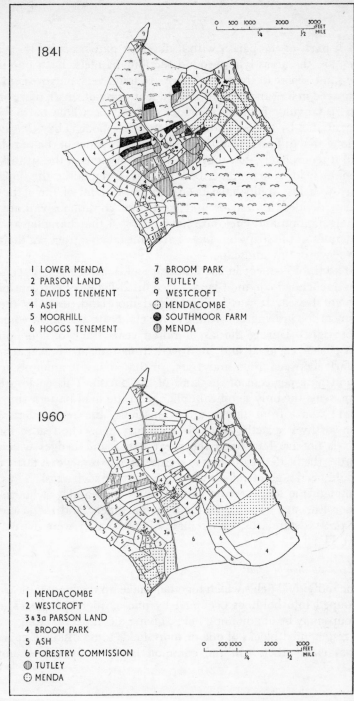

Fig. 1. Southmoor End in 1841 and 1960.

defined territorially but by rights of usage. Occupation may be by virtue of ownership or by a tenurial agreement of one kind or another.

The pattern of occupation in Ashworthy revealed by the 1841 tithe map is very complex. Farms were of all sizes, ranging from the small-holding of one or two fields to the large acreage of the substantial yeoman:

TABLE ONE

Size of holdings in Ashworthy 1841

Acres	Number of holdings	
	A	B
0–5	8	7
5–20	27	16
20–50	33	16
50–100	22	13
100–150	6	11
150–300	5	8
Over 300	3	3
Total	104	74

Column A. Holdings listed in the Tithe Award.
Column B. Holdings by occupiers.

A distinction is made in the table between farms (i.e. the land associated with a particular farmstead) or parts of farms (A), and the occupation of land by individual farmers (B). The smallest farm was one acre, the largest was five hundred and forty-seven acres. A number of men occupied two or more farms or parts of farms; for example, the tenant of the largest farm in the parish was the occupier of another farm of 83 acres, making his total holding 630 acres. Some farms were divided into three or four parts, each with different occupiers.

The pattern was complicated further by fragmentation. On the one hand, some farms were fragmented; on the other, the land occupied by an individual may have been in a number of separate tracts because he owned or tenanted more than one farm or part of a farm. Fragmentation was particularly marked around the hamlets on the land formerly under arable in strips.

The Land

At Southmoor End, for example (Fig. 1) Southmoor Farm, David's Tenement, Tutley, Broompark, Hogg's Tenement and part of Menda were all in scattered fields. David's Tenement and Hogg's Tenement were occupied by the same farmer, whose 20 acres were split up into six separate parts.

From 1841 to the present day there have been a great many changes in the detailed pattern of occupation. Fields have been added to some farms at the expense of others. Amalgamation has caused the disappearance of some farms, especially the smaller ones, while new ones have been created by the improvement of common land and by dividing up some of the largest holdings. A general effect has been to reduce the total number of holdings:

TABLE TWO

Size of holdings in Ashworthy 1960.

Acres	Number of holdings	
	A	B
0–5	7	5
5–20	10	6
20–50	17	9
50–100	27	24
100–150	13	16
150–300	12	12
Over 300	3	3
Total	89	75

The distinction between farms, or part of farms (A) and the land occupied by one person (B) still exists. The largest farm is now 377 acres and the largest holding of any farmer 396 acres.

There is still a considerable amount of fragmentation. In some parts of the parish, especially around the hamlets, there has been a tendency towards rationalizing farm lay-out by exchange or amalgamation of fields; in other parts, however, fragmentation has appeared where there was none formerly. The map of Ashworthy (Fig. 2) showing occupation by individuals reveals the complexity of the pattern of land-holding, with farms of a great many shapes and sizes and with arrows indicating fragmented holdings. As one might expect, the

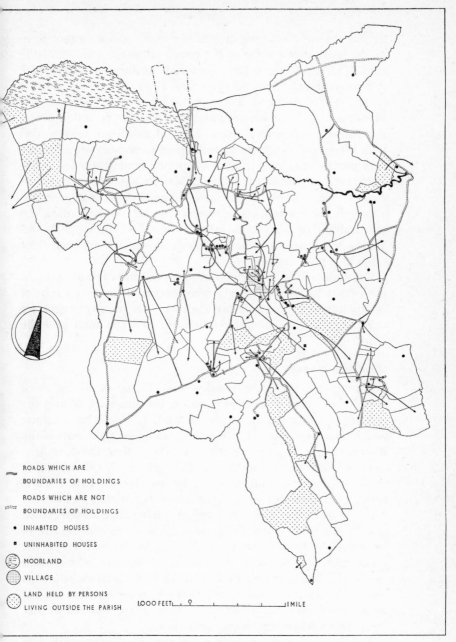

ROADS WHICH ARE
BOUNDARIES OF HOLDINGS
ROADS WHICH ARE NOT
BOUNDARIES OF HOLDINGS
• INHABITED HOUSES
■ UNINHABITED HOUSES
MOORLAND
VILLAGE
LAND HELD BY PERSONS
LIVING OUTSIDE THE PARISH

1,000 FEET   0   1 MILE

Fig. 2. Occupation of Holdings by Individuals. Ashworthy 1960.

arrows are most common around the hamlets. Southmoor End, in the south-east corner of the parish, illustrates in detail the kind of changes which have occurred during the last century. A comparison of 1841 and 1960 (Fig. 1) shows that the number of farms has declined from ten to six. Lower Menda and Mendacombe have been amalgamated into one holding and one field from Southmoor and from Menda have been added to it. Westcroft, Broompark and Menda have been considerably enlarged by enclosure from the common land: Broompark has also absorbed Moorhill, whereas Menda has lost many of its former fields. All the farms have changed to some degree and although the occupation of the narrow fields which mark the old arable strips has been greatly simplified, Broompark and Tutley still have very small isolated fields which are inefficient relics of a past century.

Southmoor End is no different from the rest of Ashworthy in the extent to which changes have occurred in the pattern of occupation since 1841. As we shall see later, these changes are significant in the general relationship between man and the land.

Ownership of land

For many centuries Ashworthy was characterized by three kinds of ownership—the large estate, the small estate and the owning of a single farm or plot of land. The only large estate, which took its name from the place, came into the hands of the Bishop family through marriage in 1692: they lived in Ashworthy House in the south-west of the parish. By the beginning of the nineteenth century the estate covered well over 5,000 acres, of which just over 1,700 acres lay within Ashworthy itself. John Bishop (1802–62) began buying land in the parish and by the time of the Tithe Award had increased the size of the estate by over 1,750 acres (Fig. 3). When he died he left his lands in the north-east of the parish to his niece, who created the Redcliffe estate and built a house in its extreme southern corner (Fig. 4). This estate passed through the hands of several members of the family and was sold in 1918. The Ashworthy estate was sold nearly twenty years later.

The Bishop family estates show continuity of ownership over

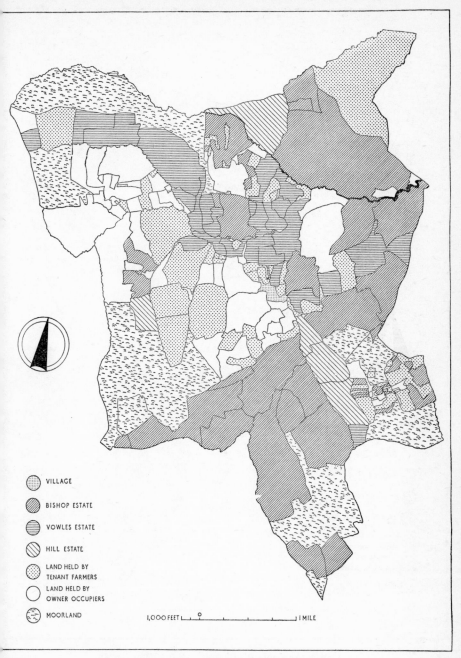

VILLAGE

BISHOP ESTATE

VOWLES ESTATE

HILL ESTATE

LAND HELD BY
TENANT FARMERS

LAND HELD BY
OWNER OCCUPIERS

MOORLAND

1,000 FEET   O   1 MILE

Fig. 3. Ownership of land. Ashworthy 1841.

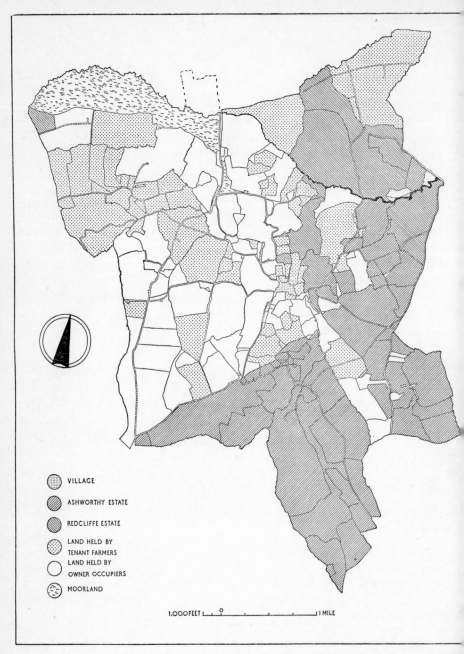

LEGEND

VILLAGE	
ASHWORTHY ESTATE	
REDCLIFFE ESTATE	
LAND HELD BY TENANT FARMERS	
LAND HELD BY OWNER OCCUPIERS	
MOORLAND	

1,000 FEET   0   1 MILE

Fig. 4. Ownership of land. Ashworthy 1918.

a long period, but—during the nineteenth century at least—acquisitions and sales of land were common. The smaller estates (for example those owned by the Vowles and Hill families in 1841) are characterized by an absence of continuity. New ones are created, last for ten or twenty years, then are sold or divided. Frequent sales or purchases cause rapid changes in their territorial pattern. Much the same is true of individual farms and plots of land, although there is some tendency towards continuity of ownership for some farms.

In geographical terms, therefore, the pattern of ownership is as fluid as the pattern of occupation: a random selection of fields would show many changes in owners and occupiers since 1800. From another point of view, however, the changes are much less haphazard. As in many other parts of England, the last fifty years in Ashworthy have seen the decline of the estate as a unit of ownership and a corresponding rise in the number of owner-occupied farms. This can be seen in the maps of ownership and in the following table:

TABLE THREE

Ownership of land in Ashworthy

Size of estate (acres)	Number of owners			
	1841	*1873*	*1922**	*1960*
Over, 1,000	1	1	1	Nil
800–1,000	1	2	Nil	Nil
400–800	Nil	Nil	1	Nil
300–400	3	4	4	3
200–300	1	3	6	5
1–200	41	33	71	84

* *Source:* Poor Rate and Special Expenses Rate Book 1922.

In 1841, the Bishop family owned 3,460 acres in Ashworthy (see Fig. 3): in 1922 they owned 2,090 acres. In the parish as a whole there were 64 tenant farmers and 19 owner occupiers in 1841; by 1922 the number of tenant farmers had decreased to 45, while at present only 7 men occupy farms they do not own (see Fig. 5). The spatial pattern of land owning is therefore much more complicated than it was formerly and tends to resemble that of occupation of land (Fig. 2).

Land-holding

When the three elements of land-holding considered above are taken together, the picture that emerges is a very complex one. While the field pattern has remained much the same during the last hundred years, occupation and ownership have been subject to a great many changes. The most striking features are the piece-meal sales, purchases and exchanges accompanying frequent and irregular alterations in occupation. The 1841 tithe map shows some evidence of a dynamic land-holding pattern in the number of farms divided among several owners and occupiers, but it is probable that changes were rather less common at that time. One of the important factors making for stability was the 'three-lives' tenancy agreement. This type of lease became common in the West Country by the sixteenth century. The normal practice was for the lease to be granted on the lives of the lessee, his wife and eldest son or for a period of 99 years, whichever was the shorter. The 'lives' had to be those of living people, but new lives could be added on the payment of a fine, should one of the original lessees die. The entry fine was usually a heavy one and tended to increase in time. The greatest advantage of this kind of lease to the tenant was the security it offered: life-hold tenure at its best provided most of the privileges of ownership for a considerable period of years, sometimes centuries, and encouraged good tenants to improve the quality of the land and the state of their farmsteads. Even the bad tenants had little fear of interference by the landlord. Under such a system patterns of occupation were likely to remain stable.

The three-lives lease was still common on the Ashworthy estates in 1841. Elsewhere in the South-west, changing conditions had brought about the introduction of short-term leases some fifty years earlier. An increase in the competition for farms had encouraged landlords to let to the man willing to pay the highest entry fine, without looking closely at his resources or ability as a farmer. More and more tenants borrowed heavily

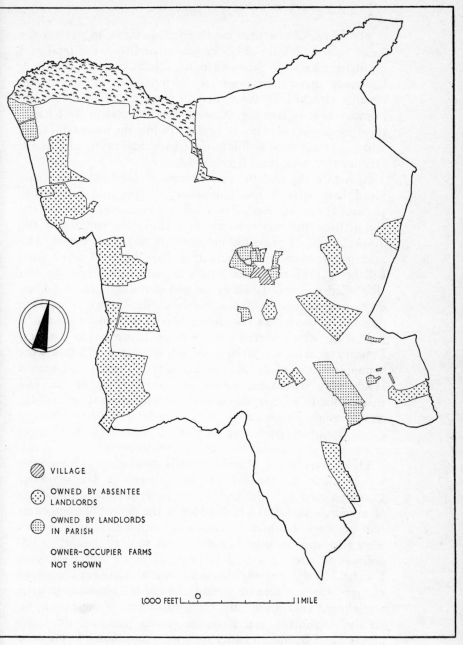

VILLAGE

OWNED BY ABSENTEE
LANDLORDS

OWNED BY LANDLORDS
IN PARISH

OWNER-OCCUPIER FARMS
NOT SHOWN

1,000 FEET   0   1 MILE

Fig. 5. Ownership of land. Ashworthy 1960.

to obtain leases and then exploited their farms to pay off the loan: they had little or no capital to improve the land and needed quick returns to make a living. The life-hold system, which had once earned the praise of all interested in agriculture, became attacked by the writers of surveys and works on the improvement of farming. Nevertheless, the system died hard: three-life leases could not be replaced while the lessees still lived and it was not until well into the second half of the nineteenth century that rack-rents became common.

In Ashworthy and the area around it, life-hold tenure survived long after it had completely disappeared from other parts of the South-west. The land was poor and therefore the competition for farms which had elsewhere stimulated the abuses of its late years did not occur to any great extent. The area was remote and conservative. New life-hold leases were still being granted in the 1870's in Ashworthy, and the last 'life' died in 1922. Towards the end of the last century, however, the comparative stability of the earlier years was breaking down. The three-lives system was being replaced by the short-term lease, which offered less security of tenure. As in the West Country generally, fourteen- or twenty-one-year leases were common, but a substantial number of farms were let on annual 'Lady Day' tenancies, which gave no security at all. The reasons for this latter practice are obscure, but its effects are clear enough. Farms and parts of farms let in this way changed hands frequently and were particularly susceptible to changes in extent and to amalgamation or sub-division.

There were other changes shortly to come to Ashworthy which made for fluidity in the pattern of land-holding. Common land was enclosed, either to form compact holdings or in individual tracts which added to the degree of fragmentation (see Figs. 3, 4 and 5). The large and medium-sized estates were sold and the sales brought about radical changes in the occupation and ownership of land. Many of the farms were bought by the existing tenants, but a significant number changed hands. More important, the old land-holding pattern was altered very drastically. Only two farms of the twenty-six on the Ashworthy and Redcliffe estates possessed the same acreage and boundaries after they were sold. Some farms were divided into as many as six parts and sold separately. A new landowner appeared in Ashworthy with the purchase of land by the Forestry Commission.

Thus during this century Ashworthy has been characterized by a constantly changing pattern of land-holding. During the last thirty years, severe economic depression, followed by war and the return of prosperity have in turn stimulated change. With very few exceptions, the farmers of the parish are accustomed to this dynamic situation. To them a farm is not so much ·a particular tract of land or group of fields which is more or less permanently associated with a farmstead, but something which can be altered in shape and disposition to suit the circumstances. As we shall see later, 'the land' is of great emotional and social importance to the farmers, but it represents to them a generalized relationship rather than a profound attachment to a single holding.

FARMS AND FARMERS

In the last section changes in the land-holding system of Ashworthy have been considered in terms of territorial patterns and with little reference to the people who are responsible for change. They are not a fixed and limited group. The individuals who buy and sell fields, who enlarge farms or split them up are not always the same individuals. This section is devoted to an analysis of change in the composition of the people who own or occupy the land.

In general, the composition of farmers and landowners as a group shows as much variety as the distribution of the land they occupy. Farms have changed hands frequently and new names appear in the County Directories and Lists of Electors almost every year. A comparison of the 1841 Tithe Award with a list of present occupiers shows that only one family has owned and occupied the same farmstead continuously throughout the period between them.

A more detailed picture can be seen from an analysis of the length of time the present farmers have occupied their holdings and the number of occupiers on each holding during this century:

31

TABLE FOUR[1]

Occupation of Holdings. Ashworthy, 1st January, 1960.

A		B	
Present occupiers: length of occupation in years	*Number of occupiers*	*Number of occupiers since 1900*	*Number of holdings*
Over 60	16	1	16
51–60	2	2	23
41–50	5	3	28
31–40	10	4	15
21–30	15	5	12
11–20	23	6	3
6–10	24	7	4
1–5	8	8	4
Less than 1	5	9 or more	3
Total	108	Total	108

[1] For the purposes of this table, holdings are defined as farms or parts of farms. Land held by individuals living outside the parish has not been taken into account. Minor changes in the land-holding pattern (i.e. of less than 5 acres) have not been included. The table does not show numbers of individuals. For example, a man may occupy two farms, acquired at different dates and with different numbers of tenants since 1900: these farms will be shown separately.

'An occupier' may be an individual or family: for the latter, close blood relationship has been used as a criterion. In the great majority of cases holdings have passed from parent to child (see below p. 61).

From the first two columns (A) it can be seen that relatively few farms have been in the hands of the same families for long periods. Fifty-five per cent of the farms were acquired by the present occupiers or their families within the last twenty years and sixty-nine per cent in the last thirty years. If the analysis is extended backwards beyond 1900, then the number of examples of continuous occupation falls sharply. Of the families occupying land in 1883, only four farm the same holdings today. Well over a third of the holdings have had four or more occupiers since 1900 (see B), and a tenth of them as many as seven or more.

Both parts of the table show substantial shifts in occupation while the differences between them point to the wide variations which occur in the histories of occupation of the individual holdings. For example, among the group of holdings which have had four tenants since 1900, there are some which were in the hands of the same family for thirty years or more and then changed occupiers in fairly rapid succession: others in the same group have been farmed by men who each stayed for about fifteen years. In a general way, however, there are chronological trends which can be related to the history of land-holding in the parish. Up until the end of the First World War there was relatively little movement between farms and most of the tenants of the Redcliffe estate bought their holdings at the sale in 1918. By the late twenties and in the thirties depressed conditions in agriculture and the sale of the Ashworthy estate brought changes. A number of men could not pay their farm rent, and more did not have the capital to buy their holdings when the estate was broken up. Thus there are considerably more occupiers in the 21–40 year groups than in the 41–60 year groups. During and after the 1939–45 war the condition of agriculture improved steadily and throughout the country men from all kinds of occupations turned to farming. Many were attracted to such areas as Ashworthy because the farms were much cheaper than in more fertile areas: established farmers who had amassed some capital looked for better holdings. As a result, a great many farms were bought and sold between 1945 and 1955 and this is reflected in the large number of occupiers in the 6–20 year groups. Many of the newcomers to farming were inexperienced or did not fully appreciate the particular difficulties of the local conditions in Ashworthy. The majority of them left after one or two years. They form a significant proportion of the 371 individuals who have occupied holdings in the parish for some period since 1900. The number of farms changing hands has declined sharply since 1955, partly because the flow of newcomers has decreased appreciably and partly because those of them who survived the crucial first two or three years have settled down to farming as a permanent way of life.

The distribution of these changes in occupation is given in Figs. 6 and 7. A comparison of the two maps illustrates in a

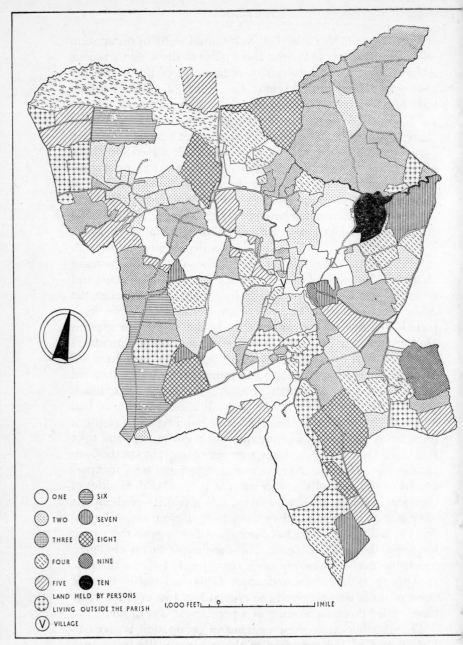

Fig. 6. Number of occupiers in holdings. Ashworthy 1900–1960.

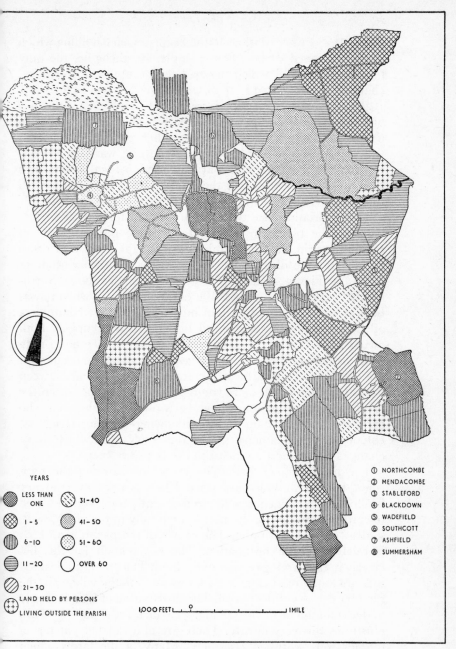

YEARS

◐	LESS THAN ONE	⊠	31-40
⊠	1-5	▦	41-50
☰	6-10	⦿	51-60
☰	11-20	○	OVER 60
⧄	21-30		

⊞ LAND HELD BY PERSONS
⊞ LIVING OUTSIDE THE PARISH

① NORTHCOMBE
② MENDACOMBE
③ STABLEFORD
④ BLACKDOWN
⑤ WADEFIELD
⑥ SOUTHCOTT
⑦ ASHFIELD
⑧ SUMMERSHAM

1,000 FEET ⌐———⌐ 0 ⌐————————⌐ 1 MILE

Fig. 7. Length of occupation of holdings. Ashworthy 1960.

different way the variations in the history of each holding which were mentioned earlier. For example, Northcombe, the only farm in the parish which has had ten occupiers this century, changed hands in 1912, 1926, 1931, 1934, 1945, 1946, 1947, 1948, 1949 and 1956. Mendacombe, at Southmoor End, has had nine occupiers, but was farmed by one man from 1900 to the Ashworthy sale in 1935. At the other extreme, Stableford, which has been sold only once this century, was farmed continuously by one family from at least 1790 to 1957, when it was bought by a newcomer to the parish. Blackdown, also with two occupiers, was acquired by its present owner in 1906.

These variations are typical and account for the differences between the two maps: they also exclude the possibility of establishing simple relationships between the pattern of occupation and the distribution of leasehold and owner-occupier farms (see Figs. 3, 4 and 5). Of the four examples above, Northcombe was part of the Redcliffe estate until 1918 when it was bought by its tenant: the eight men who came after him were all owner-occupiers. Stableford has had two occupiers, both owners: Blackdown's occupier was a tenant from 1906 to 1952 when he bought the farm. It is true that changes did occur with the break-up of the Ashworthy estate, but movement between farms has been much more common since that time, when the great majority of holdings have been owned by the men who occupied them. Tenant farms and owner-occupier farms are equally common among the extremes of those which have changed hands most and least in the last sixty years.

The distribution of changes in occupation shown on the maps is not, however, totally haphazard. There is a general tendency for holdings which change hands frequently to be concentrated towards the borders of the parish, especially in the north, west, south-west and south-east. The centre of the parish is an area of relatively stable occupation. The explanation for this lies largely in the varying quality of the land. The poorer ill-drained soils are found most commonly far away from the village, in the remoter corners of the parish. The distribution of land formerly under common or moor (see Fig. 3), which is the poorest of all, illustrates this very clearly. There are also isolated patches of inferior soils scattered elsewhere. Many of the farms which

have seen the greatest numbers of occupiers are situated on
land which was formerly common or near to its edge. Southcott,
the Southmoor End farms, Ashfield and Summersham are
typical examples. The pattern is, however, not neat or continuous, partly because the quality of the soils varies abruptly
and irregularly, or because some tracts of poor land have been
greatly improved by skilled farmers, and partly because poverty
of land is not a necessary condition of frequent change in
occupation. Wadefield, farmed by the same family for at least
two hundred years, has good land although it lies in a part of
the parish where drainage conditions are generally very bad
indeed. In contrast, Northcombe, the farm which has had ten
occupiers since 1900, is also well-favoured in its soils.

Poor land is, then, a potent factor in change of occupier.
(As we shall see later, it is by no means the only one). Men
leave these 'hard-working' farms because they are uneconomic,
because bankruptcy drives them out or because they are able
to move to a better holding. In Ashworthy, as in all the 'problem
areas' of the West Country, there is a widely recognized
'agricultural ladder' by which men climb from the poorest
farms to the good ones. In the years after the war, when the
'Up Country Johnnies' were buying farms, there was a brisk
exchange of holdings at the bottom rung of the ladder. The
newcomers were unaccustomed to local conditions and did not
realize how deceptive first appearances were, particularly in
dry weather. The prices of the farms seemed to compare very
favourably with the rest of the country. Since these holdings
would tax all the skill and energy of an experienced local man,
many of the new arrivals went bankrupt, or sold out and cut
their losses within two years. The experience of one man is
probably typical: 'I came down here looking for a place during
my summer holiday. We looked at *dozens* of farms, but they
were all too dear. Then we found one out at Padsdon (in a
neighbouring parish) which seemed the right price. It looked
all right, so we bought it. The chap was a confectioner really,
who'd taken up farming. It took me two years to find out why
it was so cheap. It was the wettest place on earth. Many times
I thought of giving up and going back to engineering. Then this
place came up and I scraped together and bought it. I was

much luckier . . . we get along now. Smith—that's the confectioner—had only lasted a year. He must have thought it was his lucky day when I turned up.'

The 'Up Country Johnnies' have an important place in changes in farm occupation, but they are still a small minority. Most of the farmers are local men and this implies—in an area like Ashworthy—that there is a considerable movement of *farm families from holding to holding*. This movement can be analysed in several ways. One is by tracing the location of the farms from which people came and to which they went for every occasion there is a change of occupier in the parish over a given period. In practice this proved to be very difficult. Farm deeds were often not available or did not give the necessary information: many of the present occupiers did not know anything about the men who had preceded them: documentary sources, such as the County Directories and Lists of Electors, were only occasionally useful. Fortunately, some of the older people of Ashworthy have a remarkable knowledge of local affairs stretching back for a number of years. With their help a list was compiled which accounted for 477 changes out of a possible total of 589 since 1900.[1] The distribution of these changes is as follows:

Within Ashworthy	205
To and from adjoining parishes	146
To and from other parishes within eight miles	72
Elsewhere in the county	25
Adjoining counties	10
Elsewhere in Britain	19

From this it can be seen that just over forty per cent of the movement has taken place within Ashworthy and nearly ninety per cent within a small area centred on the parish. Moreover,

[1] The 78 farmers of 1900 were taken as the starting point and no account was taken of previous changes of farm they might have made before that date. Each holding was then taken in turn and a list made of the location of the farms last held by the successive occupiers. Another list was made of the location of the farms to which men went when they gave up a holding. Thus every change of occupier after 1900 represented two moves, except of course for present occupiers who have made only the inward move or for men moving in who have died or retired.

the surrounding parishes did not play an equal part (see Fig. 8);[1] there is a distinct preference for some areas and a somewhat curious avoidance of others, particularly towards the north-west and west. The reasons for this irregular pattern are very obscure, since all the parishes share more or less the same natural conditions and type of farming. In part it may result from the limitations of the method of analysis, which is concerned only with movement to and from Ashworthy, and not between the surrounding parishes. Whatever the reasons, it is clear that Ashworthy is very closely linked with certain parishes, less closely with others and with some hardly at all. As farmers move from place to place they create new social ties and perhaps revive old ones. The parishes which are most important in the movement of farm families are also those which have the greatest and closest social contacts with Ashworthy. They are the places where the people of the parish have many kindred and friends. They are frequently mentioned in conversation. In short, they provide a territorial base for social and economic relations of an enduring kind within what may be called the 'Ashworthy area'. The limits of this area are not fixed: they vary considerably in different contexts. For example, the 'Ashworthy area' defined in terms of movement of farm families embraces those parishes shown within the thick broken line in Fig. 8. This is the locality within which most farmers believe they can find a holding suitable to their needs and experience in familiar conditions. The majority of farmers appear to have restricted their choice to an even smaller area—shown within the thick continuous line in Fig. 8—and it is in this narrower territorial range that social and economic relations are most widely and intensively developed.

Ashworthy is, then, part of what may be termed a *social area* much larger than itself. It may be noted that its territorial definition as given in Fig. 8 is based on one criterion and is designed to indicate its extent only in a general and convenient way. The limits of the area are arbitrary insofar as they follow parish boundaries: this is because the movement of farm families could only be calculated by parishes. In most matters

[1] The boundaries of the parishes have been altered slightly to avoid identification. The areas of the parishes are unchanged.

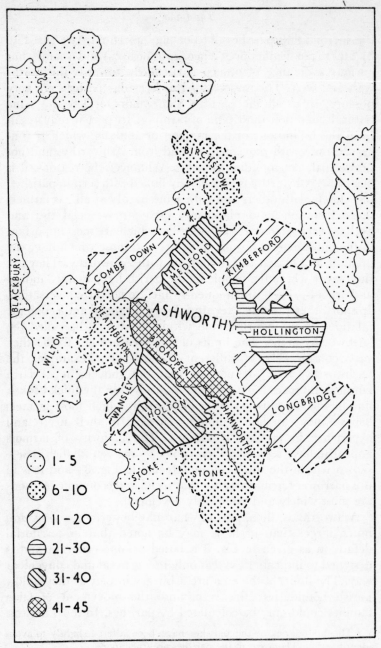

Fig. 8. Gross movement of farm occupiers to and from Ashworthy
1900–1960.

of every-day life parish boundaries are of little importance: few people know exactly where they run, even for their own parish.

This first method of analysing movement of families has shown above all that it is essentially short-distance in character and that the greatest movement occurs within the parish itself. It does not, however, tell us whether some families move more times than others, nor does it provide information about the detailed directions of movement within the area. For these an analysis by individual families is required which ideally would be based on the total moves made by every farmer who has occupied a farm in the parish. Such information is impossible to obtain and there are also other considerations which make a quantitative assessment of any kind extremely difficult. If, for example, a start is made with the seventy-five farmers at present in Ashworthy, it is soon found that many of them are young men who have been farming on their own account for ten years or less. The fact that they have not moved from one holding to another cannot be equated in significance with the permanence of those men who have occupied the same farm for thirty or forty years. Some men have begun farming in middle age, after many years in other professions: this too limits their 'potential mobility'. Since there will always be some young men, some middle-aged and some old men at any given point in time, it is necessary to limit the analysis to 'full lives', that is to farmers who have completed their working life: from the nature of the field work, information on 'full lives' can only be collected for men who have descendants in Ashworthy or—less commonly—for certain families who can be traced through documentary sources. There are too few of these to justify an attempt at quantitative analysis.[1]

The alternative is to consider selected family histories. They are intended to illustrate the kind of movement which can occur and it is known that they are each representative of several other families. The evidence cannot be taken beyond this, but

[1] The material on occupation of holdings at the beginning of this section (pp. 31–3) does, however, provide some information. For example, it is clear from Table Four that at least a quarter of the farmers have not changed holdings during their working lives and that a further proportion are unlikely to have changed more than once or twice.

it seems reasonable to suppose that the examples do in fact cover the major types of farm-to-farm change in the area.

(1) The Palmer family.[1] In 1880, John Palmer came from *Holton* as a tenant of Lower Hall Farm in *Ashworthy*. He died there in 1912. His son Robert took over the tenancy and then moved back to *Holton*, but not to the same farm as his father, in 1917. In 1922, while still in *Holton*, he bought Lower Hall (62 acres) and moved there a year later: shortly before moving he bought North Blackdown (118 acres), also in *Ashworthy*. In 1924 the family moved to North Blackdown, and Robert Palmer farmed it until 1940, when he handed it over to his second son Richard, who is the present occupier. Robert's eldest son Andrew became the owner occupier of Lower Hall on his marriage in 1937. Until that year Lower Hall had been farmed with North Blackdown.

(2) The Tapson family. Edward Tapson started farming on his own account in *Ashworthy* as tenant of Church Farm (70 acres) in 1895. He moved to Longbarrow (409 acres) in 1910 and again to Maldon (21 acres) which he bought in 1923. His son occupied it until 1947, when he retired to the village and sold the farm.

(3) James Blake. He first began farming in *Wilton St. Thomas* in 1922 as tenant of a 30 acre holding. In 1933 he moved to *Stoke* and bought his farm there in 1939. In 1941 he went to *Blackbury*, remained there eighteen months, then bought a farm in *Broadpen*. He came to *Ashworthy* in 1948 and has farmed Crowland Farm (24 acres) ever since.

(4) Edward Ackland. He moved from a farm in *Hamworthy* to Arundle Farm in 1927. He returned to *Hamworthy in* 1959.

(5) John Vallack. He first farmed at Lower East Hall from 1925 to 1931. He then moved to *Hallington* and returned to the parish in 1934, when he bought Gosseham (60 acres). In 1946 he moved to *Medford*: he retired in 1954 and returned to *Ashworthy*.

These few examples show the general complexity of movement from one part of the countryside to another. They reveal also that men move at all ages and that there is no simple progression from small farms to larger ones. When considered

[1] In order to avoid confusion, parish names are given in italics in all the examples (see Fig. 8).

in relation to the patterns of occupation and ownership it will be evident that land-holding in Ashworthy is extremely complex and subject to relatively rapid change. The significance of these changes in the social structure of the parish will be considered in the next chapter.

*   *   *

This chapter has been concerned with farming and land-holding in Ashworthy and, apart from a brief discussion of the 'Ashworthy area', little attempt has been made to relate conditions in the parish to a wider setting. As we shall see later, the relationships of Ashworthy to the world around it raise important and difficult problems; the parish does not exist in a vacuum, but neither is it 'typically English'.

Ashworthy is representative of a considerable region in its natural conditions, type of farming, general methods of agricultural practice and economic organization. Ownership and tenancy of land mean much the same in the parish as they do elsewhere in the South-west, but the particular development of land-holding in Ashworthy follows a pattern of its own, which may be broadly similar to that found in certain other parishes in the region but quite unlike many others. For example, the Bishop estate was much larger and more compact than any of the estates in the surrounding parishes; in the *Return of Owners of Land* (1873) it is shown as being over five times larger than the next estate in size. In most parishes, such as Broadpen, Hollington, Medford and Stone (see Fig. 8) the largest estates were between 700 and 1,000 acres: in Holton and Heathbury there were no holdings greater than 400 acres.

Differences of this kind between Ashworthy and the parishes which surround it are common enough and only to be expected. They reflect largely fortuitous variations in historical development which are outside the scope of this study.[1] If, on the other

[1] These variations also make comparisons with conditions in England as a whole very difficult. For example, fragmentation of holdings—which is so characteristic of Ashworthy and much of the region around it—is relatively uncommon in the West Country. According to the *National Farm Survey of England and Wales. Summary Report* (1946 p. 37) Devon and Cornwall are among the three counties with the lowest proportion of fragmented holdings (under 5 per cent).

hand, it was found that Ashworthy was unique in the changing character of its land-holding and in the movement of farm families, then this would limit the validity of the analysis to a set of special circumstances that exist only within the parish. In fact there is sufficient evidence to show that the surrounding parishes resemble Ashworthy in being characterized by relatively rapid and irregular changes in patterns of occupation and ownership. It can be inferred from the material given in the last section on movement of farmers—and can be confirmed by material gathered during the field work and from documentary sources.

For example, changes in occupation in the area can be measured with reasonable accuracy by comparing different editions of the annual *County Directories* with the *Return of Owners of Land* and *Registers of Electors*. A limited analysis of this kind for five parishes adjoining Ashworthy was made for the period 1873–1939.[1] It showed that only 13 of the 167 farmsteads remained in the hands of the same families from 1873 to 1939. Six out of the thirteen were in one parish. Between 1906 and 1939 there were 46 farms which remained unchanged. In the short period 1906–1914, over 60 farmsteads had new occupiers, 18 of whom appear to have come from within the same parish. Many of the names given in the *Directories*, etc., were of men who have farmed in Ashworthy itself.

It also seems as if the West Country generally is characterized by more rapid changes in occupation than most of England. According to the *National Farm Survey*, Devon is one of the two English counties with the smallest proportion of farmers who have occupied holdings since 1914 or earlier, while Cornwall and Somerset also have relatively small proportions.[2] It should

---

[1] The sources used were the *Return of Owners of Land* (1873), *Kellys Directory* for 1873, 1906, 1914 and 1939 and the *Register of Electors* for 1931. The parishes were Holton, Heathbury, Medford, Hollington and Broadpen.

[2] See the *Summary Report* of the Survey, pp. 31–35 and Table A9 (p. 99). In Devon, only 10 per cent of all farmers entered their holdings in 1914 or earlier: for Cornwall and Somerset the proportion is 14 per cent for both counties. This may be compared with Bedford (16 per cent) Cheshire (17 per cent) and Northumberland (22 per cent).

be added, however, that variations from county to county are very irregular and that long-term occupation is much more common in Wales than in England.[1]

Change in extent and lay-out of holdings—which, as we have seen, is very marked in Ashworthy—is much more difficult to measure for the surrounding parishes because the information is difficult to obtain and requires laborious and lengthy inquiry in the field. It was investigated as systematically as possible by asking every farmer who had occupied a holding in an adjoining parish (or who, for some other reason, knew these parishes well) to describe changes of this kind which he knew had occurred. The results were haphazard, often ambiguous or vague and did not fit into any definite territorial or chronological pattern. Nevertheless, thirty-seven farmers did mention at least one major change and many of them listed eight or nine: in all, seventy-four substantial changes, spread over six parishes, were listed. It seems certain that more detailed investigation would reveal a great many more and therefore that Ashworthy is broadly representative of the area in which it lies.

In general, then, the dynamic character of land-holding, which is so important in Ashworthy, can be found over a much larger area. Its significance in this study stems from the fact that any system of land-holding is an expression of an ecological relationship, i.e. between man and the land. The purpose of this chapter has been to document the spatial and 'structural' elements of land-holding; in the next the aim is to analyse the social elements of the 'land-man' relationship.

[1] Ibid. In Wales, ten out of the fourteen counties show 'pre-1914 occupiers' in proportions of 20 per cent or more.

CHAPTER THREE

MAN AND THE LAND (I)

The Family Farm

IN Ashworthy, as in much of Western Europe, the conjugal family is a primary unit in the social structure. All but one of the farms are 'family farms' and land-holding, land use and agricultural practice are organized around the farmer, his wife and his children. Farming and land-holding therefore share many general characteristics in common with other areas of family farming in Britain and elsewhere.

The farm family is the unit of economic production. In 1960, nearly 85 per cent of the male labour on farms was provided by farmers, their sons and other relatives, and 95 per cent of the female labour by farmers' wives, daughters and other relatives (see Appendix One, Tables One and Two). These proportions compare closely with those reported for other areas of family farming in Britain. Half the hired labour is found on four of the seventy-five farms and there are only two tied cottages in the parish. All the farmers agreed that farm workers could be found without very much difficulty: some use is made of part-time labour drawn from the village. The national decline in the numbers of agricultural workers since 1945 does not appear to have affected Ashworthy very seriously.

There are many reasons why farmers do not hire men. On some holdings the family is large enough to provide all the required labour: on others a shortage of working capital is important. It may take several years before the expense of hiring a man is returned through increased profits. The absence of tied cottages limits the possibility of hiring married men to those who live within a few miles. The mechanization of agriculture has considerably reduced the man-power required to farm a holding. These reasons do not, however, provide a full explanation for the relatively small proportion of hired labour on the farms of Ashworthy. There are many farms where the failure to employ men cannot be justified in economic or financial terms; on such farms the occupier prefers either to neglect those tasks which are not considered essential or immediately important—for example hedging and ditching —or to burden himself and his family with unremitting hard work throughout the year. In short, the farmers of Ashworthy are reluctant to use hired men and often go to considerable lengths to avoid doing so.

This situation has developed gradually during the last fifty or sixty years: in common with much of rural England, Ashworthy has suffered a steady decline in the numbers of agricultural labourers and farm servants. A hundred years ago, almost every farm had at least one hired man who 'lived in'; now there are only five in the parish. During the same period there has been a decrease in the size of the farm family, so that the total number of people who cultivate the land has fallen sharply.[1] One important result of this change is that the life cycle of the family has become closely related to its economic efficiency. In the 'normal' farm family, the cycle begins at marriage, with two adults to contribute to the working of the holding. There follows a long and often difficult period while the children are young and this in time is succeeded gradually by an improvement as they leave school to work at home. The burden on the parents increases once more as their children marry and leave the farm. Thus in a working life of between thirty-five to forty years, a family can normally expect a period of five to ten years of relatively ample labour.

This 'normal' cycle is however subject to many possible changes. Illness, death or—on very rare occasions—a broken marriage may drastically disrupt the progression. Some farmers are childless, others have no sons: some do not marry. At any given time, Ashworthy will have families at different stages in the cycle and others which are incomplete or disrupted. For example, at present sixteen of the seventy-five farms in the parish are worked by bachelors, widows or widowers and a further twelve are occupied by married men who have no

[1] See also pp. 136–39 below.

47

children. There are twelve farm families with all their children at school (seven of them have no children over six years old) and another six farmers have children who have taken up occupations other than farming. In other words, only two-fifths of the present farmers in Ashworthy approximate to the ideal family farm as it is conceived locally, i.e. 'a place of one's own' which can be worked by a farmer, and his wife and children without the assistance of hired labour. It seems indeed as if the conjugal family with one or two children is a very imperfect instrument for farming a holding over a long period. Farmers in Ashworthy, however, do not recognize this, and their reluctance to hire workers may in part result from placing a high value on the idea of a family farm and from over-assessing its economic efficiency and capabilities.

The distribution of hired labour on the farms of Ashworthy is not, therefore, a reflection of the size of the farm family or the extent of the holding. The largest farm in the parish is owned by two young brothers, both bachelors, who employ casual labour occasionally in the evenings. The older brother said that the farm was 'a bit too big for us on our own' and that 'some things have to be neglected'. He added, somewhat defensively, 'If you get a full-time man he might turn out to be no good.' Another example is a bachelor who works a farm of nearly two hundred acres single-handed, apart from part-time help with the harvest.

Ashworthy shares two other general characteristics with areas of family farming elsewhere in Britain. Firstly, its farms are medium-sized, with most falling into the 50–150 acre group and very few over 300 acres.[1] A third lie between 80 and 120 acres in size. A great many farmers mentioned 'a place of 60 to 100 acres' when talking about 'a good family farm'. Secondly, nearly all the farms are worked with somewhat modest capital resources. At the one extreme there is the established family which has inherited land, stock and money from earlier generations: at the other there is the young farmer starting his career with a heavy mortgage on his farm and virtually no working capital at all. The established farmers appear to have at least enough capital to run their farms efficiently and to buy stock

[1] See Table Two, p. 22, above.

and machinery when they feel it is necessary. Like all farmers, they are, of course, notoriously reluctant to discuss the financial aspect of farming, but their farms are sufficient evidence of adequate capital. In contrast, there are a number of farms where the signs of a shortage of capital are only too obvious in semi-derelict outbuildings, lack of farm machinery, poor roads, etc. Here the farmers were more willing to discuss their financial position and typical comments were: 'The only way I can buy *anything* is by selling something. The wife needs new clothes. I'll have to sell a calf to get them'; 'The roof of the house is leaking in six places. It all needs re-doing, but there's no hope of it for years'; 'Every penny I make goes into the farm. It's got to, it's the only way to keep going.'

The responsibilities of the owner-occupier bear heavily on many farmers and, as with hired labour and size of family, the last hundred years in Ashworthy have brought changes which emphasize the functional importance of the farm family. As we saw in the last chapter, the number of tenant farmers has declined steadily, particularly during this century, and more and more families have accepted the expense of buying their farms and of meeting all the costs of maintaining them. As one farmer put it: 'I own a farm over Birchstowe side. The tenant makes far more out of it than I do. The rent is nominal. A tenant nowadays is a happy man. . . . Half the people round here who bought places when the Bishops left have been sorry many times over.'

The replacement of the estate by the individual owner-occupier, the decrease in family size and the decline in the numbers of farm workers have together drastically changed the character of the farm household and created new stresses on the conjugal family as an economic unit. However, mechanization, the hire of agricultural contractors and new farming techniques have helped to reduce the burden on the individual farmer and, equally important, there is co-operation between groups of farms based on 'neighbourliness'. In Ashworthy, as in many other rural areas, helping one's neighbours is normally considered to be 'natural' and dozens of examples were recorded during the field work. Borrowing and lending machinery, help during the harvest, collective arrangements for sheep-dipping are typical expressions of neighbourly feelings and, as one farmer remarked; 'There's one thing about Ashworthy. If us be ill, or the tractor breaks down or anything goes wrong, the neighbours are always there to help.' Relations between neighbours join the farms of Ashworthy into a complicated network which extends outside the parish in all directions. Similar networks can be found in other parishes, joined together in an 'endless' pattern. Many of the neighbourly arrangements persist for year after year, others are short-lived; some activities, such as sheep-dipping and help in the harvest, are markedly seasonal, while some, for example borrowing and lending of machinery, take place throughout the year. There are farmers with many neighbours and a few with none at all. The network of neighbourly relations is not therefore a simple arrangement of permanent links joining farmstead to farmstead, but rather an irregular structure which changes from time to time.[1]

Neighbourliness covers many aspects of co-operation and mutual aid and there are widely recognized rules of behaviour which regularize its expression. Moreover, its scope is sharply defined : one may, for example, reasonably expect a neighbour to lend you a potato digger but never a large sum of money. Neighbours are often asked to collect parcels from shops in Longbridge but are rarely requested to witness a will. Many of these activities, which fall outside the range of neighbourliness, are considered to be 'family business', that is they take place within the kinship network. The networks of neighbourliness and kinship resemble each other in joining farm families in an endless, irregular pattern, but the kinship network, based on relationship through blood or marriage, has a much greater emotional content and exhibits regularities which enable one to talk in terms of a kinship *system*. The characteristics of this system are discussed in a later chapter: here we are concerned with its importance in the economy and in land-holding.

Many of the conjugal farm families in Ashworthy are linked together by kinship. Kindred, like neighbours, borrow and lend machinery and co-operate in many other ways in the day-to-day working of their farms; they help each other in crisis situations, such as serious illness, fire and flood. The importance of this

[1] See also below pp. 100–109.

wider network of kinship was demonstrated during the first day of the field work. The first person I interviewed was a farmer's wife who happened to be standing at the side of the road feeding chickens. I asked her how long she had lived in the farm and how she and her husband had come there. Her reply was:

'My husband was born in Wansley: his father came from there. His mother was an Ashworthy woman. His father was a hind in Wansley and he left there and rented land at Blackbury from his wife's people. He paid a proper rent though . . . John (i.e. the informant's husband) was a boy then. His father was killed in an accident when he was sixteen and he was too young to manage the farm, so his mother sold up and he went to work for John Stanlake as a labourer. It was wartime and there was plenty of overtime if you worked long hours, so he saved quite a bit. Then we got married and went to live at Marsh End with John's uncle, Thomas Graddon. We had a cottage. Uncle didn't ask any rent and I did his housework and milked the cows. He was a bachelor. My father gave me a cow and we kept a few hens and a pig.

'Then in 1952 John rented 92 acres of land and bought a second-hand tractor. He borrowed machinery from my brother at Hall Farm—over there—and started farming. My brother helped at harvest-time. . . . Then we bought this place—about six months later—when Fred Coles left, but we didn't move in because Uncle Tom wanted us to stay at Marsh End. He died in 1954 and left us some money and four cows. So we moved here and we could buy a bit of stock with the money. Now we've got 16 milk cows and 25 young animals. . . . We were very lucky. While we were at Marsh End John's grannie died in the village and left us some money . . . that was a big help. . . . When we were starting off we borrowed a lot from my brother. Now John and my brother have bought a dung spreader and a potato digger between them. We used to bale together too, but now we do it separate and the one who finishes first helps the other.'

This example is characteristic of the role of kindred in assisting the farm family and also of the range of kin from whom the greatest degree of help may be expected. Parents, grandparents, uncles, aunts, brothers and sisters—that is the people known in

Ashworthy as 'very close relatives' or 'the family'—are much more likely to be mentioned in such accounts as the one given above than 'more distant' relatives. There are, of course, many exceptions. On the one hand, closely related kin may behave in the way described by one farmer when talking of his family: 'Me father and his brother had farms next to each other at one time. They quarrelled with each other for four years.' On the other hand, a distant relationship may be invoked: 'When I was ready to retire I wanted to build a bungalow in the village here. I knew Sam Harvey had a nice bit of land, but he wouldn't sell to anybody. He sold it to me because I was a relative. . . . My grandfather and his grandfather were brothers.'

Thus kinship and neighbourliness form complementary or overlapping networks which join together the individual conjugal families and which help materially to reduce their dependence on their own limited resources. Seen from their point of view, their relations with neighbours and kin have become more and more important as the size of the farm household has declined. To return to the example of the farmer's wife once again. She and her husband farm 192 acres; their three young children are at school. In her own words: 'We would find it very hard if we didn't have my father and brother living near . . . and of course there's the other people too. Bill Ashton comes to combine for us. . . .' In contrast, there are a few families, who, for one reason or another, have no kindred in the locality and do not 'get on' with their neighbours. The extreme example is a middle-aged bachelor who farms a holding of 38 acres. He is a recluse, seldom seen by anyone. The concensus of opinion was that the farm was deteriorating rapidly in quality—'it's gone to the dogs. He doesn't farm it'. Other families, less unusual but lacking fully developed kin or neighbourly relations, are obliged to be relatively self-reliant. One such family, a childless couple who moved to Ashworthy from south-eastern England, have only one 'neighbour'. 'We get on very well with Mr. Daw over the way. He helps us a lot, although I'm afraid we can't do much in return. We hardly ever see the other farmers around here. We can manage all right as things are, but things would be bad if one of us was ill—you know, really ill. . . . As it is, it's hard work. I use the contractor of course—but it costs money.' The economic efficiency of any farm family depends in large measure, therefore, not only on its composition and its stage in the life cycle, but also on its place and participation in the kin and neighbour networks.

Family Farming and Continuity

The first section of this chapter has been concerned with the family as a unit of economic production. As one farmer remarked: 'Around here, farming is a family business.' It can, of course, only remain 'family business' as long as efficient means exist for its transmission from one generation to another. The process of transmission is of two, closely related, kinds. First, there is the handing on of skills, knowledge, experience and values within the farm family. A farmer cannot be produced overnight. As in all areas of family farming, parents in Ashworthy bring up their children to become farmers, educating them informally throughout childhood and adolescence. This is, of course, supplemented by the formal education provided by the schools. Secondly, there is the transmission of property, stock, machinery, money, etc.

Studies of other areas of family farming in Western Europe have shown clearly ways by which this continuity is achieved. A notable example is Arensberg's vivid account of the small farmers of County Clare in the west of Ireland.[1] The transmission of skills and knowledge is described in considerable detail:[2] Arensberg sums it up as follows:

'The child forms part of the productive unit which is his own family. His growing up is also an apprenticeship. He learns the techniques which will make him a full-fledged member of his class; but there is no divorce between technical and non-technical training. All he learns fits him for one end—to become a farmer-father-husband in a family of his own. . . .
The child sees his father as owner, director and principal worker of the farm. From his example, he learns which are men's tasks

[1] C. M. Arensberg, *The Irish Countryman* (London 1937). See also C. M. Arensberg and S. T. Kimball, *Family and Community in Ireland* (Cambridge, Mass. 1948).

[2] See Arensberg pp. 46–48, 55–60 and Ch. IV, 'Boys and Men'.

and he learns to value the skills they demand. In family delibera-
tions he learns too, the nice balance between the needs of household and land. . . .

This process is the daily experience of many years; it is very
gradual and is embedded in traditional social life.'

In this respect, Ashworthy is very like County Clare and
other areas of family farming. It is, for example, a common
practice for farmers to take their sons with them to the weekly
stock markets at Kimberford. As they sit through the sales, the
farmers comment almost continuously on the fine points of the
animals paraded before them and the prices which are paid.
The young men listen and learn : their turn will come when they
are fathers and farmers themselves.

The Irish farmers are a close-knit occupational group. Farmers'
children intermarry and marriage is described as a structural
'hinge' which joins the family and the land. It is at marriage
that a new farm family is created, that the land is passed on
from the older generation and its 'name on the land' is perpetuated.[1] The process begins when a farmer chooses one son
to inherit the family holding: 'His interest lies in choosing
among his sons the one he thinks will carry on most successfully.
There is no rule or norm in the matter.' In the course of time
there follows an elaborate match-making, the heir marries,
inherits the farm, and his parents retire. One daughter may
marry into a local farm family; the other children 'must
travel', i.e. they receive their share of the family fortune and
leave the family holding. 'They are not to be settled on the
land.' In this way continuity is achieved and the land is re-
tained within the family.

The main elements of this method of achieving continuity are
shown diagrammatically in Fig. 9. Both farm families in the
first generation have a son to inherit, a son who 'must travel'
and a daughter who marries into another farm household. In
the second generation one family has an only child, a son, who
will inherit, the other has a male heir and a son and daughter
who must leave the farm.

There are, of course, three possibilities not shown in the
diagram. Firstly, a man may have daughters only and 'a

[1] See Arensberg, Ch. III, 'The Family and the Land' for a full account.

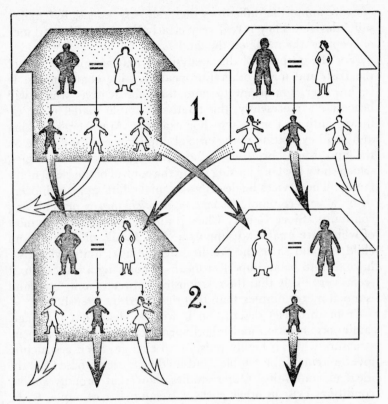

Fig. 9. Continuity and family farming in County Clare. The houses represent farms. The numbers refer to generations. The line of inheritance is shown by stippling the figures of the heirs.

stranger to the land' must be brought in by marriage. Secondly, a farmer may be childless (or remain unmarried) and, as Arensberg remarks: 'In such a situation barrenness is a curse and a disgrace.' Here the wider network of kindred becomes structurally important, and a kinsman, perhaps a cousin or nephew, comes to take over the farm. Thirdly, a farmer may die, and if his widow remarries, her second husband and his children are 'strangers to the land', who may be dispossessed by the heir whose 'name is on it'. We are told that these three possibilities are regarded as unfortunate occurrences and that the methods of overcoming the difficulties they raise are essentially 'make-shift' devices. They reveal very clearly the central importance of keeping 'the name on the land'.

(For the purposes of this analysis, we may accept this view of the Irish and many other European farming communities. It is, however, important to note that, for reasons which will become clear presently, this relatively simple model is by no means entirely convincing. For example, Arensberg's striking and lucid exposition of the crucial importance of 'the name on the land' is not borne out by the great majority of his examples, which show the land passing out of the control of the elementary family. The devices he describes as 'makeshift' appear, indeed, to be a very common, *perhaps an essential*, means of achieving continuity. Since County Clare is an area of small farms, most of which are unable to support a 'full' family of parents and children, and since the families are conjugal units, which we have seen to be an imperfect means of ensuring a succession, it seems very likely that the relationship between family and land is much more complex than that described by Arensberg.)

From this brief description it will be clear that marriage, family organization and inheritance are linked within a social structure which is highly resistant to change. Such a structure gives a remarkably stable land-holding system, based on the ideal of continuity. Other studies show that broadly similar conditions exist in other parts of Ireland. For example, R. H. Buchanan, in describing the patterns of settlement and land-holding in an Ulster townland, comments:

'Where possible the land must remain in the possession of the family. That was the accepted rule, for the people of Sheeplands display *the traditional values of all peasant societies in their passionate attachment to the family land*. If there were no children in the family to inherit the land, the farm would pass to the nearest blood relation; only in the very last resort would the owners endure the social disgrace of seeing the land sold to a stranger.'[1]

This emphasis on continuity and stability, so strikingly expressed in Ireland, is also found in works on societies with different social and economic systems in other parts of Western

[1] 'Rural Change in an Irish Townland 1890–1955', *The Advancement of Science* No. 56 (March 1958), p. 299. My italics.

Europe. In a Norwegian community, where the economic life is based partly on fishing and partly on farming, we are told that

'. . . . The territorial arrangement of the Bremnes population is fairly stable. The same fields are cultivated year after year, and new land comes into cultivation only slowly . . . land can be bought and sold, but there are several factors tending to discourage frequent sales of land. *Thus for the most part the same people go on living in the same houses and cultivating the same land from year to year. This provides, as it were, a stable environment in which social relations are maintained through the decades,* and a frame of reference by which individuals can relate themselves to other people.'[1]

Rural communities in France,[2] Sweden and other parts of Europe[3] appear to share these characteristics. They all approximate to Redfield's model of a peasant society—'one sees a peasant as a man who is in effective control of a piece of land to which he has long been attached by ties of tradition and sentiment. The land and he are parts of one thing, one old-established body of relationships. This way of thinking does not require of the peasant that he own the land or that he have any particular form of tenure or any particular form of institutional relationship to the gentry or the townsman.'[4]

When these European peasant communities are compared with rural society in England and Wales, it is clear that important differences exist. The British farmer is manifestly not one of Redfield's peasants and the great attachment to the family land appears to be absent. General comparisons are not, however, possible since there are only three published studies of British agricultural communities—one in England[5] and two

[1] J. A. Barnes, 'Class and Committees in a Norwegian Island Parish' *Human Relations*, Vol. VII, No. 1 (Feb. 1954), p. 41. My italics.

[2] See, for example, H. Mendras, *Etudes de Sociologie Rurale* (Paris 1953) on the village of Novis in the departement of Aveyron.

[3] See C. von Dietze, 'Peasantry' in *Encyclopaedia of the Social Sciences*, Vol. XII, pp. 48–53.

[4] R. Redfield, *Peasant Society and Culture* (Chicago 1956), pp. 27–28.

[5] The writer's *Sociology of An English Village: Gosforth* (London 1956).

in Wales.[1] All three are sociological surveys which analyse in some detail the system of family farming and the role of the family as an economic unit. In the Cumberland parish, a minority of the farmers—those who adhere to 'the old standards'—belong to families who have occupied the same holdings for centuries. They share with Arenberg's Irish farmers a deep feeling for the family land; as one of them put it, 'when you're born to a spot you're married to it'.[2] These families of 'the old standards' are striking evidence of the importance of continuity in land-holding and the strength of the family system, but it is clear on re-assessing the field material that their importance was over-emphasized. They amount to about twelve per cent of all the farmers, whereas fifty-five per cent had occupied their holdings for ten years or less. Gosforth is, indeed, very similar to Ashworthy in the movement of farm families within a restricted locality, as described in the last chapter.

The parish in north Montgomeryshire described by Rees seems much the same. Many of the farmers (fifty-five per cent) have acquired their holdings since 1900.[3] There appears to be little attachment to the allodial land: 'For the larger farmer economic advancement involves leaving the district. . . . The smaller farmer in Llanfihangel can better himself by acquiring a better farm within his native district.'[4] Thus in Cumberland, North Wales and in Ashworthy continuity of land-holding over a long period and the placing of a high value on the family land which goes with it are characteristic of a minority of farmers: the majority move from farm to farm, just as they probably do in the remainder of England and Wales.[5]

The difference between England and Wales on the one hand

---

[1] Alwyn D. Rees, *Life in a Welsh Countryside* (Cardiff 1950) and in A. D. Rees and E. Davies. (Eds.), *Welsh Rural Communities* (Cardiff 1960) the studies by D. Jenkins of Aberporth and T. Jones Hughes of Aberdaron.

[2] *The Sociology of An English Village*, p. 54.

[3] Rees, op. cit., pp. 184–5. Twenty per cent of the farm families have occupied their holdings for over a century and may well correspond to the 'old standards' group in Gosforth.

[4] Ibid., pp. 147–8.

[5] See pp. 44–5 above. *The National Farm Survey* figures suggest that long-term occupation is relatively uncommon.

and the peasant communities of Europe on the other in the value placed on the family holding is of fundamental importance in the social structure. In areas such as County Clare the land is, as it were, a constant to which the family organization has to be adjusted according to the logic of keeping the 'name on the land'. The need for non-inheriting sons 'to travel', or as in Norway to turn to fishing as an alternative, is—like the indemnity paid to all children but one in areas of joint inheritance such as that described by Mendras—essentially a device to ensure a rough equilibrium between the number of farm families and a given area of land. It is this equilibrium which provides the 'stable environment in which social relations are maintained' in the Norwegian parish which Barnes studied.

In England and Wales there is no such attachment to the family land to provide a 'constant', and therefore there is no need for the wider network of kindred to be used where the conjugal farm family fails to produce a male heir, but there is, nevertheless, a basic need for continuity of some kind if a family farming system is to be maintained. In the simplest terms this continuity is achieved by each farmer attempting to set up *all his sons* as farmers in their own right. Thus in Wales, Cumberland and the South-west one son inherits the home farm and the others are established in holdings elsewhere: 'The average farmer is relatively satisfied with his occupational station, and desires no better future for his children than that they too should become farmers or farmers' wives.'[1] *Now this situation is clearly inconsistent with a social structure based on the principle of keeping land in the hands of the same family from generation to generation, since—if it operates efficiently—there can never be more than a handful of farms available for non-inheriting sons in the course of any one generation.* There is moreover a fundamental inconsistency within the system itself. The farmers of Llanfihangel, Gosforth and Ashworthy firmly believe that the ideal family farm is one that can be handed on to the next generation: however, they do not necessarily attach this belief to one particular farm but rather to the holding they occupy when the son inherits. In other words, they conceive their responsibility to be the transmission of *a farm* to the heir and, for obvious

[1] Rees, op. cit., p. 147.

reasons, the last one they occupy is most suitable and convenient for this purpose. The son who inherits may, in turn, move to another farm in the course of time. While this might seem at first sight more flexible than, for example, the Irish system, its results are at least in one respect the same, i.e. that for every holding there is a son to inherit under ideal conditions. Unlike the peasant communities, therefore, there is a conflict between the ideals of family continuity and the desire to place non-inheriting sons in farms of their own.

Thus far the comparison of the two systems has been in terms of essentially simple models in order to point to crucial structural differences which have apparently not been analysed in any previous study. The analysis cannot, however, be taken much farther in this general form: it is therefore necessary to turn to an examination of continuity in Ashworthy to see how it is achieved in its particular geographical and historical context.

In Ashworthy, as elsewhere, the perpetuation of family farming requires (a) that each family maintain itself as a viable economic unit and (b) that the occupation of a farm be transmitted from one generation to the next. The first of these requirements is normally within the capabilities of the farm household, although—as we have seen earlier—it may cause hardship to individuals. Closely-related kindred outside the immediate family are of great importance in this context and they may, in such crises as serious illness or death, be the means of preventing the collapse of the family enterpise. For example, if a farmer should die leaving a wife and young children then it is usual for his widow to take over the running of the farm with the help of kindred. The people of Ashworthy regard such help as 'natural' and it is very exceptional for a family to be deprived of its livelihood in this way when there are kindred living in the locality. Only two instances could be discovered since 1900. One was the family, mentioned earlier in this chapter,[1] where the accidental death of the farmer resulted in his widow and young son leaving their farm. The holding was owned by the widow's father, who bought a cottage for her. When asked about the event, she remarked: 'Father didn't

[1] See p. 51.

think us could keep going properly on the farm. He was too old to help himself and there was nobody at home. He promised he would help when John (the son) was ready for a farm.' The second instance was that of a farmer with a large family who went bankrupt: he was forced to give up his tenancy and left Ashworthy. He found employment as a farm labourer and rented a small cottage: the older children, all adult, left home. This man has many close kindred in Ashworthy whose reason for not helping was apparently their view, widely accepted by local people, that bankruptcy is an individual responsibility. As one man remarked: 'Only fools go bankrupt.'

The second aspect of continuity—transmission of holdings from one generation to another—is very much more complex. In terms of the model described earlier, the ideal of handing over a farm to one son and placing the others on farms of their own can only be achieved, in a situation where the amount of cultivated land remains more or less fixed, by (a) some families dying out or leaving the land and (b) by some sons 'marrying in' to farm families where there are only daughters. At first sight, Ashworthy might appear to approximate to this model. In the period 1841 to 1960, ninety-six cases of direct transmission of the occupation of holdings following illness, retirement or death were recorded:

TABLE FIVE
Transmission of Occupation of Holdings.
Ashworthy 1841–1960

Transmitted to :	Number
One son	48
One daughter	12
Two or more sons jointly	12
Two daughters jointly	2
Son(s) and daughter(s) jointly	4
Wife	14
Other relatives	2
Other non-related persons	2

The table shows that in exactly half the total, occupation passed from father to son: of these, twelve were eldest sons and twenty-four were only sons. If joint occupation by sons is added, the proportion rises to nearly two-thirds of the total. Of the twelve farms which passed from father to daughter, ten were worked by the daughter's husband, who had 'married in'. The fourteen farms which passed from husband to wife are, of course, instances of transmission within the same generation, all of them designed to safeguard occupation until the children of the families were old enough to take over the farm themselves. Only four farms have passed outside the conjugal family unit.

During the same period, many of the farmers of the parish have placed their sons on holdings and helped them to start farming on their own account. Twenty instances were recorded but, for reasons which will be discussed later, there are probably many more which could not be confirmed. In contrast, evidence of families which have died out, or have left farming is relatively abundant. A superficial examination of the Parish Registers and other local documents shows that nearly all the yeoman farmers whose names appear prominently in the eighteenth and early nineteenth centuries have disappeared by the beginning of this century. Families who had lived on the same farms for at least a hundred years are now remembered only by the gravestones in the churchyard. The following two examples are representative:

(1) The Bond family. John Bond, born in 1797, was a prosperous yeoman and miller who had inherited nearly two hundred acres of land in Ashworthy. His eldest son, William, inherited his father's property in turn and farmed it during the latter half of the nineteenth century. He had six children, four of whom died as babies. The only surviving son, George, inherited the family holding. He died a bachelor in 1944 and his property passed to his spinster sister Mary: she died in 1951. The farm and stock were sold and the money realized on the sale was bequeathed to the Church.

(2) The Graves family. A family of substantial yeomen who had owned land in Ashworthy since at least the end of the seventeenth century. In the middle of the nineteenth century John Graves is recorded as owning nearly 350 acres in Ashworthy. The home farm passed on his death to William Henry, his fifth son, who had six children, one of whom died as a young man. The remaining five children inherited the farm jointly. One sold

his share to the others and emigrated to South Africa. The four left on the farm died without marrying, the last two within a few months of each other in 1924. The farm was sold and the estate passed to people who had no connection with farming or with Ashworthy.

Families who die out in this way are not confined to the yeomen: small farmers and tenants are well represented among those whose line ends with a spinster, bachelor or childless couple. The families who leave farming appear to be much fewer in number, although the evidence for the period before 1930 is very scanty and ambiguous. There have been two instances during recent years. The first, Edward Batton, who is married but has no children, sold his farm and became a haulage contractor after a serious illness. The second, George Fox, retired in 1959. He sold his farm and bought a house in Longbridge. His only child, Edward, does not wish to be a farmer and has left the district to work for an engineering firm.

It may seem, therefore, that conditions in Ashworthy have approximated to the 'ideal' situation described earlier. Many farmers' sons have taken over the occupation of their fathers' farms; others have acquired holdings which have become vacant through the dying out of a family or have married into households where there have been only daughters in the younger generation. Thus continuity is achieved by exploiting the failure of some families to reproduce or to produce sons, so that maintaining a balance between farmers and land is structurally based on or adjusted to imperfections in the conjugal family as a means of ensuring biological continuity. This is in sharp contrast to the peasant societies, such as Ireland, where— we are told—the maintenance of 'the name on the land' presupposes that the farm family does not die out, and where 'marrying in' or the resort to collateral kindred are 'makeshift' devices used to ensure continuity in 'exceptional' circumstances. In Ashworthy they are not exceptional but rather essential parts of the structure. There is a further, very important difference between the two systems. In peasant communities both the family system and the land-holding system appear to be essentially rigid: in Ashworthy, both are relatively flexible. As we have already seen, some families die out and are replaced by others; new families are created when sons leave home as farmers in their own right. This is a source of change inherent in the method of transmitting farms, but there are many more which are still to be examined. Before this can be done, however, it is necessary to approach the problem of continuity from a different starting point.

Some case histories

The evidence given in the last section of the pattern of transmission in Ashworthy as a whole must be regarded as no more than a crude measure of continuity, which tells us very little of the process as it works out in the individual family over several generations. To examine this it is necessary to describe the history of certain chosen families, which will in turn illustrate other important aspects of the general problem. The examples have been selected because they are representative of the fortunes of a large number of families in Ashworthy.

(a) *The Cornish family* (see Fig. 10). In 1835, Thomas Cornish, a fifty-year-old farmer, was tenant of Lower Arundle, a holding of forty-nine acres, and of Coombes Moor, fifty acres of rough grazing about a mile from the farm. He and his wife Elizabeth were born in Ashworthy. Two of his sons, James (born 1812) and William (born 1817), and his only daughter Mary (born 1819) lived at home: two single farm labourers made up the household. The oldest son John (born 1809) was working as a labourer on another farm in the parish.

Thomas Cornish died in 1846, three years after his daughter had married George Friend, a prosperous yeoman who owned a near-by farm. The two sons who had farmed with him became joint tenants of the two holdings. Their widowed mother lived with them at Lower Arundle. James remained a bachelor all his life. William married a local farmer's daughter in 1852 and had four sons and two daughters during the next twenty years. He died in 1880 and James became sole tenant. In 1883 William's widow, Harriet, inherited Crossfield, a farm of twenty-one acres, from her mother and moved there with her children and her brother-in-law James, then seventy-five years old. The move ended the family's association with Lower Arundle, which by this time had become known as 'Cornishes Arundle'. Changes of this kind, following inheritance, have occurred many times in Ashworthy.

Shortly after their arrival at Crossfield three of Harriet's sons appear to have left home: there is no further record of them in the parish. Probably the farm was too small to support the whole family. The remaining son, Henry James, married a local farmer's daughter in 1888, when he was twenty-one, and left home three years later to become a butcher at a village about thirty miles from Ashworthy. Like so many other men, he returned to the parish and the family farm when he inherited it: this was in 1897, when his mother died. He farmed Crossfield until his death in 1940, when his two daughters inherited it jointly. They were unmarried and had no brothers to work the farm; they leased it and bought a house in the village. Hannah died in 1942: her sister Jane sold the farm to David Cornish (see below) when the tenant died in 1959. He has split the holding, selling the farmhouse and two fields to a local smallholder: the remainder has been added to part of his own land, which adjoins Crossfield. This is a typical example of the way

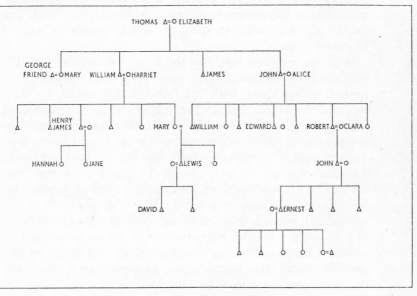

Fig. 10. The Cornish Family.

in which changes in the pattern of land-holding may be related to developments within the family.

A further branch of the family is descended from John, the eldest son of Thomas Cornish. He married Alice Blake in 1836, when he was twenty-seven and working as a farm labourer. Shortly after the birth of his first child in 1838, John obtained the tenancy of Little Southcott, a holding of 16 acres on poor land. In 1839 his first son was born and a year later the family moved to Maldon, a 'good' farm of 23 acres: three sons and a daughter were born there during the next eleven years. One son died in infancy. In 1854 John obtained the tenancy of Lower Blackbury (83 acres), the farm where his last two children were born. He is typical of the many men who have successfully climbed the 'agricultural ladder', moving to better farms as their fortunes prosper.

John's eldest son, Edward, married in 1862; he lived at home for two years and then, with his wife and first child, obtained the tenancy of Little Southcott just as his father had done. He remained there for ten years, but does not appear to have been successful for in 1875 he became a small-holder, living with his wife and eleven children in a cottage on two acres of land. The family left Ashworthy in 1882 or 1883 and nothing more is heard of them.

William, the third son, was the next to marry in 1874. His wife was Mary Cornish, his first cousin (see Fig. 10). They lived at Lower Blackbury with his father and brought up their two children there. William became the tenant but was forced to leave the farm in 1889 when the owner sold it to the Ashworthy estate. The family moved to the village and rented land near-by until William retired from farming. His only son Lewis, who had married in 1904, bought Ash Farm (62 acres) from his mother's brother in 1910. He farmed it until 1953, when he, his wife and two sons moved back into their old house in the village. Ash Farm is now rented and William's son David farms about 120 acres of land, part of it bought at the sale of the Ashworthy estate, part rented near the village and part acquired recently from Jane Cornish, his mother's first cousin. His brother is prevented from farming by ill-health.

Robert Cornish, the fourth son, was married in 1874 to Clara

Stone, daughter of the prosperous tenant of Eastbridge. When his only child John was born in 1875, Robert was tenant of Eastbridge and Pool farms, 240 acres in all. The family was living at Eastbridge by about 1880 and by the end of the century John had succeeded his father as tenant. He bought the holding (113 acres) between 1900 and 1909 and added a further 30 acres when an adjoining farm was split into three parts in 1932. His eldest son Ernest took over the running of the farm about this time and is the present owner. He had married the daughter of a neighbouring farmer in 1929: as the only child she had inherited her father's farm in 1938, so that the family now owns and works a compact holding of over 300 acres. Ernest has two sons and three daughters who live and work at home. His three younger brothers left Ashworthy as young men: two are successful farmers, the other owns a large bakery in Longbridge.

This account of the history of one family group contains most of the elements that make for change in Ashworthy—the agricultural ladder, the movement of sons from home on or shortly after marriage to begin as farm families in their own right, the change of farm following inheritance, the amalgamation of farms following marriage, the break in continuity caused by a change of landlord, the movement of individuals in and out of the parish.

(b) *The Glass family* (see Fig. 11). The Glass family have lived at Wadefield (94 acres) for at least 160 years, a record of continuous occupation which is unrivalled in Ashworthy. In the early years of the nineteenth century James Glass, a yeoman born in 1772, farmed the holding together with his younger brother William. In the 1841 Census *Schedule*, James, by that time a widower, is shown with his brother William—a bachelor —and four children, Robert (born 1808), Henry (born 1814), Jane (born 1815) and Mary (born 1817). Later that year James bought Blackdown Tenement, a farm of 42 acres: shortly after, Henry and Jane moved there and began farming. James died in 1844 and Robert, the son who had remained at home, inherited Wadefield. He was married in the same year to a yeoman's daughter from the neighbouring parish of Medford.

Robert had seven children. His youngest son Samuel inherited Blackdown Tenement when his bachelor uncle Henry died. Samuel was an improvident and intemperate man who sold his farm field by field and ended his days as a farm labourer. The third son, John, married in 1868 and moved into Heathbury parish to begin farming on his own account. He had two sons, Alexander and Nicholas. The second son, Richard, appears to have left Ashworthy as a young man but returned at the end of the century as tenant of Longbarrow. He died there in 1909.

Edward, the eldest son, remained at Wadefield and inherited the farm when his father died. Both men made considerable changes in the farm by selling parts of it and acquiring tracts of adjacent farms. Edward married but had no children. When he died in 1918, the farm passed to his nephew Alexander, who had been living at Wadefield for some years. Alexander was married and had one child, James, who inherited the farm in turn on his father's death in 1939. James, a bachelor of fifty, is the present owner.

The Glass family is representative of the small group of farmers who, in their attachment to the family holding, share a closer resemblance to the 'old standards' of Gosforth and the small farmers of Ireland than to the farmers who live around them. Continuity on the family farm is achieved by bringing in 'a close relative' as male heir when there is no son to inherit. On the other hand, the Glass family is characteristic of Ashworthy in changing the extent of its farm[1] and in the placing of non-inheriting sons in farms of their own.

(c) *The Doyle family* (see Fig. 12). There is a tradition in this family that two brothers came from Ireland to the West Country 'a long time ago'—'they were the first Doyles to come round here and we're all descended from them'. The earliest mention of the name in local records occurs in 1809, when the banns of marriage between Charles Doyle and Ann Martin were published. Charles, who was born in Kimberford, was a farm labourer who lived in a cottage near the boundary of Ash-

---

[1] Cf. the attitude of 'the old standards' in Gosforth, where even minor changes in the extent of a farm are strongly resisted: *The Sociology of An English Village*, p. 77 and *passim*.

worthy: he had two sons by 1817, when he moved back into Kimberford. A third son, Bryan, was born there in 1819. Little more is known of Charles Doyle. After a period in a neighbouring county during the 1830's he disappears, but returned to the Ashworthy area in the early 1850's as the tenant of a large farm (240 acres) in Broadpen parish. His wife and a nineteen-year-old son lived with him.

Charles's third son Bryan probably remained in Kimberford until 1846, when he acquired the tenancy of Oak Moor (in Ashworthy), a 63-acre holding. Between 1862 and 1868 he moved to Medford and returned to Ashworthy in 1876 when he became tenant of Redcliffe, a farm of 547 acres. The family moved once again in 1890, to a large farm in Birchstowe: Bryan died there in 1897, a prosperous and very successful

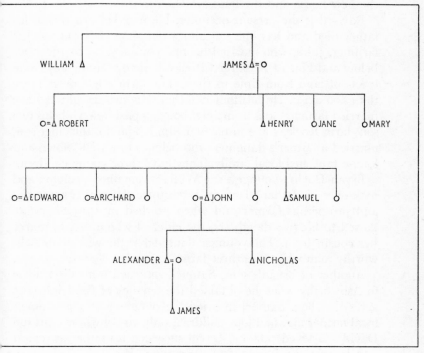

Fig. 11. The Glass Family.

farmer. He had at least seven children, but nothing is known of four of them after their births were registered in Ashworthy. The eldest son, Thomas, was born at Oak Moor in 1859. He married a local farmer's daughter early in 1890, shortly before moving with his father to Birchstowe, where his first son John was born in the same year. Thomas returned to Ashworthy about three years later and worked as a hind until 1897, when he obtained the tenancy of Rocky Lane, a farm of 125 acres. Edward, his second son, was born there in 1900. Thirty years later Thomas bought 20 acres of land about half a mile from Rocky Lane, built a house there and moved into it with his son Edward. They farmed it with a further 30 acres rented from a local landowner. The tenancy of Rocky Lane passed to John, the eldest son, who bought it when the Ashworthy estate was sold in 1935. Thomas Doyle died in 1934 and Edward inherited the new house and the land attached to it.

Edward is the present occupier. He married just before his father died and has one son and a daughter. His son has left farming. John, who married his first cousin Mary in 1924 (see below and Fig. 12), enlarged Rocky Lane by buying adjoining tracts of land from time to time. The farm now covers more than 200 acres. He has four children. His two daughters have married farmers' sons from neighbouring parishes, while his two sons farm Rocky Lane in partnership. Benjamin, the elder son, married a farmer's daughter who belongs to a well-known and long-established local family. They have three young children.

Bryan Doyle's youngest son William remained at home and took over his father's farm in Birchstowe. He was a successful and prosperous farmer and when he died in 1915 his estate passed to his two daughters, the elder of whom was to marry her cousin John. The younger daughter is the wife of an Ashworthy man who owns three farms.

Another of Bryan's sons, Samuel, returned from Birchstowe to Ashworthy when he obtained the tenancy of Eastleigh (135 acres) in 1893. Samuel married the daughter of a prominent local farmer and had four children, only one of whom—his son David—survived infancy. David suceeded his father as tenant and bought the farm a few years later. He also acquired an adjoining farm of 56 acres and other tracts of land in the parish.

He now farms over 200 acres and also owns several other holdings in Ashworthy and neighbouring parishes which he has bought or inherited. He is widely considered to be one of the most successful and wealthy farmers in the district. He has one son, who married a farmer's daughter, and two grandsons. His son works at home.

The Doyle family illustrates well how a steady climb up the agricultural ladder may be reinforced by marriage within the kin group and outside it. It also shows the relationship between mobility of farm families and the process of continuity taking place within the context of the Ashworthy area and not merely within the parish. As in the Cornish family, some branches of the Doyle family group flourish and expand, while

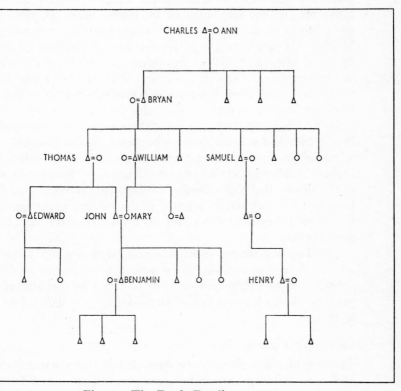

Fig. 12. The Doyle Family.

others contract or die out, leaving their holdings for kindred to take over.

(d) *The Tapson family* (see Fig. 13). Thomas Tapson, born in 1810 in a village twelve miles from Ashworthy, was a farm labourer who came to the parish as a young man. He married a domestic servant and they had three sons. The youngest son went as a young man to a neighbouring county and worked there as a farm labourer all his life. The second son, Andrew, acquired the tenancy of Poolfield, a 72-acre farm which he bought shortly before he died. His eldest daughter, Jane, inherited it and it is now farmed by her only son.

Reginald, the eldest son, worked first as a farm labourer and then as a hind. In 1895, when he was forty-five, he quarrelled with his employers and accepted the tenancy of Church Farm (70 acres), where he remained for fifteen years. In 1910 he moved to Longbarrow (409 acres) as a tenant and then bought Maldon (21 acres) in 1923. He died in 1927. Of his thirteen children, five sons and four daughters lived to be adults. One son emigrated to Australia, another—Robert—left home as a young man and worked on many farms in the district before buying a holding in Halton. Ill-health forced him to sell it and retire prematurely. The remaining three sons, John, James and Herbert worked at home. John, a bachelor, died at Longbarrow when he was twenty-nine; James, Herbert and two sisters inherited Maldon jointly when their father died. James and one of the sisters died there during the last war. Herbert sold the farm in 1947 and bought a house in the village, where he now lives with his spinster sister and his brother Robert. All three are childless.

The Tapsons are representative of a large group of families who farm land in Ashworthy for a time, perhaps two or three generations, and then give up their holdings for one reason or another—very often the failure to produce a new generation of farmers.

Continuity: a general view

The case histories given above show clearly that the continuity of family farming cannot be understood in terms of family structure alone, but only by examining the family in its particular geographical, social and historical context. As we have already noted, the milieu in which the farmers of Ashworthy live is, in many important respects, contantly changing. The sources of these changes and their significance in maintaining an equilibrium between farm families and the land must now be considered.

(i) *Changes in the farm population.* During the last hundred and fifty years the number of farm families has changed little in Ashworthy: on the other hand, the size of the total farm population has declined appreciably, largely because farmers' families are much smaller. This change will be examined in a later chapter, but it must be discussed briefly at this point because of its importance in the analysis of continuity. In the days when farm families were large, very few men succeeded in placing all their sons on a holding of their own. Occasionally, certain wealthy yeoman with a relatively small number of sons, such as James Glass, were able to do this, but in the majority of families some sons became farm labourers and others left farming to become rural craftsmen, village tradesmen, etc.

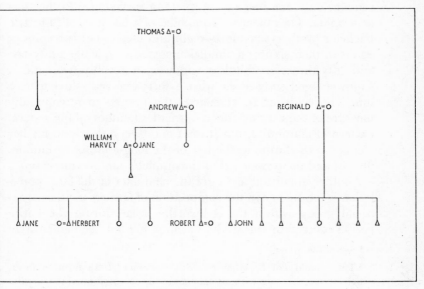

Fig. 13. The Tapson Family.

73

It may well be that the idea of 'finding a place' for every son grew up gradually with the decrease in family size and that formerly some farmers' sons were expected 'to travel'—as in rural Ireland. It seems at least to have been general among the poorer and smaller farmers, as parts of the case histories show. However, they also reveal that the decrease in family size may have different, even opposite, effects. In many families it has simplified the problem of continuity, for example where there is only one son or perhaps two. Alexander Glass and David Doyle are typical instances. On the other hand, the decrease has meant that there is an increasing number of farmers who have only daughters to succeed them or who have no children at all, for example the three surviving Tapsons and Henry James Cornish. Such a situation may result in the disappearance of a family after many generations of farming and it seems likely that the decline of the yeoman in Ashworthy is a striking aspect of this demographic change. Prosperous and long-established families like the Bonds, Graves,[1] Lobbs, Downs, Woolridges, Woodmans, Jordans and Coles died out between 1920 and the present day. Moreover, of the few yeoman families who still remain, only one has any prospect of surviving into the next generation. The others are composed of a bachelor of fifty; two bachelor brothers aged forty-eight and fifty-three; two spinster sisters in their sixties; a childless married couple aged fifty-one and fifty-three; a childless widower of seventy-two, and a widower aged sixty-seven with a forty-one-year-old bachelor son. The evidence is, of course, too limited to attempt any measure of the varying effects of smaller families on the general pattern of continuity, but it does point very clearly to further change in the future as the last of the long-established families die out and the proportion of 'incomplete' families increases.

Another important aspect of the character of the farm population is the change in the composition of farmers as an occupational group within the Ashworthy area[2] during the entire period covered by this study. Farming has not been an entirely

[1] See above p. 62.

[2] This should not be confused with movement from farm to farm, which often takes place without changes in the composition of the families who move.

hereditary occupation. Farm labourers have bought or rented small-holdings, moved to farms and become farmers. Successful and prosperous farmers like David Doyle and Ernest Cornish are descendants of agricultural workers, a distinction they share with at least twenty others out of the seventy-five occupiers in the parish. A further twenty-four belong to families who have been farmers since at least 1800, while the remainder are of unknown origin or come from families in other occupations. The rise in status from labourer to farmer is an important feature of the history of Ashworthy which, as we shall see later, has widespread effects on aspects of the social structure other than those being discussed here.

The men who have entered farming from other occupations form a separate group, which has appeared in the area in recent years, and has grown most rapidly since the end of the last war. It is composed of the 'Up Country Johnnies'. They include at present a former civil engineer, a doctor, two solicitors, an executive in an insurance firm, two solicitors' sons, one doctor's son and a professional soldier. Four are farmers' sons, but since they come from outside the West Country and appear in local eyes to speak and behave exactly like the other 'strangers' they are considered to be 'one of them' and not 'real farmers'. The newcomers have competed with the local people for available farms and the increased demand for vacant holdings in many parts of the South-west occurred quickly and was large enough to produce a miniature 'land boom'. The value of many farms rose above reasonable economic levels so that between 1945 and about 1955 many farmers were unable or unwilling to pay the high prices demanded for them. It was said in Ashworthy that 'things are better now' and that 'you'm able to buy a place for a fair price'. The period when some farms changed hands between one 'Up Country Johnny' and another at least once a year is over and the number of newcomers has declined. More and more holdings are sold at prices that are generally considered to be reasonable.

It is by no means clear how far the arrival of the 'new' farmers has upset the balance between farms and the established owners and tenants, particularly since farmers as a group have been characterized by loss and replacement over a long period.

Furthermore, their arrival has occurred at a time 'when the effects of a decrease in family size are becoming apparent. It seems certain, however, that the coming of the 'Up Country Johnnies' has considerably affected the recruitment of farmers from the ranks of the agricultural labourer and small-holder. The 'agricultural ladder' is long established in Ashworthy and some idea of its importance can be seen in the case histories. Men have moved steadily from small-holding to poor farm to better land until they acquire 'a good place'. The existence of farms on ill-drained, heavy land which is extremely difficult to work and yields little profit, but which could be rented or bought cheaply, has been an essential part of the progression. The new-comers, attracted by the relatively low prices of these farms and unaware of their serious drawbacks, bought them whenever they came up for sale and so removed a vital rung in the ladder. Many of the new men failed to farm these marginal holdings successfully and a large proportion of them have changed hands six or more times in a few years. There are still enough 'strangers' coming into the district to ensure that such farms can usually be sold above their true value and therefore there is a scarcity of 'cheap' farms for labourers and hinds who wish to become farmers.[1] Thus the opportunities for following in the footsteps of men like John Cornish and Reginald Tapson have become very much fewer.

The total effect of the demographic changes as a whole seems to have been one of intensifying the 'dynamic equilibrium' between men and land to some degree. The decrease in family size does not appear to have reduced the demand for farms by farmers' sons: very probably it is the number of farmers' sons who are *not* placed on farms of their own that has declined. At the same time, smaller families have meant that an increased proportion of farmers have been unable to provide a successor

---

[1] There are, of course, other factors which have made the progression up the agricultural ladder more difficult in recent years. Increased mechanization, for example, has considerably enlarged the amount of capital needed to start farming. Recent regulations governing the sale of milk have prevented many men from taking advantage of the monthly milk cheque as a means of financing their running costs in their early years of farming.

to follow them in their holdings. This, however, has to be set against the increased demand for vacant holdings with the arrival of the 'Up Country Johnnies', who have to some extent disrupted the entry into farming of labourers and small-holders. Thus the situation is one of a constantly changing balance between conflicting forces. The balance cannot be reduced to statistical terms because of insufficient evidence and because of the immense practical difficulties in collecting data for an area large enough to justify quantitative analysis. The problem is complicated further by the movement of farm families within the Ashworthy area: this is a further source of change which will now be discussed.

(ii) *The movement of farm families.* It was shown in the last chapter that there is a considerable movement of farmers from farm to farm, both within Ashworthy and also between it and a number of other parishes (see Fig. 8). Each parish will have its own territorial pattern of movement, extending 'outwards' in much the same way as the kinship and friendship 'networks' described by Barnes for a Norwegian parish.[1] As a result, the collection of field material for an analysis of continuity presents many intractable problems. For example, many of the families who have farmed in Ashworthy in the last century and a half have come from other parishes and have left to farm elsewhere: they could not be interviewed and the documentary sources normally provide very little information about them. Even more important, there is no statistical 'universe' which can be fixed to measure continuity, since the network has no discernable external boundary.

The case histories reveal that the movement is of two kinds. One is when a farmer's son leaves home (often with a wife and children) to begin farming in his own right. Edward Cornish and Samuel Glass are typical examples. The first acquired a tenancy, the second moved to a farm he had inherited. Of the twenty farmers' sons who have moved in this way, only four have remained within Ashworthy; twelve have gone to farms

[1] J. A. Barnes, op. cit., pp. 43–44 'This network runs across the whole of society and does not stop at the parish boundary. It links Bremnes folk with their kinsmen and friends in other parishes as well as knitting them together within the parish.'

elsewhere in the area, while four are men now living in Ashworthy whose parents live in near-by parishes. This kind of mobility is, therefore, a direct consequence of the practice of placing non-inheriting sons on holdings of their own. The second type of movement is where the farmer himself changes farms. Here the motives are much more complex. One is, of course, the progression up the agricultural ladder from a poor farm to a better one, for example John Cornish or Reginald Tapson. A second is the inheritance of a holding, either by the farmer or by his wife, as in the cases of Harriet Cornish and William Harvey, who married Jane Tapson. A third reason, which is quite as common as the first two, is where a farmer moves to a larger holding to support a growing family. John Cornish's move from Maldon to Lower Blackbury may well be of this kind, and there are many more recent examples in the parish. Again, there is the reverse kind of movement, which happens when a farmer decides he is no longer able to work a large holding and finds a smaller one, often leaving a son behind to carry on. Thomas Doyle is a typical instance.

These motives are clearly connected with or the results of the cycle of development of the farm family and the operation of the family system. The agricultural ladder is essentially a device for improving the family fortunes. There are, however, other reasons which are not directly related to the family. The most important of these has been the intervention of a landowner, particularly when a farm or estate is sold or when a lease comes to an end. William Cornish was one of a number of men who have been obliged to move in such circumstances. When the Redcliffe estate was sold, three of the smaller farms were amalgamated and their tenants were given notice to quit. All three left Ashworthy. Changes of this kind have, of course, become much rarer with the great increase in the proportion of owner-occupier farms in Ashworthy, but they still occur occasionally and are important in many of the surrounding parishes, where the number of tenants is relatively high.

The reasons which have been given probably cover the greater part of the farm-to-farm movement. Of the minority that remains, some can be accounted for in financial or economic terms—notably a high proportion of the 'Up Country

Johnnies' who have been forced to move to smaller farms after failing to succeed in large ones, some as a response to a set of unusual circumstances, while a small residue defy explanation. There is, for example, the farmer who quite recently sold a 90-acre farm and bought an adjoining farm of 93 acres. The move from farmhouse to farmhouse was less than a quarter of a mile. He gave no reason other than 'I just wanted a change' and several other experienced farmers said that they could think of no explanation. Two thought he was 'soft in the head'.

Taken as a whole, the movement from farm to farm may be regarded as a general consequence of the working of a family farming system in an area of limited good land which has experienced changes in land ownership. The movement emphasizes above all the absence of a deep attachment to the family holding and the changes inherent in the attempt to achieve continuity through all the sons of a family rather than one. The few families which place a high value on a particular farm, such as the Glass family at Wadefield, stand out in sharp contrast to the farmers around them.

The mobility of farm families also exaggerates the flexible relationship between a changing farm population and the land it occupies. Leasehold and freehold farms become available much more frequently than would occur in stable conditions: holdings for sale or rent must be relatively rare in rural communities where 'the name on the land' is of central importance. Moreover, since farm-to-farm movement takes place in the form of an 'endless' network, the working out of the process of continuity is diffused over an area much larger than Ashworthy itself.

It is, indeed, tempting to suggest that a considerable territory is a necessary condition for the operation of such a dynamic structure. From the evidence of the extent of the movement given in the last chapter it would seem that continuity must at least be considered in terms of the *social area* of which Ashworthy is part. It is for this reason that a simple model, based on conditions within the parish, is useful only in a preliminary way.

(iii) *The changes in land-holding.* The movement of farmers and changes in their composition as a group have taken place within a land-holding system which is itself changing. The latter was

79

documented in the last chapter, where it was shown that while the field pattern has altered little, occupation and owner-ship have changed very considerably throughout the period since the beginning of the nineteenth century. Some of the changes have had obvious effects on continuity in individual families. The enclosure of the common increased the amount of cultivated land in Ashworthy, and led to the creation of three new farms, as well as adding substantially to the size of many existing holdings. Some farms have been amalgamated and others sub-divided. The creation of new estates and their later division into individual owner-occupier farms has always been accompanied by changes in the occupation of farms.

In general, however, changes in land-holding have occurred without the displacement of families. Many farms have in-creased or decreased in extent through the sale or exchange of fields as often as six or seven times during their occupation by one family. The importance of changes in land-holding lies not so much in its direct effects on continuity in particular families, but rather in the way it contributes to and is a reflection of an attitude towards the relationship between family and land. In Ashworthy, continuity is seen to be the handing-on of a way of life, not of a particular tract of land. A farmhouse may have certain sentimental associations, but the land that goes with it is, as it were, a means to an end, to be sold or transformed according to circumstances.

*   *   *

The main purpose of this chapter has been to examine the way in which family farming is perpetuated in Ashworthy in terms of the ecological relationship between man and the land. The conditions described are, of course, peculiar to a small area of the West Country, but it is believed that they are broadly characteristic of a great part of England and Wales, and that they differ considerably from other areas of family farming in Western Europe. In the peasant communities of countries such as Eire, the logic of 'keeping one's name on the land' enforces a sequence to which the family must conform. The balance between farm families and the land, expressed through the land-holding system, is, we are often told, essentially stable and highly resistant to change. The family is part of a wider kinship system, which is structurally important in ensuring continuity.

In Ashworthy, as in most of England and Wales, the social and economic environment in which the farm family operates is made up of complex elements subject to rapid or radical change and often in conflict with each other. This dynamic situation is exacerbated in Ashworthy by the nature of the geographical conditions, which make considerable demands on the farmer and stimulate mobility. Moreover, the conjugal family which lasts only one generation is an imperfect instrument for ensuring continuity and it is only rarely that the wider network of kindred is called upon to maintain 'the name on the land'. Seen as a whole, therefore, the equilibrium between family and land is achieved in a complicated way, characterized by irregular shifts and internal changes in structure.

In Fig. 14 an attempt is made to represent this situation in a much simplified form. Four farms are shown in the first generation, from left to right, the large farm, Three Chimneys; a rather smaller one, Two Chimneys; the small farm Gable End; and One Chimney Farm. In Three Chimneys the only child is a son, who inherits when his parents die. In Gable End the farmer is childless and his family dies out. In One Chimney the only child is a daughter. In Two Chimneys there are three sons, one of whom inherits the family holding: a second marries into One Chimney and the third is bought Gable End. Thus in the transition from the first generation to the second, the absence of a deep attachment to the family land and the weaknesses of the conjugal family as a means of ensuring continuity are clearly apparent.

In the second generation further changes occur. The bachelor in Three Chimneys dies, the holding comes up for sale and is bought by the owner of Two Chimneys, moving up the agricultural ladder. Two Chimneys becomes vacant and is sold to an 'Up Country Johnny'. The family in Gable End are childless.

In the third generation Three Chimneys passes to the only son and the daughter leaves home. Two Chimneys passes to the only son and the daughter marries into Gable End, bought for the son of One Chimney when the farm came on the market on the death of the childless couple. With no son at home in One Chimney the daughter inherits and the farm is run by a man who 'marries in'.

The fluid relationship between family and land is seen clearly in the changes which occur in the original family of Two Chimneys (the men are 'stippled') over three generations. The 'breaks' in continuity are seen as families composed of a bachelor or childless couple die out, and in the entry of the 'Up Country Johnny'.

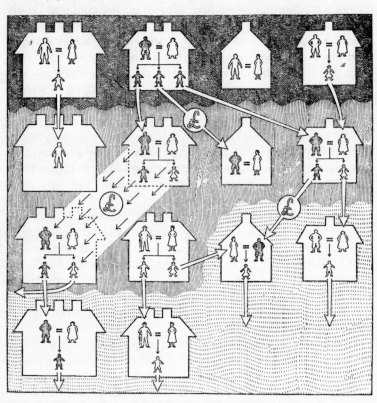

Fig. 14. Continuity and family farming in Ashworthy. The houses represent farms of different size. Each type of background shading represents one generation. The '£' sign indicates the purchase of a farm. The figure in the bowler hat with an umbrella is an 'Up Country Johnny'.

The essential difference between the situation shown in Fig. 14 and that found in County Clare, shown in Fig. 9, is that while the Irish system is stable and self-perpetuating and can be seen to 'work' as a simple model, in Ashworthy the balance between family and land is dynamic, partly for structural reasons and partly because of elements independent of family farming as such. Fig. 14 is not, therefore, the representation of a non-mathematical model, but only perhaps of part of one, the operation of which cannot, from the evidence available, be fully described at present. For this reason also it is not possible to examine further the doubts which were raised briefly above (p. 56) concerning the validity of the widely accepted model of the extremely stable and simple structure of the family-land relationship in peasant communities. It can at least be said, however, that most of the vivid case histories quoted by Arensberg—to take one example—are entirely consistent with the situation which has been described for Ashworthy. Perhaps further research will show that even peasant farming is characterized by the complex internal changes in equilibrium which are so striking a feature of the social structure of an English parish.

CHAPTER FOUR

MAN AND THE LAND (II)

THE starting point of the last chapter was that the farm family is both a social and economic unit. Decisions and actions which affect the size, layout and economy of a farm also affect the lives of the individuals in the family who live on it and, equally, changes in the family bring about adjustments in the control and operation of the economy. The countryman makes no distinction between these two aspects. The most striking changes occur when one generation succeeds another: the first part of this chapter examines these changes and their relationship to the family structure.

In all the rural areas of the British Isles which have been studied, the 'complete' farm family is composed of a farmer, his wife and unmarried children. This elementary family lasts for one generation and is broken up and replaced by a new family when one son, who is to inherit his father's farm, marries and begins farming in his own right. Thus in Eire,[1] central Wales[2] and Cumberland,[3] marriage and inheritance go hand-in-hand. In all three, the marriage of the inheriting son is the focal point of the transition from one generation to another. There are, however, important differences between them. In County Clare, the parents retire to the 'West room' of the home farm when their son marries.[4] In Montgomeryshire, farmers rarely retire, so that a son cannot inherit the farm until his father dies and cannot marry while his mother is alive or while there are brothers at home.[5] In Cumberland, the parents normally retire

[1] Arensberg and Kimball, op. cit., p. 107. 'It (marriage) is a central focus of rural life, a universal turning point in individual histories.' See also Chs. VI and VII.

[2] Rees, op. cit., Ch. V.

[3] *Sociology of An English Village*, pp. 45–58.

[4] Arensberg, op. cit., p. 78.

[5] Rees, op. cit., pp. 68–69.

to a house or cottage near the home farm, but the rule that a
son may not marry while his mother remains at home is strictly
observed.[1]

In spite of these differences, the cardinal relationship between
marriage and inheritance—and therefore between family and
land—lies at the centre of any explanation of continuity in these
three areas. Ashworthy is quite different. Marriage is *not*
necessarily associated with inheritance : there is no rule that a
son many not marry while his mother lives at home : the
transition from one generation to another does not unite the
transfer of economic control, ownership of land, the creation
of new family ties and a change in status into one interlocking
whole when the inheriting son marries. In Ashworthy these
changes are spread over a variable period of time and they are
therefore much less spectacular. This can be seen from the case
histories of farm families given towards the end of the last
chapter. William Cornish (p. 64) did not marry until six years
after he had taken over the family holding jointly with his
brother on his fathers' death. His widowed mother lived with
him after his marriage. Henry James Cornish (p. 65) married
while living with his widowed mother, and although he was
the only son remaining at home, he left three years later : he did
not inherit the farm for another six years. David Doyle (p. 70)
married and lived with his parents for about ten years before
he took over his father's farm : David's son, who has two children and has been married for nearly eight years, lives with his
father.

The apparent lack of a relationship between marriage and
taking over a farm of one's own extends also to the sons who do
not remain at home. Whereas in Eire, Wales and Cumberland
sons who are placed on farms of their own marry when they
leave their parents to start farming in their own right, in Ashworthy they sometimes marry and remain with parents for
several years before moving into a new farm. Edward Cornish
(p. 66) is a typical example.

In order to understand this difference between Ashworthy
and the other British communities, it is necessary first to examine

[1] *Sociology of An English Village*, pp. 46–47, 51.

the means by which farms pass from one generation to another. In Eire and Wales at least, the farmers are owner-occupiers, so that a son who takes over his father's farm also inherits it in the strict sense. Thus in County Clare, the 'writings' which form an essential part of the match-making that leads to the marriage of the heir are in effect a legal conveyance of the land from father to son.[1] In Ashworthy, transmission is a rather complicated procedure, which may take several forms. The first, and simplest, is when a farmer retires and conveys his holding to a son, who therefore inherits and assumes control of the farm at the same time. A second form is when a farmer dies while still in control of the farm and a son or daughter inherit. Thirdly there is the partnership agreement between a farmer and one or more of his sons. When the farmer dies, occupation and possibly ownership pass to the other partner or partners. Much more common than these three, however, is the form in which control and inheritance are separated. Here the *control* of the farm passes to the inheriting son when the farmer retires or dies: the son does not *inherit* the farm until both his parents die, since it is customary in Ashworthy for a farmer to leave his holding to his widow during her lifetime or until she remarry. Moreover, as we shall see later, there are very often complications in inheritance itself which emphasize the separation between it and the transference of economic control.

These forms of transmission apply only to owner-occupier farms. On tenant farms, possession normally passes from father to child on death or retirement, but the son (or daughter) does not *inherit* the farm in the strict legal sense. Under the former 'three lives' system and more recently under a short lease, many farmers' sons have negotiated a new tenancy agreement with the owner of the farm. Instances have occurred of a landlord refusing to allow a farmer's son to take over the tenancy on his father's death; the last was in 1954.

Thus transmission of occupation with control and inheritance are not necessarily identical in Ashworthy. It is likely that the two have become more closely related in recent years as the proportion of owner-occupiers has increased, making it possible

[1] Arensberg and Kimball, op. cit., pp. 115–18.

for more men to convey their holdings to their children when they retire; but in general, marriage, the taking over of the home farm, and its inheritance are still quite separate events which take place over a considerable period of years. Some idea of their relationship may be gained by examining in detail the cases of direct transmission of holdings given in Table Five above (p. 61): for convenience we will first consider marriage and the taking over of a farm, without distinguishing between transference of control and inheritance.

Of the forty-eight sons who succeeded their fathers, twenty-three were married at least one year before they took over the home farm. A further fifteen were, or still are, bachelors. Of the remaining ten, seven were married after they took over the farm, four of them after a period of several years. Only three were married immediately before taking over a farm owned and worked by their parents: they are unusual instances because their families each owned two holdings which were farmed as a unit. When the sons married they left home and moved into the 'second' farmstead and began working the land attached to it on their own.

Of the twelve examples of joint succession by sons, six were or are both bachelors; three were sets of bachelors when they took over the home farm but one married later in each set; three were instances where one brother was already married and one a bachelor when they obtained possession. In the four instances of joint succession by brothers and sisters, all but one man were single when they succeeded and have not married up to the present. The two examples of joint succession by daughters are much the same: all were single when they took over and all have remained unmarried. In contrast, ten of the twelve daughters who succeeded alone were already married; the other two remained spinsters all their lives.

It will be clear, therefore, that in Ashworthy marriage and the transference of control are not associated with each other as they are in other parts of Britain. On the other hand, there may be a tendency for sons who are placed on holdings of their own to marry near the time they leave home. The number of recorded instances is small, but of the twenty men in this category, fourteen married shortly before moving into their own farms, four were already married at least one year before, one was and has remained a bachelor, and one married two years after he left home.

Marriage on the farms of Ashworthy is not a structural 'hinge' linking family and land as it is in other parts of Britain. It does, of course, mark a change of status for the individual, but it does not bring about the striking changes in economic and social relations within the family which are so important in other communities. Indeed, if the farmers of Ashworthy are to be believed, the changes which occur are very small:

'I think it's a good thing for a lad to marry. It makes 'e more responsible and he'll work with his father all the better. It's good for the old fellow too—he knows his boy is growed up. When my boy married I made 'e a partner but us still go on as us always did.'

'It doesn't make much difference to the farm. The men still work the same and do the same jobs. Of course it's different in the house. They (i.e. the son and his wife) have to be in separate rooms and if his mother don't get on with his wife then there's trouble. Most times they gets on with their own washin' (i.e. mind their own business) and make a good go of it.'

'When my boy married it made no difference. His wife is a lovely girl. Us have had no trouble. Mind you, us have always got on—the boys and me. I think it all depends on the family. If the father wants to be boss and won't let his boys do anything for theyselves, well, getting married won't make much difference. The boy is still treated the same.'

These comments, from men whose sons have married and live with them, are typical. Farmers' wives, sons and daughters-in-law said much the same, but they were, of course, being interviewed by a stranger and one could expect little else. It seems reasonable to suppose that the change in status of a son and the introduction of his wife may, from time to time, cause conflicts and friction within the family, but only within the sphere of personal relations: the balance of economic and social relations remains much the same. Moreover, since farmers' sons and daughters may marry while their mother and their unmarried siblings are at home, and since marriage is more or less independent of control of the holding and its inheritance, the average

age of marriage in farm families is not notably different from England and Wales as a whole. In this respect it differs sharply from the other areas of family farming, where loyalty to parents and the close relationship between marriage and succession delay the age of marriage quite considerably. Thus in Ashworthy, the average age at which farmers' sons married in the period 1880–1960 was 27·5; this may be compared with 28·3 for Gosforth in Cumberland (1900–1950) and 31·3 for Llanfihangel-yng-Nghwynfa, Montgomeryshire (1890–1940). Similarly, the average age of marriage for farmers' daughters in Ashworthy was 23·8, in comparison with 27·7 for the Montgomeryshire parish. In Cumberland and Wales most farmers' sons marry between twenty-five and thirty, with a considerable proportion between thirty and thirty-five.[1] In Ashworthy, the majority of farmers' sons also marry between twenty-five and thirty, but the next largest group is between twenty-one and twenty-five and there is a marked decrease after the age of thirty :

Age at first marriage (percentage)[2]

	−21	21–4	25–9	30–4	35–9	40–4	45+
Farmers' sons	3·9	23·9	45·8	16·4	9·1	·9	Nil
Farmers' daughters	22·4	46·4	19·4	9·0	1·4	1·4	Nil

As the table shows, most farmers' daughters marry between twenty-one and twenty-four, while over a fifth are married before they are twenty-one; since they play a smaller part in the family economic unit than farmers' sons they are freer to marry at an early age.

The age at which farmers' sons take over control of their parents' farms is difficult to determine and does not lend itself easily to statistical treatment. Some farmers' sons take over when their father retires and leaves the farm; others take over while their father is still at home and here the amount of

[1] See Rees, op, cit., pp. 65–68 and *Sociology of An English Village*, pp. 45–46.

[2] This table is based on 110 first marriages of farmers' sons and 134 first marriages of farmers' daughters, taken from the Ashworthy parish register and from data collected during the field work. The period covered is from 1880 to 1960, but over 70 per cent of the marriages fall between 1900 and 1960.

control which the son is granted may vary enormously. Some young men are said to have become 'their own masters altogether': others are reputed to have taken over only in a nominal way: 'That young chap down the lane is supposed to be running the place now, but the old man is really the boss.' Then there are men who gain control when they are relatively young because of the untimely death of their father, while others are partners with their father and may not become fully in control until they are well into middle age. Of the sixty men who succeeded their fathers singly or jointly, only twenty-three are clear-cut examples of direct and full transference of control: the average age at which they took over is 31·3, nearly four years later than the average age of marriage.[1] Obviously, much significance cannot be given to this figure, but it may be compared with an average age of 28·7 for young men beginning as farmers in their own right on holdings found for them by their parents. It seems as if the sons who remain at home can expect to wait for a few years longer than their brothers before achieving full status as a farmer.

On the majority of farms, the transition appears to be a protracted process, which may take as long as ten years or more. This applies particularly to farm families where the parents remain on the farm until they die, even when the holding is legally conveyed to a son long before the father's death, and on farms where father and son are partners. Unlike marriage, the transference of control does bring about important changes in the structure of social and economic relations within the family, and the time it takes in Ashworthy is a result of the conflict between the pattern of authority within the family and the necessity to maintain the farm economy. This conflict is made all the more difficult because farm and family are so very closely related. When his children are young, a farmer makes all the important decisions: he is the sole authority within the family. As his sons grow up, their economic importance

[1] Among the twenty-three are nine bachelors and four pairs of men who took over jointly. The average may be compared with the figure of 'about thirty-two years' given for the country as a whole (based on Census Returns) by A. W. Ashby in 'The Farmer in Business' *Journ. Proc. Agri. Econ. Soc. X* No. 2 (Feb. 1953).

increases steadily as they provide more and more of the man-power needed for the farm. The point is reached where the father sees that his sons do much more work than he can and that the loss of their labour and skills would be far more serious to the running of the farm than his own. Moreover, one or more of his sons may be married and have children of their own; they are fathers themselves and have assumed many of the rights and duties of the head of a family. But he is still their father and therefore the head of the household. Above all, he decides who shall inherit the home farm and how his other children are to receive their share of the family fortune. It is easy to see that in this situation a farmer is reluctant to hand over full economic control to a son, and that even when he does, he may still retain at least some of his authority as a father.

Seen from this point of view, the legal conveyance of a farm and the partnership agreement are largely concessions to conditions which exist outside the family and which affect its economic and financial status. The farmers of Ashworthy are members of a larger society, with complex laws which must be observed. They are obliged to pay taxes and to comply with a great number of regulations which affect every aspect of their farming. The conveyance is thus not only a recognized means of transferring control but is also a device for avoiding the payment of death duties, which would diminish the value of the family's wealth. The partnership agreement may affect the amount of income tax a family has to pay. Therefore, resort to such legal practices does not necessarily indicate that the economic well-being of the family has been given complete priority over the wish of the head of the household to retain his position of authority. Some farmers hand over formally to their sons and still keep complete control of the family's affairs. The length of time which the transference of control takes is broadly a reflection of the degree of patriarchalism within the family: the more authoritarian the father, the longer the son has to wait to become master.

As one might expect in this difficult situation, the pattern of authority varies considerably from one family to another. Two examples may be given to illustrate the extremes:

Man and the Land (II)

The Smith Family

William Smith is a retired farmer. He lived at home with his father and two younger brothers, John and Edward: when his father died the three sons inherited the home farm jointly. He spoke at length of his life at home: 'I had no wages as a boy but then us got into trouble over income tax, so all four of us went into partnership—with a proper deed. Us was all supposed to get so much each year. Of course us didn't—the money was used for the farm. Father believed in giving us responsibility, he wasn't independent. Of course I asked father about most things—but if I was at a sale and saw two good bullocks, I just bought them. Edward was very clever at figures. He always did the accounts. Father used to rely on him. But John—he was just a servant—he never took responsibility. He never did anything himself. . . .

'One day I said to father: "Father, us are killing ourselves here. I'd like Dellcombe." So he said: "Well get on your pony and go and ask Farmer Dark if he wants to sell or rent." So I went over and he were hedging. I said: "Now don't get mad at me for what I want to ask you" and he said "all right". So I said: "Do you want to sell or rent this place?" He said: "There's been a lot here asking that question and I've always said no, but if I do sell it, you shall have the first chance." It were a Tuesday, the day of the fatstock sale in Longbridge, so I said: "Well you talk it over and let me know on Friday." On Saturday a letter came from the lawyer. So I went over on my pony again and saw him. I said: "Well, how much do you want for it?" He said: "I gave twelve hundred for it and I'm asking two thousand two hundred and fifty." I said: "We're not gipsies, we won't haggle over it—I'll give you two thousand two hundred." He didn't like it much but he agreed. He said: "You won't be able to give me a deposit", but I did, I gave him two hundred pounds. Then I went home and told them what had happened. . . .'

'When we was at Parr Down, Mary (his sister) was in service away. One day her husband came to visit. He went round the farm with me. He said: "Is all this yours?" I said: "Every bit." He said: "We will want a share you know." I said: "Will

92

you? Well you'll be well off then, won't you!" I went straight
to father and said what he'd told me and I said: "What's here
is the work of the four of us and if he gets a share, father, I'm
off down the road tomorrow." Father said: "When I'm gone
you and Edward will be the bosses, you don't have to worry."
But when he died he *did* leave them something after all.'

These extracts from William Smith's account show that his
father was prepared to hand over a great deal of the economic
control of the farm to his sons while they were still young men.
The fact that William initiated the move to Dellcombe and
negotiated its purchase (when he was thirty-six years old) is
particularly striking. Even in this egalitarian family, however,
there is one son who is unprepared to accept responsibility
and whose status is therefore very much lower than the other
males in the family. The account also reveals that in one respect
the father's authority and decisions are absolute, i.e. in inheritance. In virtue of his position as head of the family, the father
in Ashworthy may retain some measure of control—often a
very considerable one—over the running of the farm and the
affairs of his children long after he has retired, because of his
unchallenged right to decide the way in which the family
wealth and property is apportioned among his heirs.

The Caley family

When the farmers of Ashworthy discussed patriarchal families
they nearly always quoted three examples which were said to
be extreme instances; one of them was the Caley family. David
Caley is a middle-aged bachelor whose father died about ten
years ago. The concensus of opinion was that David was
completely subordinate to his father. Typical remarks were:
'When his father was alive he wasn't allowed a say in anything. He had to do what he was told'; 'I doubt if his father
ever told him anything about the farm or gave him a penny to
spend on himself. His clothes was bought for him and he never
went anywhere on his own'; 'When his father died, David had
no idea at all how to run the place. A proper mess he's made
of it.'

One farmer, who knew the family well, said: 'I've always
felt very sorry for David. His father always treated him like a

"home boy". I was there one day and David was trying to catch a calf. His father—and he was over eighty—pushed him out of the way and said: "Get out of it, son—you'll never catch 'e," He treated him like a child of three—and he was a man over forty then.'

It must be stressed that this degree of subordination is rare in Ashworthy, but there is certainly a considerable minority of farm families in the parish who approximate more closely to this extreme than they do to the Smith family at the other. Surprisingly enough, however, sons of authoritarian fathers marry at about the same age as other farmers' sons, which is, perhaps, further evidence of the lack of relationship between marriage and the transmission of farms.

The change from one generation to another becomes complete when one or both of the parents die and the children inherit. In Ashworthy this is normally marked by the proving of a will: very few farmers die intestate. Like the partnership deed and the conveyance of land, the will is a formal recognition of the family's place in the greater society of which the parish is a very small part. As such, its provisions represent a compromise between the wishes of the head of the family, which are informed by the immediate circumstances of his dependents, and the demands of English law. Occasionally these may conflict, as, for example, when a farmer makes a will which prohibits an heir to sell or mortgage his farm after his death: clauses of this kind are sometimes found in wills made by farmers who place a high value on the family land and who wish to ensure that it remains in the hands of their descendants. In English law there is no means of preventing such land being sold, except during the lifetime of the owner with his consent. Under the Settled Land Act of 1925, which enables a tenant for life to sell settled land, even a strict Family Settlement is not a safeguard against sale.[1] Such conflicts are, however, uncommon and in general, of course, the provisions of the law serve to protect the interests of the family.

The information contained in wills provides invaluable data

[1] Provided that (a) the market price is obtained and (b) that his trustees receive the purchase money. See Public General Acts, 1925, Ch. 18 and especially pp. 427–8.

on the structure of farm families and on the detailed working of the process of continuity. Variations in detail exist between one will and another, but they share certain important general characteristics, which will be considered in turn.

The first is the provision made for the farmer's wife. It is a firmly accepted principle in Ashworthy (as it has been in England for centuries)[1] that a husband must provide for his wife in the event of his death and that this provision will continue until the wife's death or until she remarry, whichever is the earlier. The most common means of ensuring this is either to leave the estate to the wife during her widowhood or to set up a Trust Fund, the income from which goes to the wife until her death or remarriage. Another method is to leave the estate to a child or children with the proviso that they pay the wife a stated sum of money at certain times until her death or remarriage. Where there are no children, the estate is normally left entirely to the wife. Occasionally, a farmer's will provides that his estate is divided between his wife and children.

The particular method used to ensure provision for a wife has important consequences within the family. Where a farmer bequeaths his farm to his wife for her lifetime, the ownership of the land remains vested in the older generation and—in a formal sense at least—so does economic control. In practice the widow takes one of two courses of action. She may hand over effective control of the holding to a child or children, who take all the decisions in the everyday working of the farm: or, alternatively, she may assume the role of head of the family and exercise considerable direct and indirect control herself. When the latter happens there is a conflict between her status within the family and the more general status of women in this farming community. 'Farming is a man's job' in Ashworthy as else-where and, apart from certain recognized and well-defined activities such as helping at the harvest or rearing poultry, it is generally accepted that women are unsuited to or incapable of performing the everyday tasks of a farmer. When, therefore, a farmer's widow inherits the control and possession of a farm she must exercise her authority through her sons, who work the

[1] See, for example, G. C. Homans, *English Villagers of the Thirteenth Century* (Harvard 1942).

land and who attend the sales to buy or sell livestock according to her instructions.[1] There have been a few examples of women taking over control in this way during recent years. The farmers of Ashworthy spoke of them with somewhat reluctant approval, qualified with such remarks as: 'Of course it's a bit hard for the boys' and 'You can't *really* expect a woman to run a place properly, though I suppose 'tis her right.'

The other common means of ensuring provision for a widow —by either setting up a Trust or charging the heirs to provide for her maintenance—are both an explicit recognition that farming is 'a man's job'. Farmers almost always choose Trustees from their sons, brothers or other male relatives and transfer control and possession to men who are both farmers and kindred. By such means, the farm is maintained as a viable unit, the widow is cared for, and the children are certain of receiving their inheritance when their mother dies or marries again.

The second general characteristic of farmers' wills is the parity of treatment which is accorded to 'close' kin or, if they should die, to their children. In this context, close kin are those persons who are considered to be eligible for inheritance. For example, where there are children the estate is normally shared in equal parts between them or, if any one of them should die before the will becomes effective, his or her share is equally divided among his or her children. Where there are no children to inherit, the estate is normally divided equally between nephews and nieces. Very often, however, this simple procedure is very misleading, since the estate apportioned by the will may be a relatively small part of an individual's total property. The most common instance is where a farmer conveys his holding to a son some years before his death, or buys a farm for a son who is not to inherit the family land. When this occurs the equality of inheritance in a will may well conceal great disparity in a farmer's treatment of his children. Furthermore, it is quite common for a person who qualifies as close kin by blood relationship to be omitted from the list of heirs. This happens most

[1] And in the same way a daughter who succeeds (in the absence of male heirs) is expected to hand over control of the farm to her husband if she is married.

often when sons or daughters emigrate to some distant part of the world, such as South Africa or Australia: they have become so remote that they lose the right to inherit. On the other hand, remote kin may qualify for inheritance because they have performed some service or have come to be regarded as members of the family circle.

There are, in effect, two kinds of will. The first is one which accurately represents the disposal of a farmer's property and reflects the values of the family farming system. The second is essentially designed to apportion the residue of an estate which remains after a farmer has ensured continuity by gift or conveyance to his child or children. Both kinds are, however, important in that they complete the transition from one generation to another. Sometimes, indeed, the second type of will marks a very important stage in the transition, i.e. where a farmer conveys his farm and stock to a son but keeps his money or other financial assets. The farmers of Ashworthy are, like family farmers elsewhere in Britain, most reluctant to invest their surplus capital (which is normally small in amount)[1] in shares, bonds or other means of obtaining an income from it. They 'lock their money up' in bank accounts. These assets are hardly ever transferred to sons when they become farmers in their own right, although certain sums may be handed over in times of need. Thus a son who has received his father's farm by conveyance may be seriously short of working capital and must wait until his father's death (or even his mother's death) before he has access to it. Such a state of affairs is, of course, a further factor in delaying or interrupting the full transfer of economic control from father to son.

In general, therefore, the transition from one generation to another is—for many different reasons—a protracted affair lasting several years on the farms of Ashworthy. Seen from the outside, it has many disadvantages: it stifles or at least discourages initiative in the younger generation; it can separate control of the working of the farm from control of the family capital reserves and so hamper improvement or innovation; it allows young men to achieve adult status as married men and

[1] As in all farming, the proportion of capital invested in the actual running of the farm is very high.

fathers long before they obtain economic independence and the status of farmers in their own right. However, seen in terms of the values of the family system and of the aim of ensuring continuity in a complex and changing situation, the lengthy transition may be regarded as a response to the demands of the relationship between family and land.

*   *   *

In considering the relationship between farm families and the land, particular attention has been given to the effects of changes in land-holding and in the composition of the farm population. There remains the influence of these changes on other aspects of the social life of Ashworthy.

As a starting point it is useful to recall the conditions which are found in peasant farming communities, where '. . . the same people go on living in the same houses and cultivating the same land from year to year. This provides, as it were, a stable environment in which social relations are maintained through the decades, and a frame of reference by which individuals can relate themselves to other people'.[1] Clearly these conditions do not apply to Ashworthy. Farm families have long been accustomed to the arrival of new neighbours, some of whom may be acquaintances of long standing from a near-by parish and some complete strangers; a farmer's kindred may change in territorial disposition many times in the course of one generation. Enduring social relations of a 'face to face' character over a long period of years between people who live near each other are therefore not the general rule.

Nevertheless, the social structure does have a territorial basis. Farm families may move from holding to holding but, as we have already seen, most of this movement occurs within the group of parishes which has been called 'the Ashworthy area',[2] and much of it within the parish itself. A neighbour or relative who leaves a near-by farm may move to one a mile or so away and is unlikely to be more than six or seven miles away. The countryman sees his social environment as a series of concentric

---

[1] Barnes, op. cit., p. 41.

[2] See above, pp. 38–41.

tracts. First, there is the small territory around his home, where his friends, neighbours and possibly some relatives live: they will certainly include a number of people with whom he has close social relations. Secondly, there is the parish, centred on the village with its church and chapel. The parish is recognized as the formal territorial unit and the community to which the individual belongs. In conversation with outsiders a man identifies himself by naming his parish, and he normally feels a vague loyalty to it which is reinforced by all kinds of formal and informal links. It is the place where he buys his food, goes to church or chapel, has his children baptized, is married and buried; if he is gregarious he may belong to its Social Club or visit its one public house. He 'knows' the majority of the people who live in the parish, some of whom will be 'friends' and relatives.

Thirdly, there is the Ashworthy area. This is the group of surrounding parishes which the individual knows well and within which he may have lived at some time or another. It is familiar territory, many of its everyday happenings are discussed in conversation, and a number of the people who live in it are relatives, former friends or neighbours. Fourthly, there is the remainder of the county, where most of the people are 'strangers', but where the way they behave and speak is not very much different from Ashworthy, and where—as one farmer put it—'us still almost feels at home'. Last comes the remainder of England, most of which is remote and unknown.

The Ashworthy folk, do not, of course, see their social horizon delimited in a precise way; they think rather in terms of particular people or of specific places and houses. For example, a farmer may say he knows Hollington well because he has relatives or former neighbours living there, or because he once farmed there himself. Another may feel loyalty to several parishes largely because of fortuitous geographical arrangements which affect his everyday life: some of the farmers living near the boundary of Ashworthy send their children to school in Broadpen, and have their letters delivered by a postman from Combe Down, the parish they use as their postal address. Hardly anyone in Ashworthy knows where the parish boundary runs, and two separate groups of its cottages and farms are popularly held to be in Broadpen and Medford respectively.[1]

The distinction between Ashworthy parish and its social area is, therefore, vague and uncertain; this is reflected in the content and particularly in the territorial arrangement of social relations. The social area, rather than the parish, is the locality within which the great majority of an individual's past, present and future friends, relatives and neighbours live. To illustrate this and to describe some of the other important factors which affect social relations, four examples have been chosen which will be examined in terms of relations between neighbours. In Ashworthy, a farmer's neighbours are those people who co-operate with him and with his immediate family in certain well-defined ways during the every-day running of the farm and household. Some of the people who live near him may not be neighbours simply because they do not behave in a neighbourly manner. Some, but not all, of a man's neighbours will also be 'close friends' or relatives: in the examples which follow, close friends and relatives who are not neighbours are not included.[2]

(i) *Edward Dean* (1 in Fig. 15). Edward Dean is the owner of a large farm which he took over from his father in 1954. He is thirty-five years old and has always lived in the same farmhouse. The men he recognizes as neighbours are scattered over several parishes, three of them living more than six miles away by road. Of the eleven individuals, three (B, F and H) are men he knew at school, although H left Ashworthy as a boy and did not return until he obtained the tenancy of his present farm in 1953. M and N were neighbours of Edward Dean's father and 'came with the farm when I took it over'. K and L are neighbours because 'they are close friends of my father-in-law (J) and when he came here to dip his sheep, they came as well'.

---

[1] This is in sharp contrast to Gosforth and certain Welsh rural communities, where the closely-knit community has a sharply defined territory, i.e. the parish, the boundaries of which are known in detail by the majority of the inhabitants. See *Sociology of An English Village*: p. 168 and Rees, op. cit., Ch. IX.

[2] The effects of the movement of families on social relations between kindred are examined in Ch. Six below.

A, O, P and Q are 'Up Country Johnnies' who have bought their farms since 1954: A has only been at his present farm since the end of 1959, but has rented land elsewhere in Ashworthy since 1956. D lived most of his life in an adjoining county before he bought his farm in Ashworthy in 1948.

In addition, there are Edward Dean's four relatives who act as neighbours. His father (E) bought an adjoining tract of land before he retired; he now farms it 'to keep myself occupied'. His sister (G's wife) married a farmer's son; they moved to their present holding in 1954 and G's father (J) became a neighbour of Edward as a result. D, who is Edward's father's first cousin, came to live in his present home when he married its owner's daughter in 1922 and 'has been a neighbour ever since'.

Thus of the sixteen families whom Edward Dean recognizes as neighbours, only four were neighbours of his father (C, D, M and N). There have also been important changes in the nature and intensity of neighbourly relations, which are best summarized in Dean's own words:

'The war made a big difference to neighbours. Machinery came in and changed everything. Ask my father how it was in his day. . . . Take threshing. It was a big day round here. Now I combine most of mine and rick the rest. I have four people in for two days and I pay them. . . I'd rather do that than keep going back (i.e. to neighbours' farms for their threshing). The only big thing left here is the dipping; ten farmers came to that: (A, B, E, F, H, J, K, L, M, N) most of them keep about thirty sheep and it isn't worth fixing up a bath because it costs five or six pound.

'If it wasn't for dipping I wouldn't hardly see my neighbours, although I sometimes ride round on a pony. . . . I do my own hay with the baler. . . . These days you only see a few neighbours—those who are friends or you borrow things from. I borrow O's potato digger and he borrows a disc harrow. . . . I lend him more than I borrow from him. . . . Of course I see a lot of my father and brother-in-law—with they being near-by, us work like a family. . . .

'There have been a lot of changes round here. . . . I would visit a new farmer, but most (farmers) wouldn't bother these days. Us have always lived in Ashworthy, so us generally like to meet them. Mind, a lot depends on what they be. . . . If they'm a bit bit—um—well, if they've studied farming in a book and class theyselves higher than farmers, they don't get mixed in very much . . . but a happy-go-lucky sort mixes in very well. I think I'm lucky, the new ones are a nice lot.

'Farmers these days can't *afford* the old-fashioned ways. I prefer to pay older men and such for jobs. . . . If I held a proper threshing I'd be bound to go round all the farms and I can't afford the time. . . . There's still a few of course.'

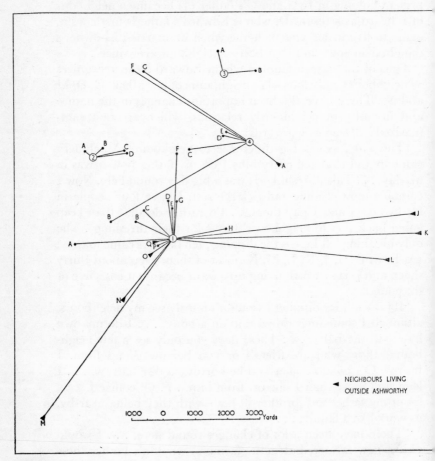

Fig. 15. Neighbour networks on four farms.

(ii) *David Thompson* (2 in Fig. 15). David Thompson is an 'Up Country Johnny' who came to Ashworthy in 1954: 'I'd worked in an office all my life, but I had to leave for health reasons; I didn't expect to live more than a year.' He bought a 60-acre farm, which he works with his twenty-six year old son. His four neighbours are local men. A came from Blackbury to his present farm in 1934: B is A's son and has been farming on his own account since the beginning of 1959; C farmed in his native parish about twelve miles from Ashworthy before buying his farm in 1946: D has always lived in Ashworthy and inherited his farm from his father. Thompson said 'they are all local farmers, born and bred'. (D, on the other hand, spoke of A and his son as 'not *real* Ashworthy people'; of C as 'a local chap, but he hasn't been here long'; and of Thompson as 'an Up Country Johnny'.)

The pattern of neighbourliness was quickly established: 'When I bought this place I met A and arranged for Bob (his son) to come down a week early and stay there. It was one of the best moves we ever did. They took to him and he took to them in every way. That man (A) is a born diplomat: he taught Bob without *telling* him. Then we came down and things started going wrong. The weather was bad, everything was hopeless. We had no hay and didn't know where to turn. Then Bob met C in the lane—didn't know who he was—they're as charming a family as you could meet—and mentioned the hay. Nothing was said. Then that afternoon, out of the blue, D rang up and said "I believe you're short of hay, I've got a bit you can have." I didn't know who he was, I didn't know how he knew, I'd never met him. From that day on they've been marvellous neighbours, absolutely marvellous. If there was any trouble it was positively *uncanny* how one or other of them appeared on the doorstep.

'I think the thing that happened was that I was willing to admit ignorance. I was rather worried about Bob at first, but inside a year he was "in". He's more in the community than I am now.'

David Thompson is aware that he has been fortunate in his neighbours: 'We have been very lucky here. Other people have had much more difficulty. Our neighbours have helped us far more than we have helped them in return. . . . We are really pleased when we can lend them machinery.' At the same time his circle of neighbours is small and he has practically no social relations at all with the many other farmers who live near-by.

(iii) *Edward Ames* (3 in Fig. 15). Edward Ames, who is twenty-five years old, inherited his farm when his father died in 1957. In his father's day the farm was linked with at least nine others in ties of neighbourliness, but of these only two remain. This change was explained as '. . . a sign of the times. This place is a bit too big for us, but us do get casual labour in the evenings and week-ends, railwaymen and retired farmers and such. . . . Farmers with lots of neighbours be on the move all the time . . . they spend more time on other farms than on their own place. I can't get on with that, I just pay for a job and that's the end of it.' In spite of this, neighbourly relations with A and B, both very experienced local farmers, are very close and cover many aspects of farm work; in particular there is considerable borrowing and lending of machinery.

(iv) *John Robertson* (4 in Fig. 15). John Robertson, who is thirty-four years old, bought his 90-acre farm in Ashworthy in 1957. He is a farmer's son, who has worked in several counties in southern England, but to the local people he is an 'Up Country Johnny' and therefore not 'a real farmer'. This distinction was prominent in his own account of the first few months in Ashworthy and the way in which relations were established with his neighbours: 'I got married when I was working in the south of the county and started looking for a farm. After we had looked at dozens, we found this place. We bought it from the Harveys, who claimed their family had lived here for a hundred and fifty years. If they had, they hadn't done much to it in that time. . . .

'The day we arrived, the D's came over and we've been good neighbours ever since. They've been very kind to us. . . . If they have a machine I haven't got I go to borrow it, and if I've got one they come. They are very nice people: they take a great interest in us. Of course you know they are related to the people we bought this place from, and they are cousins—or something like that—to C and E. It's like that on nearly all the farms round here. . . . Well C and E are good neighbours, but we don't see as much of them as D. They are very old-fashioned and I have to go to help them in harvesting and threshing and things like that. . . . It's an awful waste of time, but you have to do it. They're always willing to help. . . .

'The rest of the local farmers we hardly ever see . . . they're not neighbours. . . . After we'd been here about nine months I met A in Longbridge. He's a "foreigner" like us. We met a lot of people through him, people like ourselves. . . . That's how we met B, F and G. They are up-to-date in outlook, so we see a lot of them and we help each other because we farm the same way. . . . I often talk about farming with B and we swop ideas—and machinery. We help each other a lot really. . . .'

These four examples show clearly that the territorial patterns of neighbourliness which radiate from each farm to form a complex network change fairly frequently and that there is an important element of chance in determining the pattern for any one farmer at a given time. Once established, neighbourly relations tend to persist and are normally broken only by movement to another farm, death or retirement.

Neighbourliness in Ashworthy appears to be different in many important respects from that found in other British rural communities. In Wales[1] and Cumberland[2] a newcomer's neighbours are largely pre-determined by the existing pattern of relations between farms, and the total network thus remains more or less static; the number of neighbours varies roughly with the size of farms, and the content of neighbourly feelings is much influenced by the fact that a farmer 'has known most of them (i.e. his neighbours) and their relatives all his life, and this common experience ensures a wide measure of social intercourse'.[3] In Ashworthy the neighbourhood network changes often, and the number of neighbours a farmer recognizes is not related to the size of his farm. Edward Ames (3 in Fig. 15), with his two neighbours, farms over 300 acres; John Robertson (4), with 90 acres, has seven. Edward Ames's father had nine neighbours, while the man who preceded John

[1] Rees, op. cit., pp. 91–100, and T. J. Hughes in Rees and Davies, op. cit., pp. 159–162.

[2] *Sociology of An English Village*, pp. 144–54.

[3] Rees, op. cit., p. 98.

Robertson in his farm had fourteen. Moreover, while many of the Ashworthy farmers—like those in Wales—share 'a common experience', they have not necessarily known each other all their lives. The Ashworthy area, within which so many families move from farm to farm, is too large for an individual to know more than a minority of its inhabitants really well. Almost certainly this has resulted in a restriction of neighbourliness, both in scope and content.

It does indeed seem doubtful if neighbourliness has ever been as well developed in Ashworthy as it has among the dispersed farmsteads of Montgomeryshire and Cumberland. In this West Country parish, rural craftsmen, retired farmers and villagers have provided an important source of casual labour for many decades and have thus greatly reduced the need for neighbourly assistance in the fields or at threshing and sheep-shearing. Farm mechanization has lessened the dependence on neighbours very considerably and—when allied with the use of casual labour and the occasional hire of an agricultural contractor's services—has made it possible for individuals like Edward Ames and his young brother to farm over three hundred acres on their own. The important occasions in the farming year—harvesting, threshing, sheep-shearing and dipping—at which the attendance of neighbours was at one time a clear necessity, are nowadays rapidly losing their social importance.

The change is, however, by no means complete. As the four examples above indicate, some farmers are 'old-fashioned' and still hold threshing days and the like in the traditional way. The 'progressive' farmers, usually younger men, resent having to give up their time: 'Old Jack has always stuck to the old ways. His threshing lasts three days. You don't get paid—paying don't enter into it—you get all your meals—but it's time you can't afford. Then he still carries his hay—that means five men have to be taken off their farms. The worst of it is—us don't *want* he back for that amount of time. This backwardness —t'is as big a stumbling block as anything—particularly if you'm got just the one odd man out. It'll have to change.' On the other hand, the increased use of machinery has created a new dependence on the goodwill of neighbours. Borrowing and lending of machinery is very well developed in Ashworthy, and

106

although Income Tax concessions have encouraged farmers to
buy their own equipment, there are still many large and expensive machines which are beyond the means and needs of
the average farmer. For example, only one man in the parish
owns a combine-harvester. He remarked: 'Once I've done my
own, the combine is out every day for weeks and weeks. Of
course I can't do it for nothing—it's dear to run and it's a man's
time as well. So I make them pay the usual rates. . . . *So many
ask me, I only go to neighbours and friends.*'

The conflict between the 'old-fashioned' and 'progressive'
farmers is complicated by the existence of the 'Up Country
Johnnies', who are 'progressive' to a man but who are also
relatively inexperienced farmers and who lean heavily on the
skill and knowledge of the local people. As newcomers, they
resent the burden of neighbourliness and are angered by its
apparent wastefulness; yet without the help of neighbours they
would be—in the words of one of them—'lost, lonely and in a
hell of a mess sometimes'. Their difficult and confusing position
is clearly reflected in their comments on neighbours:

'In the place we lived before we came here, people were
very much friendlier. They thought you were all right until you
did something wrong; up here they won't have anything to do
with you until you do something right. . . . These people think
all the time about money. They've stopped having children so
there's nothing else for them to do. Take X across there. (An
Up Country Johnny.) They all believe he's bought his cows on
H.P.—and he probably has—but they don't say that—oh no!
They say he *rents* them.

The trouble here is that people are far too interested in you.
Take my neighbours. There's Z in the farm down the road. A
very nice family and they've helped us more than you'd believe.
I honestly don't think we could manage without him: but the
trouble is he *expects* me to drop everything when he's saving hay
or something like that. Sometimes I don't know whether to
thank him or punch him on the nose. He'll come round to say
our bullocks are straying on the road, or there's a parcel from
London for us down at the village. He must watch this place
with binoculars. I told him once if we ever catch fire to nip
over to tell us, because he'd be sure to know before we did!'

'Our nearest neighbour is Q. When we came here he was a great help. . . . He knows this area backwards. . . . Mind you, he's like all the chaps around here—very conservative. He bought a cow at Longbridge once and tried to milk it. It kicked him. So he thought it must be used to a milking machine and sent his boy over to ask us if we would try it on our machine. We did and the cow gave two gallons. I took the milk over and said: "You need a bigger bucket." Old Q said: "Good God, have you milked it already? We tried for three hours!" Well, it wasn't long before he bought a milking machine himself. . . .'

'M still holds the old-fashioned threshing. They kill a pig for it. You have an enormous meal of pork before and after. When I was there last I told the thresher: "Don't expect this when you come to our place, all you'll get is sandwiches." He said "Then we won't come"—but he did, you know.'

These comments, with their characteristic mixture of resentment and friendliness, illustrate how the wide differences in background and outlook between the Up Country Johnnies and the local farmers affect the content of neighbourly relations. The last of the examples shows particularly well how such differences may be perpetuated through misunderstanding. The Up Country Johnny regarded the threshing as an economic activity of little social value and thought of the large meals as 'extravagant and ostentatious'. The local farmers—even the 'progressive' ones—believe that if one does hold a 'proper threshing' then one's reputation as a farmer and as a man is judged by the hospitality offered. The Up Country Johnny who provided sandwiches was described as 'mean', 'ignorant' and 'tight-fisted'.

Thus recent technological changes in farming and the arrival of the Up Country Johnnies have together affected the strength of neighbourliness in an area where changes in the farm population have for many years inhibited the development of a stable network covering the countryside. The effect of these changes is, of course, most marked on neighbourly acts between farmers at work, and is much less apparent in aspects of neighbourliness which are not directly connected with the economy. In Ashworthy when a farmer talks of his neighbours, he is normally referring to the limited group of people who co-operate with him in farming; he may, however, use the term in a wider sense, for example: 'Us never saw much of 'e but us went to his funeral because he was a neighbour.' Funerals are, indeed, the most striking expression of neighbourliness in this more general meaning. Even the Up Country Johnnies attend them: 'People around here attach a lot of importance to showing up at a funeral. I went to one; it was a chap I'd never met. I couldn't recognize anyone there, so I tacked on the end of the procession.'

On the other hand, many of the small acts of mutual aid which in other rural communities are characteristic of neighbours are performed by kindred or 'close friends' in Ashworthy. Typical examples are looking after children while the parents are away and help in time of illness. Kindred may come from considerable distances in family crises and 'close friends' are usually people who have known each other for the greater part of a life-time, so it may be that this too is a reflection of the changing character of the farm population at large. Neighbours come and go, kindred and close friends are 'always there when they are needed'. Ties created by kinship or long acquaintance are strong enough to withstand the many changes which are so typical of the social system.

Taking the social area as a whole, then, it can be seen that (with the exception of the Up Country Johnnies) the composition of the people who inhabit it remains largely the same, while their territorial disposition changes very frequently. Some social relations, such as those based on kinship and close friendship, may be continuous; or they may be 'dormant' for periods of separation produced by movement of individual families, to be revived at times of need or when a further move brings families into physical proximity again. Other social relations, such as those arising from neighbourliness, acquaintanceship, or working for the same employer, are much more likely to be episodic or short-lived. These make up some of the discontinuities which give the social structure its particular flexibility.

PART TWO

PART TWO

INTRODUCTION

THE first part of this study has been concerned with the relationship between man and the land. It was shown that the farm family is a primary unit in the economy and in the system of land-holding. In order to understand how the land is occupied from one generation to another, the farm family was considered as an instrument for ensuring continuity, and the way in which the transmission of farms is related to family structure was examined. The analysis was based on the period between the Tithe Award of 1841 and the begining of 1960, with particular emphasis on this century.

During this period of about one hundred and twenty years there have been marked changes in the population structure of Ashworthy, which have affected the whole parish. In common with most of the English countryside, it has suffered a marked decrease in its total number of inhabitants. The process of rural depopulation and 'the drift of the towns' have been written about at length—and most commonly in terms of decline and the decay of a long-established way of life. To look at Ashworthy in this general context is to raise a number of questions which so far have not been considered. Has population loss affected the balance between people and land? Has rural depopulation brought about changes in the structure of the farm family and in the means of transmission of farms? Are groups other than farmers affected by population decrease and to what extent? Does 'a stake in the land' keep people in the countryside?

In order to answer these and other questions, it is necessary to examine in detail the changes in population which have taken place in Ashworthy and the effects of these changes on different groups. Farmers' families account for less than half the total population of the parish. There are also a small number of craftsmen and tradesmen, who, like farmers, have property and skills to pass on from one generation to another: a much larger number of the inhabitants are villagers or cottagers—farm labourers, forestry workers and the like—who do not own or occupy land, who have little property to leave to their children and who do not normally teach them occupational skills. It will be shown in Chapter Five and the first part of Chapter Six that these three broad occupational groups have been affected differently by population decrease. Farmers and their families have tended to remain in the countryside; farm labourers have tended to leave; rural craftsmen and their families form an intermediate group, in some ways resembling farmers and in others the landless manual workers.

It appears therefore that the particular relationship which farmers have with the land—the basis of rural life—is of a kind which largely counteracts those pressures which cause others to leave the countryside. On the other hand, as we shall see later, 'the drift to the towns' is only one aspect of population change. The people who remain in the countryside do not necessarily live all their lives in the same house or in the same parish. Short-distance migration, almost completely ignored by students of rural demography, is an outstanding characteristic of the Ashworthy area during the last hundred and twenty years, and one which again has brought about differential changes within the total population. Long-distance and short-distance movements of people, taken together, have had far-reaching effects on family and kinship structure and on social and economic relations in general, bringing further elements of change into country life. These effects are examined in the second part of Chapter Six and in Chapter Seven.

The aim of this second part is, then, to analyse the close-knit life of Ashworthy as a social system which, like the relationship between farmers and land, is in a state of 'dynamic equilibrium'. Particular attention is paid to social relations between kindred largely because this is a convenient way to show how rural life 'works'. We shall see that the kinship system of this remote rural parish is in many respects strikingly similar to that found in a London Borough, and in other ways significantly different. These differences and similarities need to be elaborated by further sample studies, to enlarge our knowledge of our own way of life.

CHAPTER FIVE

POPULATION CHANGE

Ashworthy 1800 to 1960 : a general view

THE demographic history of the English countryside has been studied for many years and it is now a commonplace that the population of rural areas rose rapidly from 1800 to the middle of the nineteenth century and has been declining ever since. 'Rural depopulation' is nowadays a familiar phrase. Ashworthy and the parishes around it appear to be little different from the rest of the English countryside:

TABLE SIX

Population 1801–1951.

| Year | Totals | | Percentage Change | | 18 South† Devon parishes | 112‡ Rural Districts |
	Ashworthy	Nearby parishes*	Ashworthy	Nearby parishes		
1801	659	2,797	—	—	—	—
1811	753	3,157	+14·3	+12·9	+11	+ 7
1821	942	3,709	+25·1	+17·5	+14	+14
1831	1,054	4,348	+11·9	+17·2	+ 3	+ 7
1841	1,116	5,054	+ 5·9	+16·8	+ 4	+ 6
1851	1,117	4,582	+ 0·09	− 9·3	− 7	+ 3
1861	1,010	4,134	− 9·6	− 9·8	− 9	− 0·2
1871	911	3,996	− 9·9	− 5·7	+ 4	− 0·04
1881	810	3,340	− 11·1	−16·5	− 7	− 0·6
1891	783	3,181	− 3·3	− 4·7	− 0·4	− 0·7
1901	712	2,928	− 9·1	− 8·0	− 10	+ 2
1911	713	2,835	+ 0·14	− 3·2	+ 4	—
1921	682	2,886	− 4·3	− 1·09	− 8	—
1931	613	2,770	−11·1	− 4·0	− 0·1	—
1951	611	2,746	− 0·03	− 0·87	+ 3	—
§1960	519	—	−15·0	—	—	—

As the table shows, the population of Ashworthy and of the surrounding parishes increased rapidly from 1801 to 1841. Between 1841 and 1851 the number of people in Ashworthy remained almost stationary, but in the neighbouring parishes a decline had already begun after 1841, as it had in the South Devon parishes. The first half of the nineteenth century was therefore a period of remarkable population growth. In Ashworthy the number of inhabitants rose by just under 70 per cent between 1801 and 1851, while in the near-by parishes it rose by over 80 per cent between 1801 and 1841. During the second half of the century the trend was reversed. The population of Ashworthy declined in every decade between 1851 and 1901, so that the total returned to near that of the early years of the century. A similar change took place in the near-by parishes. Ashworthy has continued to lose people in the present century, although the loss has been less regular than before 1900, a characteristic which is shared with the neighbouring parishes. Therefore, as a result of over a century of population decline, there are now fewer people in the Ashworthy area than there were at the beginning of the nineteenth century.

Table Six shows also that the rate of population growth and decline in the English countryside varies in time from place to place. For example, between 1841 and 1851 the population of Ashworthy increased slightly, in contrast to a sharp decrease in the neighbouring parishes and the 18 South Devon parishes: in the 112 Rural Districts—the location of which is not given in the *Census*, but which are presumably scattered throughout the English countryside—the population rose quite appreciably. Between 1911 and 1921 the population of Ashworthy and of the South Devon parishes declined sharply, whereas in the area around Ashworthy it increased slightly. These variations may

---

* The parishes are—Broadpen, Heathbury, Combe Down, Medford, Hollington, Holton and Stone. (See Fig. 8, p. 40.)

† John Saville, *Rural Depopulation in England and Wales 1851–1951* (1957), Table XXV, p. 176.

‡ 1901 *Census, General Report* (1904), pp. 25–27.

§ Survey carried out during field work. Unlike the *Census*, it does not include visitors.

be related partly to general changes, such as periods of wide-spread economic depression in agriculture, for example in the 1880's, or to circumstances which affected certain small areas at particular times. Thus, while the decade 1861–1871 was a relatively prosperous one for the farmers of south-west England as a whole, the Ashworthy area experienced depressed conditions. In Ashworthy itself, many small farms were amalgamated and young men left the parish to seek work elsewhere.[1] The neighbouring parish of Heathbury provides a more spectacular example. In the last thirty years of the nineteenth century, when all the other parishes in the area were suffering severe losses, the population of Heathbury increased by 32 per cent between 1871 and 1881, 31·8 per cent between 1881 and 1891, and by 3·8 per cent between 1891 and 1901. This sharp rise was the direct result of the construction of a new railway in the 1870's.

This analysis of change in population totals is useful as background information and also insofar as it confirms the importance of migration from the countryside as a factor in the demographic history of the Ashworthy area. However, recent studies have shown that rural emigration has considerable effects on the ratio of males to females and on the age structure of the population as well as on total numbers. In particular, this is argued very convincingly in John Saville's authoritative study *Rural Depopulation in England and Wales 1851–1951*. And since both these aspects of population change might be expected, *a priori*, to have effects on family structure, they must be examined in the light of the evidence for Ashworthy and the surrounding area.

The sex ratio and age structure

It is now well known that there have been more females than males in England and Wales since the beginning of the nineteenth century. The sex ratio (expressed as females per 100 males) has varied between 103·6 in 1821 and 108·8 in 1931.[2] However, in the rural areas generally a pronounced lack of employment opportunities for women and their consequent

[1] According to the marginal comments given in the *Census* of 1871.

[2] Saville, op. cit., pp. 90–98. See also Appendix Two, Table One.

migration has produced a surplus of males over the years; most Rural Districts in 1951 had sex ratios ranging from 96 to 101.[1] Ashworthy and its neighbouring parishes show much the same picture, with ratios that are well below the national average throughout the period from 1801 to 1951. (See Appendix Two, Table One.) In 1901, for example, Ashworthy had 97·7 females to every hundred males, which may be compared with 100·3 for the neighbouring parishes, 101·1 for all Rural Districts in England and Wales, and 106·8 for the country as a whole. In 1951, the figures were 94·6, 95·5, 98·3 and 108·2 respectively.

In general, therefore, more females have left the countryside than males to seek work in the towns. In the Ashworthy area the movement has been particularly marked since 1911 and this can be attributed to the sharp decline in the practice of employing female house servants on farms. This change is as typical of Ashworthy as it is of the parishes which surround it, but the 1914–18 War brought about a temporary surplus of women, reflected in the high ratio of 103·5 for 1921.

Now, as Saville points out, the proportion of males and females is not distributed equally throughout the age range of the total population. Among the more important factors which affect the distribution are the relative numbers of male and female births, differences in the male and female mortality rates—particularly for children and in the older age groups—and unequal rates of migration between the sexes. These factors, together with several others, notably age of marriage and the number of people who marry, are also important in determining the age structure of the population. Ashworthy is, of course, far too small to make an analysis in such terms profitable or meaningful, but a description of the changing age structure of the population is necessary, both in relation to the process of rural depopulation and to a consideration of the family structure.

The distribution of the population of Ashworthy in five-year age groups for selected years is given in Fig. 16. The most striking feature is the sharp difference between the age structure in the nineteenth century and the twentieth century. In

---

[1] *1951 Census. General Tables* pp. 84–95. The lowest county is Wiltshire with 77·2, the highest is East Sussex with 116·4. Both are exceptional.

1841, 1851 and 1861 we can reasonably speak of an 'age pyramid': there is a more or less consistent decrease in the numbers in each successive age group, for both males and females. Well over half the population is found in the 0–24 age group, within which children of nine years or less are roughly equal in number to young people of between 10 and 24. This is clear evidence of a high birth rate. At the other extreme, the number of people age fifty or over forms less than a fifth of the total. By the end of the century this pyramidical structure had vanished and the diagram for 1901 shows broad resemblances to that of 1951. The birth rate has declined, so that the proportion of young people (i.e. under twenty-five) is nearer a third than a half. There are corresponding increases in the numbers of people in the late middle- and old-age groups. This change is summarized in the following table:

TABLE SEVEN

Age distribution for selected years (percentages).

	Ashworthy							1951 England & Wales	Rural Districts
Age Group	1841	1851	1861	1901	1921	1951	1960*		
0–4	14·9	13·7	13·0	8·3	8·2	8·2	5·0	8·5	8·4
5–14	25·6	24·6	23·9	19·1	15·2	14·2	11·7	13·7	14·0
15–24	17·9	18·2	17·3	17·7	17·6	14·2	9·8	12·9	14·5
0–24	58·4	56·5	54·2	45·1	41·0	36·6	26·5	35·1	36·9
25–44	24·2	22·3	21·7	26·6	27·4	24·8	N.K.	29·8	28·6
45–64	12·6	15·4	15·9	18·6	22·0	28·5	N.K.	24·1	23·1
65 and over	4·8	5·8	8·2	9·7	9·6	10·1	N.K.	11·0	11·4

* Based on a survey carried out during the field work. The Ashworthy figures for the census years are calculated from information supplied by the Registrar General. The figures for England and Wales and the Rural Districts are based on the *1951 Census: General Tables*, p. 84.

In general, then, the population of Ashworthy has been 'growing older', with a steady decline in the number of young people during the twentieth century. People are living longer and there has been a consistent increase in the relative size of the older age groups. In this respect, of course, Ashworthy is a tiny but representative example of national changes in our population structure. In 1951, the proportions of young (under 25) and old (65 and over) people in Ashworthy were much the same as those found in Rural Districts as a whole and in England and Wales. On the other hand, as Table Seven shows, this was not true of the 25–44 and 45–64 age groups. In

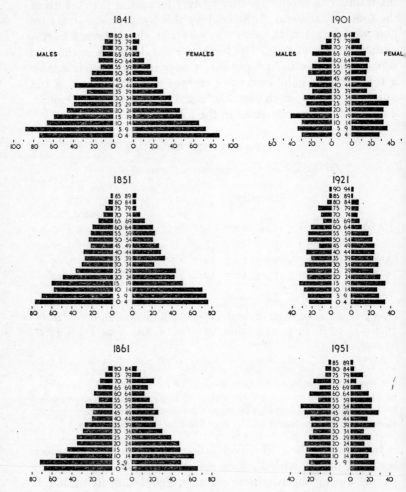

Fig. 16. Age structure in quinary groups for selected years.

Ashworthy there are more people in the older group than in the younger: indeed, 50–54 is the largest of the quinary age groups in the parish.

It is, therefore, the young adults and people in early middle age whose numbers are relatively low. Saville, speaking of the rural areas generally, has suggested that this reflects the fact that migration from the countryside is most marked after the age of 25, particularly among women.[1] Thus while women aged between 25 and 44 account for 15·1 per cent of the total population in England and Wales, they make up 14 per cent of the population in Rural Districts. In Ashworthy they account for 12·1 per cent. The equivalent percentages for men are 14·7 for England and Wales, 14·6 for Rural Districts and 12·7 in Ashworthy.[2] It might seem, therefore, that Ashworthy has suffered particularly from rural depopulation in the years preceding 1951; but, as we have already observed, there are other variables to be taken into account. All that can be said at this point is that migration has taken place and is reflected in the age structure. Census statistics, however detailed, cannot take us farther and it is necessary to turn to other kinds of evidence.

Ashworthy in mid-nineteenth century

Three important documentary sources are available which provide a great deal of information about Ashworthy in the middle years of the nineteenth century: they are the Tithe Award of 1841 and the Enumeration Schedules for the 1841 and 1851 *Censuses*.[3] The Tithe Award gives the ownership and occupation of land by holdings and by individual fields. The 1841 Enumeration Schedules list the full name, age, sex and occupation of each inhabitant, grouped in households: the ages of persons under fifteen are given exactly and those of persons aged fifteen and over in five-year groups. The 1851

---

[1] Saville, op. cit., pp. 118–25.

[2] Calculated from the 1951 Census, *General Tables*, p. 84, and from information supplied by the Registrar General.

[3] The Tithe Award, with its accompanying map, is in the custody of the Rector of Ashworthy. The Enumeration Schedules are part of the Home Office Records kept at the Public Record Office.

Enumeration Schedules give full names, exact ages, the relationship of each member of a household to its head, and the sex, occupation and parish of birth of the inhabitants who have been enumerated. The Ashworthy Schedules also contain information on the amount of land occupied by farmers and the number of men they employ.[1] This section is based very largely on these three sources.

Throughout the nineteenth century the economy of Ashworthy was based almost exclusively on agriculture. In 1851, farmers and their families made up 26·9 per cent of the total population (167 males and 136 females); agricultural labourers and their families accounted for a further 39·5 per cent (239 males and 202 females), so that two-thirds of the inhabitants were directly dependent on farming. Of the remaining third, the great majority were craftsmen and tradesmen in occupations closely connected with the land, such as blacksmiths, wheelwrights, millers, millwrights and saddlers, or were men who provided essential services for the community as a whole, for example shoemakers, tailors, masons and shopkeepers.

The bare fact given in the *Census* Schedules do not include explicit information on economic conditions, but there are clear indications of the poverty of the area. Most of the Ashworthy folk lived very modestly and many suffered considerable hardship. A dozen or so of the farmers recorded in 1851 are prosperous yeomen, owning two to three hundred acres of land, employing seven or eight labourers and three or four house servants. The majority, however, are tenant farmers, employing one or two men, who barely supported their families by unremitting hard work. To these families, a bad harvest, disease among livestock, illness or death in the household were often catastrophic. Two examples from the *Census* Schedules speak for themselves:

> (1841) *Jackman*, John (40) farmer, Sarah (45), Bettsy (10), John (8), Sarah (6), Richard (4), William (1).
> (1851) *Jackman*, John (52) pauper, 'retired farmer—ill', Sarah (54) wife, pauper; Sarah (16) daughter—glover.

[1] For example 'A farmer of 90 acres. Three men'.

(1841) *May*, George (40) farmer, Elizabeth (35), William
(5), Susan (1); John Dennis (35) farm labourer,
Richard Weekes (15) servant, Susannah Woolridge
(15) servant, John Friend (12) servant, Elizabeth
Cowle (10) servant.

(1851) *May*, Elizabeth (43) widow, pauper, deaf, Susan (11)
daughter, servant, Ann (9) daughter; Mary Hill (60)
widow, lodger, pauper.

Both families had left farms of about a hundred acres between
1841 and 1851, to live in cottages which they shared with other
families. Some of the children have been sent from home to
work.

Farm labourers and their families were in an even more
precarious situation: illness or the death of the chief wage-
earner invariably resulted in a move to the poor-house or a bare
existence on parish relief. In the 1851 Schedule, fifty-three
paupers and their dependents are recorded.

The majority of the people living in Ashworthy in 1851 were
born in the locality. Just over 72 per cent (404 males and 401
females) were native to the parish, and a further 15 per cent
were born in adjoining parishes. Over half the remaining 13
per cent were born within a ten-mile radius of Ashworthy
village, while—in contrast—less than 3 per cent were natives
of other counties. Of the farmers, 67·8 per cent were born in
Ashworthy, 17 per cent in adjoining parishes and the remainder in places within a ten-mile radius. The figures for
agricultural workers are, however, rather different. Of the
male farm workers and servants, 59·6 per cent were native to
the parish and 22·2 per cent were born in adjoining parishes:
over four-fifths of the remaining 18·2 per cent are natives of
other neighbouring parishes. Of the female farm servants, 62·5
per cent were born in Ashworthy and 21·9 per cent in adjoining
parishes. The significance of these figures will be considered
later: here it may be noted that even in the middle of the nineteenth century there was considerable short-distance migration of countryfolk within the Ashworthy area.

The age-structure of the 1851 population is typical of rural
parishes which had experienced rapid growth throughout the

first half of the nineteenth century (see Fig. 16). Over a quarter of the inhabitants were children in the 0–9 age group and well over half the population (56 per cent) were under twenty-five years old. The death rate was relatively high and only one-sixth of the population was aged fifty years or older. There was little difference between the numbers of males and females in the various age groups. (See Appendix Two, Table Two.) The relatively small proportions of men and women aged between twenty-five and forty suggest that emigration was already important by 1851, but was concealed by a high birth rate.

In 1851, there were two main types of household in Ashworthy,[1] (a) the 'simple' household composed of a single group of persons related by blood or marriage and (b) the 'composite' household composed of a single group of kindred together with one or more individuals employed by the head of the house.

TABLE EIGHT

Types of household. Ashworthy 1851.

	Villagers		Outside Village		
	Craftsmen	Other Villagers	Craftsmen	Others	Farmers
Simple	19	50	12	42	16
Composite	10	1	3	1	40
Others	3	3	—	3	3
Total	32	54	15	46	59

Table Eight shows clearly that the composition of households was closely related to the three-fold division of occupations within the parish. At the one extreme there were the farm labourers and other hired workers who lived almost entirely in simple households: at the other there were the farmers who employed single men and women as labourers or servants and provided accommodation for them along with the family. This custom of 'living in' is, of course, long established in the

[1] For the purposes of this study 'a household' is defined as a group of persons occupying a structurally separate dwelling.

English countryside. Between these two groups were the craftsmen and tradesmen, many of whom employed resident inden-
tured apprentices. The other twelve households shown in the
table were made up of eight families who had lodgers living
with them and four households composed of two or more
families occupying the same dwelling. One household had four
families under the same roof.

The practice of 'living in' contributed substantially to the'
size of households, particularly on farms. (See Appendix Two,
Table Three.) Of the 59 farm households, 25 had 8 members or
more, and 12 had 11 members or more; in contrast, only one
of the 98 hired workers' households had more than 7 members,
and over a half of them were composed of 4 people or less.
Once again the craftsmen's households fell in an intermediate
position, with about half made up of 5 or more people. The
two large households which were not occupied by farmers or
craftsmen were those of the Bishop family (14 members, including 10 servants) who owned the largest estate in Ashworthy, and of the Rector (12 members, including 4 servants).[1]

The picture which has emerged from this brief analysis of
Ashworthy in 1851 is, then, one of a relatively poor agricultural
parish, inhabited by people born in the locality: birth and death
rates are high and there is some evidence of the beginnings of
emigration. This picture is, however, a static one: it tells us
very little of demographic change. Fortunately, it is possible to
compare the situation in 1851 with that in 1841, by using the
information contained in the Enumeration Schedules of the
Census: by this means, some of the more important factors
which influenced population structure and distribution and the
composition of households and families is revealed.

Population Change 1841–51

As we noted earlier, the Enumeration Schedules allow the
identification of every individual living in Ashworthy at the
time of the *Census*. By comparing the Schedules for 1841 and

[1] The size of household at any one time, was, of course, determined by
the number of resident servants and the number of family members;
variations were largely accounted for by children or by relatives of the
head of the household and his wife. This family element in the household
is considered in the next chapter.

1851 it is therefore possible to discover those individuals who have remained in the same dwelling over the ten-year period, those who have moved within the parish, those who have come to live in Ashworthy from elsewhere, and the children who have been born. It is also possible to list the people living in the parish in 1841 who are not recorded in 1851, but the Schedules do not, of course, tell us if they have left or died. Many of the deaths are given in the Burial Registers of the Church; others may be inferred with confidence from the age of the individual in 1841; some persons can be traced to other parishes through local documents; the remainder must be characterized as 'uncertain' although it seems probable that many of them have left the parish and not died.

In addition, it is often possible to make inferences about the movements of individuals and families during the inter-censal period, so that, taken as a whole, the comparison of Schedules provides a detailed record of population movement over the decade. One example may be taken to illustrate the method of analysis. In the 1841 Schedule the following entry occurs:[1]

> 'Blackdown. *Graves*, John (40) farmer, Catherine (40), John (15), Edward R. (10) Catherine J. (9), William Henry (5), Selina (3), Eleanora (9 months): (servants) Thomas White (30), John Hemmet (15), Frederick Saunders (15), John Ellicott (10), Grace Jay (20), Mary Hanking (15), Grace Coles (13).'

In 1851 there are two entries:

> 'Blackdown. *Graves*, John (27) farmer, Harriet (25) his wife, John (1) son: (servants) Susan Davies (21), Elizabeth Luxon (14), Richard Jackman (46) widower, John Friend (21), John Down (16).'
> 'West Hall. *Graves*, John (54) farmer, Catherine (51)

---

[1] The surname of the farm family and the names of the farms have been altered, since they are used elsewhere in this study. The form of the entries in the Schedules has been modified and compressed for convenience of treatment. It will be recalled that the ages given in the 1841 Schedule are in five-year groups (and always listed as the lowest figure) for persons over fifteen. There are therefore some discrepancies between 1841 and 1851.

his wife, Catherine (18) daughter, William (17) son, Selina (13) daughter, Eleanora (11) daughter: (servants) Mary Anne Painter (18), William Pengelly (24), Enoch Vanstone (19), Thomas Littlejohns (20), William Martin (17), Thomas Veale (15), Thomas Painter (15).'

It will be evident that these entries alone contain a considerable amount of information about change in the ten years between the *Censuses*. John Graves senior moved from Blackdown to West Hall, taking his wife and four children with him. The Tithe Award records that he owned both farms in 1841. His eldest son, John, married the daughter of an Ashworthy yeoman in 1847 and took over his father's farm in the summer of 1849.[1] The second son, Edward, died in 1848.[2] Of the farm servants at Blackdown in 1841, Frederick Saunders married and went to live in Ashworthy village, where he is recorded as a farm labourer with one child in 1851; Grace Jay moved from Blackdown to Summerfield and is shown as a cook there in 1851; the others are not recorded in 1851 and their names do not appear in the Marriage or Burial Registers of the Church. They probably moved to farms in near-by parishes.

Of the farm servants at Blackdown in 1851, Susan Davies, a housemaid, was born in a large town about thirty miles from Ashworthy and, like Richard Jackman who was born in Holton, is not recorded in 1841: both probably came to Ashworthy during the inter-censal period. Elizabeth Luxon, John Friend and John Down were natives of Ashworthy and are shown as children living in the village in 1841. Similarly at West Hall, Mary Anne Painter and Thomas Painter, born in Longbridge, William Pengelly, born in Broadpen, Enoch Vanstone, born in Thrushelton and Thomas Veale, born in Combe Down, are young people (not recorded in 1841) who came to Ashworthy to work. Thomas Littlejohns was a native of the parish, living with his parents in the village in 1841. William Martin was the son of a farm labourer who lived in a cottage near Blackdown.

[1] According to the Marriage Register and documents in the possession of a descendent of the family.
[2] Recorded in the Burial Register.

This one example of a farm household between 1841 and 1851 shows one birth, one death, fourteen people moving from one dwelling to another within the parish, five people who have probably left and seven who have come to Ashworthy. As we shall see presently, this example is typical in so far as it shows considerable migration within the Ashworthy area, particularly of farm servants, as well as movement within the parish itself.

The total changes in Ashworthy are summarized in the following table:

TABLE NINE

Intercensal movement of population 1841–1851.

	Farmers' families	Craftsmen's families	Farm labourers' families	Others
Living in same dwelling	161	76	115	66
Moved within Ashworthy	42	32	102	34
Came to Ashworthy	19	27	123	38
Changed status*	10	—	—	—
Children born in Ashworthy	71	55	101	23
Total 1851†	303	190	441	161
Living in Ashworthy	213	108	317	
Probably moved from Ashworthy	64	31	202	
Died	21	11	73	
Changed status‡	9	—	—	
Not known§	—	11	36	
Total 1841	307	161	628	

* Two families of farm labourers in 1841 who had become farmers by 1851.

† Does not include twenty visitors in 1841 and twenty-two visitors in 1851.

‡ Two farmers' families in 1841 who had become paupers by 1851 following the deaths of the heads of the family.

§ Individuals who have died or left the parish, for whom no documentary evidence could be found. All were over 40 in 1841.

The table shows very clearly that population totals may conceal considerable movement of families and individuals, both within the parish and between it and other parishes. In 1841 the resident population of Ashworthy was 1096; in 1851 it was 1095. Yet of the 1851 population, 18·9 per cent had entered the parish since 1841 and a further 19·1 per cent had changed their dwelling within it, that is, well over a third of the total. In the same way, just over 27 per cent of the 1841 population had probably left by 1851,[1] and this proportion does not include those people classed as 'Not Known', at least some of whom must have moved out of Ashworthy. The importance of this movement in comparison with birth and death rates may be seen from the fact that natural increase in the ten-year period accounted for just over 13 per cent of the total population.

However, the table shows that there are significant differences in migration rates between the main occupational groups. Farm families were clearly the most stable group. The families who occupy the same farms from 1841 to 1851 make up nearly three-quarters of the total (73·3 per cent).[2] A further 15·2 per cent changed farms within Ashworthy and 8·2 per cent came to live there. Farmers and their families who left the parish account for 20·8 per cent of the 1841 total. At first sight the latter might seem a high proportion, but a further breakdown shows that of the sixty-four individuals, twenty-two were farmers' sons who left their families in Ashworthy, and a further four were farmers' daughters who left on marriage. Complete farm families who left amount only to 15·6 per cent.

Among the families of craftsmen, 54·7 per cent occupy the same houses between 1841 and 1851.[3] A further 24·7 per cent

[1] The great majority were young men and women aged between fifteen and thirty. It seems unlikely that more than a few died.

[2] Including children born in Ashworthy between 1841 and 1851. There were sixty-one children born to parents who remained on the same farms, four children to parents who moved within the parish, and six children to parents who entered the parish. The second and third groups are largely young married couples, moving into their first farms.

[3] Including children born in Ashworthy between 1841 and 1851. There were twenty-eight children born to craftsmen who did not change dwellings during the ten years, fifteen children to parents who moved within Ashworthy, and twelve children to parents who came to the parish.

moved from one house to another within Ashworthy, usually in the village, while families entering the parish account for 20·5 per cent. As one might expect, farm labourers and their families show the greatest movement, many of them being single young men and women. Only 37·4 per cent remained in the same dwelling between 1841 and 1851,[1] 30·8 per cent moved within the parish and 31·7 per cent came from elsewhere. Roughly the same proportion, 32·1 per cent, left Ashworthy during the same period.

A clear picture emerges from these figures. The population as a whole is surprisingly mobile, but—as the data on place of birth shows—largely within the restricted limits of the Ashworthy area. At the same time, farmers—as owners and occupiers of land—were a relatively stable group, nearly three-quarters of them remaining in the same farm during the ten years. Craftsmen, many of whom had workshops attached to their homes, were rather more 'foot-loose', with roughly equal proportions occupying the same house and moving elsewhere. Farm labourers, with no stake in the land or in workshops and equipment, were relatively free to move, and the proportion living in the same dwelling fell to just over one-third. Thus the three-fold occupational division is reflected as clearly in the population movement as it is in the composition of households.

This analysis places rural depopulation in a new perspective. Since there was an excess of births over deaths between 1841 and 1851 and the total population remained almost unchanged, some loss by migration did occur. In later decades of the nineteenth century this loss became more and more important. However, it can now be seen as part of a much more complex pattern of migration, in which short-distance movement within a well-defined area is very significant. The Enumeration Schedules and other local documents do not, unfortunately, reveal the destinations of emigrants, but as the

---

[1] There were fifty children born in farm labourers' families who occupied the same houses in the intercensal period, thirty-four children to parents who moved within the parish and seventeen children to people who came to live there. The number of unmarried individuals was, of course, highest in the last group.

great majority of immigrants are local people it seems reasonable to assume that the outward movement is of largely the same kind. Moreover, some of the people who left between 1841 and 1851, particularly farm families, reappear in Ashworthy within the next twenty or thirty years, having come from near-by parishes.[1] Secondly, it is equally clear that migration from the countryside in the mid-nineteenth century was very largely confined to farm labourers and their families and that farmers and their families were little affected.

Previous studies of depopulation have ignored this aspect of rural demography. They have dealt with population totals, age and sex differentials and the like. It is true that they deal with large areas, for which the detailed and very laborious method of analysis used for Ashworthy is inappropriate: but in ignoring the value of sample studies it is also true that rural depopulation as a process has been much over-simplified and even misunderstood.

The years 1841 and 1851 were chosen because the very full records of the Enumeration Schedules were available. The same kind of analysis for later years in the nineteenth century would presumably show short-distance migration continuing, but with the numbers of those leaving the parish increasing steadily to bring about the fall in the total population. In order to assess the long-term effects of these changes and to examine the situation in the immediate past an analysis must be made of the population in 1960 and of change during the previous decade.

Ashworthy in 1960

As we saw in Chapter Two, Ashworthy is still essentially an agricultural parish. There are seventy-five households whose main occupation is farming and a further twenty-four households whose heads are in occupations ancillary to farming or largely dependent upon it. Of the remaining fifty-three households, thirty-five have persons 'not gainfully employed' at their head, many of whom are retired farmers and farm labourers or their dependents. The full occupational pattern is shown in the following table :

[1] This emerged from the analysis of land-ownership and changes in occupation of farms. See pp. 31–43 and 64–72 above.

TABLE TEN

Occupations in Ashworthy 1960.

Occupation	Heads of households	Others
Farmers	75	64‡
Craftsmen or tradesmen in business on own account	15	—
Railway and road transport	15	6
Agricultural workers	5	12
Forestry workers	3	4
County Council roadmen	3	—
Quarrymen	2	—
Postmen	2	—
Journeymen in crafts or trades	4	1
Old age pensioners, widows or retired persons	32*	2
Others not gainfully employed	3	2
Unemployed	1	—
Domestic servants	—	6
Shop assistants	—	7
All other occupations†	12	3
	172	97

* 15 men and 17 women.

† Includes 4 managers of shops, 2 'general dealers', 2 clergymen, 1 schoolmaster, 1 policeman, 1 clerk and 1 Water Board employee.

‡ Does not include farmers' wives.

The table shows that out of 229 people who are gainfully employed, 139 are farmers and a further 17 are farm labourers, i.e. over two-thirds of the working population are directly engaged in farming. The present condition of agriculture in Ashworthy has been discussed earlier in Chapter Two and need not be considered further here. The table also reveals clearly the importance of the village as a service centre for the surrounding district. The large number of pensioners and retired people reflects both the age structure of the population and the role of the village—where most of them live—as a place to end one's days.

As in the middle of the nineteenth century, the majority of people living in Ashworthy in 1960 were born in the locality. Just over a half (51·6 per cent) were native to the parish and a further 10·8 per cent were born in adjoining parishes. A slightly larger proportion (11·2 per cent) were born in other parishes lying within a ten-mile radius of Ashworthy. As for the remainder, 9 per cent were born elsewhere in the county and 17·4 per cent were natives of other counties.[1] Thus nearly three-quarters of the present inhabitants were born in the Ashworthy area. The proportion of 'strangers' has, however, risen considerably since 1851, particularly among farm families and those in occupations other than agriculture and rural crafts:

TABLE ELEVEN

Place of Birth by Occupational Groups 1960.

Place of birth	Farmers' families	Craftsmen's families	Farm labourers' families	Others
	%	%	%	%
Ashworthy	59·6	58·9	25·0	50·0
Adjoining parishes	8·3	5·4	58·4	7·5
Neighbouring parishes	9·0	25·3	8·3	13·1
Elsewhere in county	8·6	10·4	8·3	10·6
Other counties	14·5	—	—	18·8

Craftsmen's families and farm labourers' families resemble each other in being entirely composed of people born within the county and with over nine-tenths born in the Ashworthy area. At the same time, the mobility of farm workers is reflected in the small proportion born in Ashworthy itself—viz. half that or less of those in other occupational groups. Farmers and craftsmen show large percentages born in and around the parish, but the 'Up Country Johnnies' are a significant element in the farm population. In general, place of birth accurately reflects the pattern of movement of individuals and families, and the table confirms the significance of short-distance migration, which, as we have already seen, was important in the middle of the nineteenth century.

[1] Includes thirty-five individuals whose place of birth was not recorded. Most of them were almost certainly born outside the county.

The age structure of the 1960 population is almost certainly 'top heavy'. For a number of reasons, one of the most important being the limited time available for field work, the ages of all inhabitants were not recorded. The date of birth of everyone under twenty-five was obtained and of about half those of older people.[1] As Fig. 16 shows, however, there is a distinctive trend in the age structure of Ashworthy during the present century and there is no reason to suppose that this trend has ceased between 1951 and 1960. Therefore it appears that about a quarter of the 1960 population were aged 24 or less, a slightly smaller proportion were aged 25–44 and nearly a third were aged 45–64.

The composition of households in 1960 shows a very sharp contrast with that described for 1851. The decline in the practice of 'living in' on farms and the almost complete disappearance of the lodger from the village as economic conditions improved have together reduced the number of composite households to negligible proportions. In 1960, there are seven farm families with resident labourers or servants and a further four composite households in the village, each with one lodger. All the craftsmens' families and farm labourers' families live in simple households.

One result of this change has been a reduction in the size of households, particularly on farms. The large composite households of 1851 have disappeared and it is now rare to find more than six people living in the same dwelling. (See Appendix Two, Table Four.) However, farm households are still the largest and those of farm labourers the smallest. With the disappearance of the composite household, family size is now the main determinant of household size.

Population Change 1951–1960

Curiously enough, the documentary information available for the middle of the twentieth century is much more limited and scattered than that which exists for the nineteenth. The Enu-

[1] Many of these could be confirmed from documentary sources, such as the Parish Registers, but a significant number could not; since some people refused or were very reluctant to give their date of birth and others gave a false one, it was decided not to attempt a complete record.

meration Schedules for 1951 are not accessible; there was no *Census* in 1941; the records of the 1931 *Census* were destroyed by enemy action during the last war. A comparison of 1941 and 1951 would be vitiated by the abnormal conditions of wartime; many families from London and the south-east of England were evacuated to Ashworthy. It is, however, possible to make an effective analysis by using such sources as the annual *Register of Electors*, which gives the names and addresses of all adults living in the parish, together with the survey material collected during the field work.

The comparison is made between 1951 and 1960. The first of these was a Census year, so that some data are available: it is also exactly a century later than the end of the decade analysed in the last section. The field-work material has been revised to early in 1960, so that the period covered is slightly less than nine years.

TABLE TWELVE

Changes in population 1951–1960.

	Farmers' families	Craftsmen's families	Farm labourers' families	Others
Living in same dwelling	153	32	10	91
Moved within Ashworthy	46	22	4	31
Come to Ashworthy	44	4	22	60
Total 1960	243	58	36	182
Living in Ashworthy	199	54	14	122
Moved from Ashworthy	75	19	26	67
Died	20	2	2	11
Total 1951	294	75	42	200

Children born between 1951 and 1960 are included with their parents in the appropriate category. Less than 5 per cent of the children were born outside the parish.

As in the nineteenth century, there is considerable migration.

Of the 1960 population, 55·1 per cent occupied the same dwelling for the nine-year period; a further 19·8 per cent moved within the parish and 25·1 per cent came to live there. During the same time 30·6 per cent of the 1951 population left Ashworthy. These proportions are broadly similar to those found in the years between 1841 and 1851 and in both periods there is a net loss of population by migration. However, while this loss from 1841 to 1851, amounting to about 15 per cent, is counterbalanced by the excess of births over deaths, so that the total population remains almost unchanged, between 1951 and 1960 deaths exceeded births and loss by migration accounts for 9·3 per cent out of a total decline of 15 per cent.

There are also close similarities in the degree of movement of the different occupational groups in 1841–51 and 1951–60. Farmers' families are still the most stable element in the population, with 63 per cent occupying the same farms during the nine years. A further 18·9 per cent moved within Ashworthy and 18·1 per cent came to the parish from other places. During the same period 25·5 per cent of the 1951 total went elsewhere. Craftsmen's families show somewhat greater mobility, particularly within the parish: 55·2 per cent occupied the same dwellings, 37·9 per cent moved within Ashworthy, 6·9 per cent came there and 25·4 per cent left between 1951 and 1960. The proportions for agricultural labourers' families are 27·8 per cent, 11·2 per cent, 61 per cent and 62 per cent respectively. The movement of farm workers has increased considerably since the nineteenth century, particularly between Ashworthy and other parishes. The factors which brought about these variations between occupational groups in the nineteenth century are still relevant in the twentieth.[1]

The analysis of the two sample periods has shown, therefore, that migration within the parish and between it and other parishes near by has been an important feature of population history for over a hundred years. From 1951 to 1960, as in the nineteenth century, the great majority of the families move within the small limits of the Ashworthy area. However, in the century or so covered by the two sample periods there have been many significant changes. The total population of Ashworthy

[1] See above pp. 130–31.

has fallen from just over 1100 in 1851 to less than half that number in 1960. The number of farm labourers and their families has decreased from 441 in 1851 to 42 in 1951: in Ashworthy, as elsewhere, the mechanization of agriculture and the 'drift to the towns' have been important reasons for their decline. The dying out of many rural crafts and trades has reduced the number of craftsmen and their families from 190 in 1851 to 75 in 1951; the continuing role of the village as a service centre has prevented a more marked decline. Farm families have declined from 303 persons in 1851 to 294 in 1951, a small decrease, while 'others', in such occupations as forestry and public transport, together with retired people and pensioners, have shown an increase from 161 in 1851 to 200 in 1951. Thus farmers, the most stable group in the parish and the backbone of its economic and social life, have grown from just over a quarter of the total population (26·1 per cent) in the mid-nineteenth century to nearly a half (48 per cent) in the middle of the twentieth. The 'drift to the towns' has had little, if any, effect on farm families.

This can also be seen very clearly in an examination of local school-leaving records.[1] Between 1947 and the end of 1959 there were 55 young people who left school: 51 attended the Secondary Modern School and 4 the Grammar School, both at Longbridge. Three of the Grammar School children left at sixteen; the remainder all left school at fifteen. Farmers' sons and daughters accounted for 24 of the 55: 22 of them went to work at home with their parents. One left the parish to become a police cadet, the other became a shop assistant in Kimberford. Of the 31 craftsmen's and villagers' children, 14 have left Ashworthy to work in shops and factories in other parts of England; a further 6 have found work in other parts of the Ashworthy area and have gone to live in places within 10 miles of the village. The remaining 11 live at home, but 6 of them work outside Ashworthy. Thus nearly all the children of farm families live and work at home when they leave school, while two-thirds of the children from other families leave the parish to work elsewhere.

[1] These records were compiled by the Headmaster of Ashworthy School, whose help is gratefully acknowledged.

The reasons for this contrast are quite straightforward. In an area of family farms such as Ashworthy, farmers' sons and daughters are nearly always assured of work at home, indeed, as we have seen in an earlier chapter, their labour is essential to the economic well-being of the farm. One of the two farmers' sons who have left agriculture belongs to a family with three other sons working at home on a holding of some 80 acres. On the other hand, there is little work in Ashworthy for villagers' children and no daily public transport service from the village. The six young people who found employment in the local area find their own way to work each day. In general, therefore, distance to work places an effective limit on the numbers who can remain at home, and although there have been and will be opportunities for employment on the farms of Ashworthy and in the crafts and trades of the village, the majority of young people who do not live on farms must leave the parish sooner or later.

This situation is somewhat complicated—at least in statistical terms—by the general pattern of short-distance migration. Young men who live and work in Ashworthy may move with their families to other parts of the area. Some may remain as lodgers, others find jobs near their new homes. Families moving into the parish may have sons and daughters who seek employment. Here again, however, the broad occupational division is crucial. The children of farmers and craftsmen are normally assured of work with their parents wherever they move: agricultural labourers' children, if they follow their fathers into farm work, or into other kinds of work on the land such as forestry, have little difficulty in finding employment near home. In contrast, the daughters of the quarrymen, the sons of council roadmen, the children of craftsmen's journeymen, i.e. the children of the 'others' who make up the fourth occupational category are most often obliged to leave home when their parents move.

The analysis of records for the mid-nineteenth and mid-twentieth centuries has shown the existence of short-distance migration as an important characteristic of the demography of Ashworthy. It has also shown significant differences in the rates of migration between different occupational groups. This aspect of rural life has been almost completely neglected in earlier studies[1] although it is clearly important in an understanding of population structure and in the study of rural depopulation. Its particular significance to this study is that it confirms the general view of rural social life as in a state of 'dynamic equilibrium' and, secondly, it serves as an essential preliminary to the analysis of family and kinship which follows in the next chapter.

[1] An important exception is Dr. J. Sheppard's paper 'East Yorkshire's Agricultural Labour Force in the mid-ninetenth century', *Agricultural History Review*, Vol. *IX*, Pt. 1 (1961), pp. 43–54.

CHAPTER SIX

FAMILY AND KINSHIP

THE demographic changes which were analysed in the last chapter, particularly the change in age and sex structure, the effects of migration, the reduction in the size of household and the virtual disappearance of the composite household, are closely related to the dynamics of family organization and the operation of the kinship system. The methods used to study population change, based on sample periods in the mid-nineteenth and mid-twentieth centuries, can also be applied to analyse family and kinship structure within an historical framework.

Family and kin in 1851

The data given in the Enumeration Schedule make it possible to classify the family types found in Ashworthy in 1851. (See Appendix Three, Table One.) The most common type was the elementary family composed of parents and children, accounting for just over half of all the families in the parish, and also of farmers', craftsmen's and villagers' families respectively. Other families were variants of the elementary type, notably childless couples and 'denuded families'.[1] The childless couples were mostly young people, married for a relatively short time, who may be regarded as 'incomplete' or 'potential' elementary families. The denuded families were composed of a widowed parent and children: those denuded by the death of the husband were in a large majority. Taken together, these three types amounted to 62 per cent of all the families in Ashworthy, and it is clear, therefore, that the elementary family and its 'normal' variants were dominant in the middle of the nineteenth century.

[1] See R. Firth, *Two Studies of Kinship in London.* (London 1956), 'Kinship in South Borough', p. 35.

Family and Kinship

The bare facts of the *Census* do not, of course, tell us very
much about family life in Ashworthy; for example, how near
did it approximate to the stereotype of the patriarchal Victorian
family? It is possible to go a little way towards answering such
questions, by using the *Census* data in conjunction with other
local records. Firstly, if family life was dominated by the father,
then at least his dominance was not always reinforced by
seniority in years. An examination of the disparity in the ages
of spouses shows somewhat surprising results:

TABLE THIRTEEN

Difference in age of married couples 1851.

	Farmers %	Craftsmen %	Others %	All %
Wife older than husband by 1 year	16·8	25·0	22·8	21·6
Husband and wife same age	14·2	16·8	10·8	13·1
Husband older than wife by 1–3 years	23·1	30·6	28·8	27·5
Husband older than wife by 4–7 years	25·1	22·0	24·0	24·0
Husband older than wife by 8 years or more	20·8	5·6	13·6	13·8

In over a fifth of all marriages, the husband was the junior
in years, and only among farmers was marked seniority apparent.[1] In contrast, a quarter of the married craftsmen were
younger than their wives. The reasons for the differences between occupational groups cannot be inferred from the available data, but it may be relevant to note that membership of
each group tended to be perpetuated by marriage. Farmers'
daughters married farmers' sons and so on.

It appears possible, therefore, although the evidence is
slender, that farm families were more patriarchal than others.
This was accompanied by significant differences in size of

[1] In the extreme case among farmers, the husband was twenty-one
years older than his wife: for craftsmen the extreme was twenty-three
years and for the other married couples eleven years. One farmer's wife
was thirteen years older than her husband.

141

family between occupational groups. Farmers' families were the largest, followed by craftsmen's families and then the families of other villagers.[1] This can be seen clearly from the number of children living at home in each family. (See Appendix Three, Table Two.) Thus 11·4 per cent of village couples were childless and just under 70 per cent had one to three children living at home. There was only one family with six children, the largest in this group. Of the craftsmen's families, 9·3 per cent were childless and 67·4 per cent had one to three children at home; again six children was the largest number and there were only two families of these. Farmers had the highest proportion of childless couples, 12·5 per cent, but far fewer families with one to three children, 43·8 per cent; 20·8 per cent of married or widowed farmers had six or more sons and daughters at home, the largest being a family with ten children. It would seem therefore, that the families of farmers came nearest to the stereotype of the large patriarchal Victorian family.

However, it must be noted that size of family was not a simple reflection of number of children. There were also 'additional kin', that is relatives of the head of the household other than his wife, sons and daughters. Their distribution gives a somewhat different picture from the number of children in the family:

TABLE FOURTEEN

Additional kin of heads of households 1851.

Number of added kin	Villagers	Craftsmen	Farmers
1	14	15	10
2	7	1	4
3	1	2	1
4	—	—	2
5	1	—	—

Additional kin were more common in craftsmen's families than in those of farmers and villagers, 38·3 per cent, 28·8 per cent and 22 per cent respectively having at least one additional kin member. The main reason for this appears to be the fairly

[1] In this respect they resemble differences in size of household.

common practice among craftsmen to accept nephews as resident apprentices. The total number of additional kin (a hundred) was not, however, large enough to disturb the general pattern of family size.

There were in all fifty-eight families who had kindred living with them, i.e. well over a quarter of all the households in Ashworthy. Their existence qualifies the dominance of the elementary family, and indicates that some extension of kinship was important in the parish. (There were, in addition, a small number of bachelors and spinsters living alone and a few families of unmarried siblings, but they form an insignificant proportion of the whole. In nineteenth century Ashworthy marriage was the normal basis for setting up a household. (See Appendix Three, Table One.) Most of the additional kin were closely related to the head of the family:

TABLE FIFTEEN

Relationship of additional kin to head of household 1851.

Father	2	Brother	6	Nephew	10
Mother	9	Sister	1	Niece	6
Father-in-law	7	Brother-in-law	4	Uncle	1
Mother-in-law	7	Son-in-law	6	Aunt	1
'Cousin'	1	Daughter-in-law	2	Grandson	14
		Great-grandson	1	Grand-daughter	22

Over a quarter of the relatives were affinal kin of the head of the family, but perhaps the most striking aspect of the relationships is the high proportion of grandchildren. They were, with very few exceptions, the children of a widow or widower living with parents. Two principles appear to underlie this arrangement: firstly, when one spouse dies in a family with children, the parents of the survivor may provide a home and care for the denuded family. Secondly, and following from the first, where the children are young there should be a female relative to look after them. For example, some families were composed of a widower, his widowed daughter and her children, and others of a man and wife, their widowed son and his children. A few were composed of a widower, a widowed son and his children, together with a sister, niece or unmarried daughter of the head of the family. In these families at least there is evidence of a strong link joining three generations and possibly alternate generations. Such links may also have been created or merely reinforced in those families where the additional relative is a parent, nearly always widowed. In Ashworthy, as elsewhere, a widow or—less commonly—a widower might look to one of his or her children for a home and security.

The *Census* material and other documentary evidence tell us nothing further about the extension of kinship nor about social relations between kindred. In a general way, however, the importance of the elementary family and the closeness of relationships found in extended family households suggest that the kinship system was relatively narrow in range and shallow in depth. Moreover, it operated in conditions where, as we have seen earlier, individuals and families were likely to move quite often from one place to another. In such circumstances the members of a person's immediate family and his close and distant relatives might at one time be scattered over a large area of countryside and at another be gathered together quite near to each other, with important effects on social relations between them.

The Enumeration Schedules provide ample evidence of this mobility. As we saw in the last chapter, over a quarter of the people living in Ashworthy in 1851 were born outside the parish. Of the 164 married heads of families, over a half had wives born in different parishes from their own.[1] Farm labourers' sons and daughters normally left home between the ages of ten and fourteen to become resident farm servants.

The family in 1960

The analysis of family and kin in Ashworthy in 1851 was largely quantitative in its approach because of the limitations imposed by available documentary evidence. In comparing 1851 with 1960 and examining the changes which have taken place, these quantitative data will once again be useful, but

[1] The proportion was 53 per cent. As one might expect, farmers had the lowest proportion, 43.7 per cent, followed by craftsmen, 52.9 per cent, and other married couples, mainly farm labourers, 58.7 per cent.

they may now be supplemented by first-hand material gathered during the field work.

We begin with the types of family found in the parish in 1960, summarized in Appendix Three, Table Three. The table shows that the elementary family and its incomplete or denuded variants are dominant, amounting to just over 75 per cent of all families. There has, therefore, been a significant increase since 1851, when 62 per cent of all families were of this type. On the other hand, the proportion of 'pure' elementary families has decreased from just over a half in 1851 to less than a fifth in 1960, with a corresponding increase in the numbers of denuded families and childless couples. Other types which show important increases are spinsters and widows living alone. As one might expect, these changes have been accompanied by a sharp decline in the proportion of families with added kin, which decreased from 27·4 per cent in 1851 to 4·1 per cent in 1960.

In general terms, then, it is clear that the elementary family and related types, already dominant in mid-nineteenth century Ashworthy, have increased their pre-eminence during the last hundred years. At the same time, the extension of kinship, at least as manifested in family type, has declined in importance. In more detail, the comparison of the family types in 1851 and 1960 reflects in striking fashion the relationship between demographic change and family organization. As we saw in the last chapter, the proportion of middle-aged and old people in the population has increased steadily during the last hundred years and the proportion of young people has decreased. More and more, therefore, the likelihood of childless couples, of widows and widowers, and of married couples whose children have left home forming a significant part of total family types has increased. Thus elementary families denuded by the loss of children who have married or left home to find employment have become an important new category. Widows living alone provide an equally good example.

Now as we saw in the last chapter, demographic change has had differing effects on the main occupational groups in Ashworthy and one might expect this to be reflected in family types. It may be recalled that villagers, particularly agricultural labourers, have been the most mobile group, followed by craftsmen, with farmers as the least mobile. It is not surprising to find then, that the proportion of denuded families in the village[1] (23·7 per cent) is higher than that of farmers (20 per cent) and that the proportion of true elementary families in the village (30·2 per cent) is considerably lower than that on farms (46·6 per cent). On the other hand, in this respect craftsmen's families no longer form an intermediate group in the way that they did in the nineteenth century. Their proportion of denuded families (25 per cent) is the highest of the three groups, while their proportion of true elementary families (45 per cent) closely resembles that of farmers. It is clear that farmers' sons and daughters tend to stay at home much longer than villagers' children, principally because inheritance, continuity and the role of the family as an economic unit are so important in farming. The craftsmen are still in an intermediate position in that some of their families are economic units with father and son working together, while others are one-man businesses that cannot support two people. This difference within the group, together with the very small number of craftsmen's families, probably accounts for the statistical variation noted above. Widows and widowers living alone are much more common in the village (13·1 per cent of all families) than on farms (2·7 per cent) and among craftsmen (5 per cent).

The one family type which does not appear to fit conveniently into the general picture is the childless couple, accounting for 11·8 per cent of village families, 15 per cent of craftsmen's families and 16 per cent of farmers' families. (Here, as in the proportion of true elementary families, craftsmen and farmers closely resemble each other.) At first sight one might expect fewer farmers to be childless than villagers. The situation is, in fact, largely a result of differences in age between the two groups. A number of childless couples on farms are young people, married for less than five years: far fewer of the village families are of the same kind.

Another simple index of the effect of demographic change on the family is the number of children living at home. (See Appendix Three, Table Four.) As a comparison with 1851

---

[1] Craftsmen also live mostly in the village, but are not included in the village totals.

shows, the number of children living with their parents has decreased considerably during the last hundred years. In the mid-nineteenth century, families with four or more children were relatively common; nowadays they are quite rare. The change is partly the result of the general decrease in family size and partly a consequence of the migration of young people to find employment. Together these have greatly reduced the differences that once existed between the three occupational groups, with the important exception of the category with no children at home: the latter includes, of course, many couples whose sons and daughters have all left home.

In other respects, however, there are still significant differences between families in the three occupational groups, seen, for example, in the disparity between the ages of husbands and wives:

TABLE SIXTEEN

Difference in age of married couples 1960.

	Farmers %	Craftsmen %	Villagers %
Wife older than husband by 1 year or more	6·5	5·9	14·2
Husband and wife same age	21·0	11·8	26·2
Husband older than wife by 1–3 years	25·8	29·4	14·1
Husband older than wife by 4–7 years	12·9	35·3	22·9
Husband older than wife by 8 years or more	25·8	Nil	11·8
Not known	8·0	17·6	10·8

As in the nineteenth century, husbands who are older, sometimes considerably older, than their wives are more common in farm families than in others. Just over a quarter of farmers are at least eight years older than their wives. Farmers and craftsmen tend to favour seniority in marriage, about two-thirds of them being at least one year older than their wives: among villagers, on the other hand, rather less than a half have a year's seniority or more. Once again, therefore, similarities appear between farmers and craftsmen.

The difference in age between husband and wife is, of course, a reflection of the age at which the two sexes marry. This is shown in the following table:

TABLE SEVENTEEN
Age at first marriage (percentage)[1]

	−21	21–4	25–9	30–4	35–9	40–4	45+
Farmers	3·9	23·9	45·8	16·4	9·1	·9	Nil
Craftsmen	6·3	28·1	43·8	14·4	7·4	Nil	Nil
Villagers	3·2	41·5	34·4	13·3	2·3	2·3	3·1
Farmers' wives	22·4	46·4	19·4	9·0	1·4	1·4	Nil
Craftsmen's wives	33·4	40·0	21·0	5·6	Nil	Nil	Nil
Villagers' wives	25·4	42·2	19·9	9·2	3·3	Nil	Nil

The figures show clearly that women tend to marry earlier than men and do not differ greatly from one occupational group to another. On the other hand, farmers and craftsmen generally marry later than men in the village. The peak age for marriage of farmers and craftsmen lies in the 25–29 age range, for village men in the 21–24 age range.

The comparison of family type and organization in 1851 and 1960, using relatively simple criteria, has shown that the differences between the three main occupational groups, which were so important in the nineteenth century, have been to some extent reduced or changed in emphasis during the last hundred years. The process has not been consistent, partly because demographic change and migration have had irregular effects on the family, and partly because family life itself does not follow an orderly pattern through time. It must be remembered too that the numbers of craftsmen and their families have declined much farther than those of farmers and villagers. At the same time, the analysis has shown that there are still

[1] This table is based on 128 first marriages of villagers and 121 first marriages of villagers' wives, 32 marriages of craftsmen and their wives, taken from the Ashworthy parish register, and from data collected during the field work. The period covered is from 1880 to 1960, but over 70 per cent of the marriages fell between 1900 and 1960. For data on farmers and their wives see pp. 88–9 above.

important differences between farmers and villagers, with craftsmen lying in an intermediate position, but with a strong tendency to resemble farmers rather than villagers in their family type and organization.

Thus the comparison confirms the expectation, arrived at on other grounds, which was stated in the Introduction to Chapter Five (p. 113). This expectation was based on the analysis in Part One of the relationship between man and the land and the importance of continuity in the structure of the farm family. The transmission of property and skills, so crucial in farm families, is also found in certain craftsmen's families, which therefore tend to resemble them. In contrast, some craftsmen and tradesmen, and nearly all villagers have little property or skills to transmit to their children and so differ in their family type and organization. The majority of farmers' sons become farmers on land they have inherited or otherwise acquired with help from their fathers: just over a half of the present craftsmen are the sons of craftsmen, while less than one-sixth of other villagers follow the same occupations as their fathers.[1] Thus farmers and some craftsmen tend to marry 'late', to be some years older than their wives, to have at least one child living at home, because as young men their interests and future prospects are inseparable from family interests: in contrast, other craftsmen and most villagers have much less to keep them at home when they are young adults; they must make their own way in the world. On farms, therefore, the tie between father and son is particularly strong, as it is in some craftsmen's families. In other households it is very much weaker, although it is my impression that even there it is stronger than in the urban families described by other sociologists.[2]

---

[1] A number of villagers, like their fathers, are 'labourers', some of whom work on farms, others in quarries, etc. Many have changed their place of work several times. They have been classified as following a different occupation from their father if their place of work is clearly different, e.g. a farm and railway line.

[2] See, for example, M. Young and P. Willmott, *Family and Kinship in East London* (London 1957), and *Family and Class in a London Suburb* (London 1960). For further material on the link between father and son see *Sociology of An English Village*, p. 42 *et. seq.*, and *The Country Craftsman*, pp. 136–41.

The distinction is, then, fundamental in the social structure, but it must be remembered that the relationship between man and the land is much less rigid in Ashworthy than it is in other areas of family farming. Therefore, as we saw in an earlier chapter, the more spectacular features of farm family life, such as a high proportion of bachelors and marked parental dominance, which are found elsewhere, do not occur in Ashworthy and so the distinction between farm families and others is less striking.

Kinship

It was noted in the last section that one of the most marked changes in family organization during the last hundred years was the decline in the numbers of additional kin. In 1960, only seven families in Ashworthy had relatives living with them, numbering fourteen in all, and there were five three-generation families. It might seem, therefore, that the extension of kinship has diminished considerably in importance. All the added kin are closely related to the head of the household[1] and there is only one household which can be regarded as a particularly good example of kinship extension. It is composed of the head, his wife, four single children, a married daughter and her husband, the head's widowed mother, and his wife's brother and sister. They are a family of substantial farmers.

From the evidence of family type alone, therefore, it appears that extension of kinship—which was not particularly well developed in Ashworthy even in the mid-nineteenth century—has become functionally unimportant. In a general way it might be argued that the social provisions of the Welfare State, which have made it easier for widows and widowers to live alone for example, have replaced many of the functions of kindred. In addition, decades of migration and an ageing population have together reduced the possibilities of kindred conveniently coming together to form a household. Several of the widows in the village have sons or daughters living in distant parts of England: to them there is a great deal of

[1] They are related as follows: mother—2; mother-in-law—2; brother-in-law—2; sister-in-law—2; daughter—2; father-in-law—1; grandson—1; son-in-law—1; sister—1.

difference between making a home with a child who lives in the next village and with one who lives in Kent or Essex.

On the other hand, it has been shown elsewhere in this study that kinship is an important factor in the everyday lives of Ashworthy folk. It would, indeed, be a great mistake to suppose that, because the majority of people in Ashworthy live in elementary families, they therefore ignore the ramifications of kinship. Family type and membership are only two aspects of the kinship system: for other aspects we must leave the documentary material used so far and turn to the data collected during the field work.

The Range of Kinship

In a small rural community like Ashworthy it is possible to construct a genealogy extending over several generations for most individuals, using information collected from informants together with documentary evidence of various kinds. It is also possible to establish the actual kin connections that join up households, so that a comprehensive genealogical structure or 'map' can be produced for the community. This is a basic procedure which can be used in the analysis of many aspects of social activity, providing a frame of reference to which a great deal of day-to-day social behaviour may be related. It is, however, extremely important to realize that such kinship data are consciously collected and arranged by the field worker and that the result differs in a number of very significant respects from the kinship information available to and used by the countryfolk themselves.

In general, the people of Ashworthy are very interested in kinship and possess a considerable amount of knowledge about relationships by blood and marriage, which embraces not only their own kindred but also includes an impressive number of their friends, acquaintances and neighbours. A number are 'experts', who can effortlessly trace their way through the kin ramifications of dozens of families over several generations. This interest in kinship is a direct reflection of the fact that it is a genealogical system operating in a community where 'everyone know everyone else'. It is largely in terms of this system that the people of Ashworthy organize their lives. However, the most expert of the local people have a great many gaps and irregularities in their knowledge and there are others who express little interest in kinship and know little even about their own kin relationships. Moreover, there is considerable variation from individual to individual in the use of kinship terms and in the range of recognized relationships. Terms such as 'my family', 'my relatives' or 'my in-laws' are employed in a great many ways to cover quite different groups of people in different contexts. Some people regarded remote affinal kin as 'distant relatives', others excluded the husbands and wives of first cousins—'they are not related to me'. Therefore, just as every individual has an unique set of *actual* kin so too does he have his own unique view of which persons do or do not constitute his kindred and of their particular relationships. As one might expect, in the close-knit Ashworthy system the individual's conception of his or other people's kin networks approximates more or less to the actual networks, while the differences between them are important in giving a rich variety and flexibility to the social relations between kin.

Now, up to this point, no distinction has been made between *knowledge* of kin and *recognition* of kin, although it can be seen from what has already been said that an individual may be able to trace a relationship by blood or marriage without necessarily recognizing it as part of his own kinship network.[1] In a community like Ashworthy, where kin relationships are constantly cropping up in conversation, kinship information frequently extends beyond the range of recognition. This distinction poses both practical and theoretical problems for the field worker. Informants in Ashworthy were asked to construct a 'family tree' to include all the people who were related to them by blood or marriage. It might seem at first sight that the individuals they described were those, and only those, they recognized as kindred and it is almost certainly true that the vast majority of them were in this category. There are, however, a number of difficulties, arising partly from the interview

[1] This point is considered at some length in the important recent paper by K. C. Rosser and C. C. Harris, 'Relationships through Marriage in a Welsh Urban Area', *Sociological Review*, Vol. 9, No. 3 (Nov. 1961).

situation and partly from the nature of the kinship system. First, some informants were very proud of the fact that they could 'claim' a large number of kindred, and may therefore have included individuals as kindred whom they did not recognize in practice. Secondly, it was fairly common for informants to remember additional relationships some days or weeks after the interview, and it is quite probable that many of the genealogies are incomplete. Thirdly, recognition of kinship implies a very wide range of social relations from close and continuous association to the most tenuous and irregular links: it is indeed a feature of kinship in Ashworthy that people claimed as relatives others with whom they had no overt social relations at all. (The latter may, however, be brought into close social contact by a change in circumstances or some fortuitous event.) In sociological terms, therefore, there seems little difference between an individual known to be related to Ego but not recognized by him as kin and an individual recognized by Ego as kin but with whom little or no social relationship is maintained.

These difficulties make generalization about kinship difficult and in order to make it possible certain assumptions must be made about the data which have been collected. They are (a) that all the kin given by informants in their genealogies are recognized kin; (b) that the genealogies are complete in so far as they include all the individuals with whom the informant has social relations of any kind; and (c) that kindred who are known but not recognized are not included in the genealogies and are of negligible importance in the analysis of kinship as a basis for social activity.

With these considerations in mind, we may now turn to the general characteristics of kin recognition in Ashworthy. The first is that recognition is relatively shallow in depth. Most people in Ashworthy could cover five generations—from grandfather to grandchild—and a small number, particularly persons in late middle age, could extend over six generations. There were some individuals whose recognition of kin stretched over four generations only, but I could find no more than one person whose range extended farther than six generations. He was a bachelor in his late forties, greatly interested in his ancestry, who had made some attempt to trace them through a family Bible and the deeds of his farm. His recognition covered, in an irregular fashion, seven generations—from his father's father's father's father to a second cousin's grandchildren. The family Bible provided most of the information about the more remote ascendant generations and there were many gaps in the descendant generations, particularly of affines. He is not representative of the parish in range of kin, nor, strikingly enough, in the fact that he is the last member of the only farming family in Ashworthy which has occupied the same holding for more than a hundred years. Here there is at least a hint that depth of kinship recognition, particularly of ascendant generations, is often linked with the pride in family *and family land*, found particularly in stable systems of landholding. The evidence from Gosforth in Cumberland strongly supports this suggestion,[1] and it must be remembered that farmers whose families have occupied the same holding for generations frequently have detailed records of their ancestors in the form of farm deeds and wills. In contrast, farmers—and others—whose families have moved frequently from one place to another, as they have in Ashworthy, rarely have such records and lack a strong emotional attachment to the past as symbolized by a particular house or farm.

On the other hand, there is generally a wide lateral extension of kinship recognition, taking in the different categories of kin as far as second cousins once or twice removed[2] among blood relations. Recognition of affines is less wide as a rule, although it often extends as far as the spouse's first cousin once or twice removed. In general, the lateral range is greatest in a person's own generation, followed very closely by the generation of his parents. The first generation below, i.e. that of his children, usually extends less widely, largely because—as one man put it— 'there's children being born all the time and you just can't keep up'. The second ascendant and descendant generations are

[1] See *Sociology of An English Village*, Ch. IV *passim*.

[2] As Firth has observed, this is consistent with a depth range of five generations, two ascendant and two descendant from Ego. (Firth, op. cit., p. 37).

very much narrower in range, and quite often next to nothing
was said about them.

There are further variations according to the age, marital
status and sex of the individual. Broadly speaking, the range of
recognition increases with age, particularly after marriage and
the arrival of children. Women have a wider range, and more
detailed and accurate knowledge within it, than men.[1] It
appears that the concentration of a woman's interests within
the home and family leads to collecting information about
other families who are linked by blood or marriage. At the same
time it is common to find widows and spinsters who are experts
in genealogy, perhaps as a form of compensation for the in-
completeness of their own family situation. Finally, there are
variations which result from particular family circumstances
and differences in temperament.

These variations are accompanied by wide differences in the
number of kindred that a person 'claims'. In Ashworthy, the
extremes were a farm labourer brought up in an institution,
who recognized no kin at all, and a villager who listed over 200
people. The construction of a full genealogy is a lengthy and
laborious procedure, and within the limited period of the field
work it was impossible to collect more than a small number.
Fourteen individuals were asked to describe their full 'family
tree' without assistance; nine 'claimed' between 126 and 214
people. This gives some idea of the size of the 'kin universe'[2]
possessed by the people of Ashworthy. However, in the collection of these data and in gathering other information on kinship,
it was very common to find that informants expressed a strong
wish to have their spouses or other members of their family
present to help them. This is in keeping with Firth's view that
the household acts as a unit within the kinship system—'Husband and wife share their kin; they tend to act together in kin
relations.'[3] and also with the observed behaviour of Ashworthy
people on many occasions. When the spouses of those of the
thirteen informants who were married added their contributions to the genealogies the totals rose by as much as 76, giving

[1] Cf. *The Sociology of An English Village*, p. 72.

[2] A term used by Firth, op. cit.

[3] Op. cit., p. 27.

one household a kin universe of 242 persons. In one of the households, husband and wife described their respective kin universes separately (see below, p. 157) but, although information was collected on differences between members of the same household in kinship recognition and in social relations arising from it, no attempt was made to investigate the topic systematically.

In general, then, the numbers of recognized kin were large, but not surprisingly so to the people of Ashworthy: most of them expected 'hundreds' of kindred before beginning to construct their genealogies. Dead kin were included as a matter of course, often without mentioning that they were no longer alive. Some were links between living kin and were mentioned for that reason, but many others were recognized who were not links; very often the mention of their name was the occasion for an anecdote or circumstantial detail which showed clearly that their inclusion is to be seen in terms of affection and sentiment. Dead kin are, as it were, parts of the collective social background, which—in the eyes of Ashworthy folk—makes a person what he is. If they are famous, or outstandingly clever, or otherwise of high status, then the person who claims them as kin can share their social prominence to some degree.

In the full genealogies which were collected, dead kin accounted for between sixteen and twenty-seven per cent of all kindred. The variation was partly a result of difference in age among informants, since the older the person the more likely it is that there will be a high proportion of dead kin in his own and his parents' generations. It was also related to the size and range of the kin universe, since dead kin who linked living relatives were mentioned (and perhaps recalled?) more often by people with a large number of kin. Quite commonly too, people did not know if a particular relative were alive or dead: 'I haven't heard of 'e for years, I expect he'm dead.' It was indeed usual to find death equated with no knowledge of a person: 'He and his family went to Australia. I don't know anything about them now. They might just as well be dead.' When social relations of any kind have been completely severed, then the recollections of ties and associations which bind a man to another are 'frozen' in much the same way as when a death occurs.

In short, then, recognition of kin in Ashworthy is relatively shallow in depth, extends rather widely within the relevant generations, and normally includes large numbers of persons. There are many variables which affect the total range of kin an individual recognises, and within this range his knowledge varies from possessing a great number of detailed facts about one person to merely recognizing that another exists—often not even knowing his name. These general characteristics can conveniently be illustrated by the example of a married couple, John and Edna Brown. They are not so much 'an average type' as an 'apt illustration'[1] which provides a useful focus for discussion.

The Brown Family

John Brown is forty and his wife Edna is thirty-eight; they live in a small house in the village. Their two children, John and Reginald, are eight and five respectively. It took four conversations of over three hours each for these two people to describe separately their respective kinship universes, and a further four evenings were devoted to discussing their kindred with both of them present. Their combined kinship universe is shown in Fig. 17. It covers six generations in depth, their own, two descendant and three ascendant but, largely because of their age, there are only three people in the second descendant generation—the grandchildren of one of John's sisters.

Edna's recognition of her consanguineal kin extends laterally as far as 'Margaret', a second cousin once removed on the paternal side, and includes several second cousins, Brenda Green, Belinda White, Jack Edwards, Heather Black, etc. However, while a considerable amount of detail is known about the lives and activities of most second cousins, all that Edna knows of Margaret is her one Christian name and the fact that she is a schoolteacher in Westmorland. Edna could not identify all the necessary kin who link her with these distant relatives, but, on the other hand, she recognized all the affinal kin acquired by her marriage to John. This recognition does not mean that her social relations with 'John's side of the family'

[1] See M. Gluckman, 'Ethnographic data in British Social Anthropology', *Sociological Review*, Vol. 9, No. 1. (Mar. 1961), pp. 5–18.

are identical to his, but rather that they are people she had come to accept as 'relatives' and has learnt about through conversation and social intercourse. Since they are 'relatives' her behaviour towards them will be different, if only perhaps very slightly different in some instances, from that towards other people.

John's recognition of his consanguineal kin extends also as far as second cousin once removed, but he claims only two relatives at that distance—'Ernie' and Bill Grey's daughter. He is, however, able to relate a fair amount of circumstantial information about them and knows considerably more about his second cousins. His recognition of 'Edna's people' does not cover all the individuals shown in Fig. 17; with one or two exceptions, to be discussed later, it includes only Edna's parents, grandparents, parents' siblings, siblings and their children, and first cousins and their children. He has met or knows of some of Edna's more remote kin but does not recognize them as 'my relatives'.

The Brown's recognition of kin is widest in their own generation and in that of their parents. Their recognition of the first descendant generation is rather more limited in range and there is a sharp contraction in the second generation removed from their own. The second descendant generation is, of course, thinly peopled because of the Brown's age and because 'we can't keep up with the children of really distant relatives'. The second ascendant generation is constricted because 'they died when we were very young' or because 'we've forgotten all about them'. There are, nevertheless, 214 people shown in Fig. 17, representing a remarkable body of kin knowledge and recognition. Edna recognized them all, John recognized 138 of them. Of the total universe, 21 of 'John's side' (19·1 per cent) and 28 of 'Edna's side' (27·5 per cent) are dead, and some of them, for example John's mother's brother and sister, Annie and Bert, are remembered and recognized by both the Browns as personalities and not as links with living kin.

The collection of individuals who are recognized as kin by the Browns, as shown in Fig. 17, represents their kin universe at a particular point in time. New persons appear as children are born to kindred and, perhaps less commonly, others are

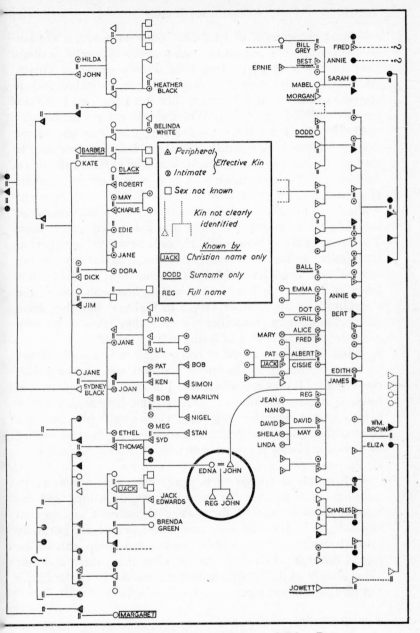

Fig. 17. The kinship universe of John and Edna Brown.

no longer recognized, or forgotten. Sometimes too, a chance event may add one person or even a group of people to one's kindred. For example, when John Brown visited a village about thirty miles from Ashworthy in 1944, he stayed with a married woman named Morgan. 'She just happened to be the person who put people up. When she heard my name and where I came from she started asking questions and in no time at all she was treating me like a long-lost relation. It turned out that her maiden name was Mabel Grey; she was a daughter of "cousin Sarah"—a first cousin of my mother. Honestly, I never even knew "cousin Sarah" was married! While I was there I found out that there was another daughter too—a sister to Mabel, who had married a chap called Best. Their son, Ernie, delivers milk. He calls on several members of the family, so the news soon went round about my staying down there. Then I met Mabel's brother Bill; he lives a few doors away. Now *he* has a married daughter who lives in the same block as my brother David in Oakton! But they have never claimed any connection—even if they knew of it; they never treated each other as if they were related.'

(Edna was quite explicit in recognizing these kinfolk of her husband's although she has never had any social contact with them at all: 'If they are relatives of John's, they are relatives of mine. It stands to reason . . . If they came here to Ashworthy I would treat them like relations. How would John feel if I treated them like strangers?' We see here a powerful motive at work for giving husband and wife at least a *potential* joint kinship universe.)

Such instances appear to be quite common: almost every informant had at least one account—usually a long and extremely involved one—of the chance discovery of unsuspected kindred. As in John Brown's case, these people are normally somewhat distant kin, whose exact relationship cannot be traced through all its links. At the same time, these accounts point clearly to the interest which Ashworthy folk take in the ramifications of kinship.

Kinship grouping

The Browns, like the other people in Ashworthy and in

England as a whole, adhere to what has been called the 'patrinominal' principle of kin grouping.[1] A wife takes her husband's surname on marriage, and children have the surname of their father. Since these surnames are transmitted from one generation to another, the system is in one sense patrilineal, reinforced by law and reflected in such social practices as referring to a collection of kin as 'the Browns', or 'the Joneses'. Thus, in Fig. 17 all the male and unmarried female descendants of William Brown have Brown as their surname and together with the women who have married male descendants, are known collectively as 'the Browns'.

In terms of kinship recognition, however, the picture is somewhat more complicated. As Fig. 17 shows, some individuals are known by their Christian names only, some by their surname only and some are recognized as kin whose names are not known at all. For example, in describing his consanguineal kin, John Brown said: 'When I was in Bigtown in 1941 I met a young lad called Jowett. It's an unusual name, so I went home and asked mother about him. It turned out he was a grandchild of a brother of my granny—my father's mother, Eliza. . . . No, I never saw him again and I don't know what his first name was.' Here is a clear example of the initial identification of kin through a surname, and it may be noted in passing that the kin link was established through John Brown's mother. Again, speaking of other kin, he said: 'My brother Albert's girl Pat, she's married to a chap called Jack—he's a compositor. They have no children. I don't know what her married name is. . . . My father's brother Charlie is a widower. I haven't seen him since my father died in 1943. I don't know what his wife's name was and I've never seen any of his children to speak to.'

There are in all seven persons recognized by the Browns as kin who are known by their surnames only, five on 'John's side' and two on Edna's. Six of the seven are affinal kin, as are two of the three persons known only by their Christian names. The number of people whose names are not known appears to be much larger, but it must be remembered that the statement,

[1] See Firth, op. cit., p. 40.

'I don't know what his (her) name is', when applied to blood kin, may often refer only to Christian names. For example, Edna Brown said of her mother's father's father: 'I know nothing about him, I don't even know his name'; from the diagram it is clear his surname was Black, and when questioned, Edna promptly mentioned it. On the other hand, Christian names and surnames of affines are often not known and one may include here the maiden names of female affines. This point is considered further below.

Other genealogies for people in Ashworthy show a somewhat similar picture, but with a larger proportion of individuals known only by a Christian name or, less commonly, a surname. The Browns are more knowledgeable about kin than most. Nevertheless, the system is clearly patrinominal and in this respect it is consistent with the position of the father in the elementary family and his relationship with his children. As we saw earlier, the farm family may reasonably be described as patriarchal and the links between father and sons are particularly strong. Even on farms there are close ties between mother and daughters, but these are subordinated within the family structure. The ties between mother and sons are weakly developed. In craftsmen's and other villagers' families the dominant position of the father is less sharply defined, but it is strong enough to make it possible to describe kinship in Ashworthy as *patri-central*. At the same time, it must be noted that the links between the individual elementary families which make up the kin network are not maintained entirely by the father. Farmers and their sons frequently meet other farmers and their sons who are kindred at markets and on other occasions, while farmers' wives and daughters see much less of their kindred.[1] They are tied to the home and have fewer reasons for leaving it. Nevertheless, a married daughter does visit her mother often, thus maintaining a particularly close link between families. A married daughter's husband or a married son are much less likely to visit. Moreover, since women tend to have greater knowledge of kinship than men,

[1] This has been noted in other rural communities. See, for example, *Sociology of An English Village*, p. 150, and the reference cited on p. 235 (for Monmouthshire).

it is the mother rather than the father who is repository of kinship information.

One might expect from this that there would be greater knowledge of maternal than paternal kin, but examination of the genealogies collected in the field shows otherwise:

TABLE EIGHTEEN

Knowledge of Ascendants' Names

Father's father	17	Mother's father	12
Father's mother	12	Mother's mother	9

In addition, father's father's father was known five times, FFM, MFM, MMF, MFM each three times, MFF twice, but MMM only once. Quite often it is the wife who knows of her husband's ascendants, prompting and correcting him when necessary.

There is, therefore, a clear orientation towards the patri-central-patrinominal in Ashworthy kinship, but it is not developed enough to consider the system in terms of simple patrilineal descent groups. There is some continuity over generations, but, as we have seen in the chapter on farm families, there are many breaks and shifts in the pattern with an emphasis on the elementary family.

Kin Differences

The kinship universe of the Browns shows that kin are of differing importance to the individual. Some are 'close relatives' who are seen regularly, others are 'very distant relatives' whose names or sex may not be known and who are not seen for year after year. Since the Browns are particularly well informed about and interested in their kindred, it may be useful to summarize the kin range of other informants, using in modified form Firth's distinction between 'recognized' and 'nominated' kin.[1] Recognized kin are those people who are claimed as related by blood or marriage, including those not known by name: nominated kin are those persons recognized

[1] Op. cit., p. 42.

as kin whose Christian names are known if consanguineal kin, or whose Christian names and/or surnames are known if affinal kin.[1]

TABLE NINETEEN

Range of Kin

Individual	Recognized Kin	Nominated Kin	Household*	Recognized Kin	Nominated Kin
A	202	165	A	242	179
B	149	109	B	217	143
C	180	101	C	215	116
D	151	112	D	183	127
E	132	108	E	154	120
F	126	73	F	152	109
G	129	104	G	146	117
H	99	64	H	141	108
I	92	61	I	92	61
J	42	40	J	42	40
K	16	16	K	16	16
L	0	0	L	0	0
John Brown	138	138	The Browns	214	159
Edna Brown	214	159			

*Where an informant was married, only his/her spouse was asked for further information to give the kin universe of the household.

The variations in the kin range of the individuals shown in the table are brought about by circumstances in their life history rather than by a difference of interest in kinship. Obviously, married persons are likely to have a much larger range than unmarried ones, such as J, K and L. K is a bachelor in his late forties: his parents died suddenly within the same year and since then he has lived more or less as a recluse. He has no brothers or sisters, his father was an only child, his mother had only one sibling and all his grandparents were dead before he was born. Generally, the early loss of one or both parents, the isolation of the elderly who have outlived

[1] Firth does not make this distinction, which is employed here because, as shown above, the surnames of consanguineal kin may often be inferred.

their own generation, and migration over a considerable distance are the most common reasons for the contraction of an individual's kinship universe. Short-distance migration, so important within the Ashworthy area, has little effect on kin recognition.

In the same way, special circumstances may produce an assymetry in the 'family tree' of an individual or household. For example, D's father's father was said to have come from a distant county and 'no one ever knew anything about his family. He was a mystery man'. D's father's mother was 'a home girl' (i.e. an orphan) and his two siblings died as young children. On the other hand, his mother's family was 'normal' and has lived in the Ashworthy area for many years: there is therefore a marked maternal bias in his kinship universe. However, to judge by the individuals and households in Table Nineteen, such asymmetry is not general. As we have seen, women tend to have greater kin knowledge than men and, associated with it, a greater range of recognition. At the same time, information about patrilineal kin and their affines is greater than about matrilineal kin and the persons married to them. It appears as if the two cancel each other out, so that a wife who might be expected to know more about her own consanguineal kin and their affines than her husband does about his, also acquires a knowledge and recognition of her spouses' 'side of the family', largely perhaps because he is a man in a patri-central kinship system. The 'joint' kinship universe of a married couple is therefore likely to be symmetrical rather than otherwise.

There is, then, an important element of *chance* in the make-up of any individual's kinship universe and this is strongly reinforced by the flexibility of the kinship system as a whole. In Ashworthy, as elsewhere in England, there are few rigid rules of behaviour which oblige a person to behave in a particular way towards a particular person by virtue of his kin relationship. People can *choose* those kindred they wish to associate with and those they wish to ignore. Equally important, kinship sentiments and associations are often not strong enough to overcome such obstacles as distance, differences in social status and the like, particularly among people who are cousins or

more distantly related.[1] However, where relationships are fully
developed, they are, of course, of great emotional strength and
are not easily broken. Moreover, although the element of choice
is fundamental and far-reaching in its consequences, there are
certain occasions or circumstances when what may be termed
a vague sense of kinship overrides all 'normal' considerations.
Thus a person may attend a first cousin's funeral after long
years during which all social contact was absent: as one man
put it: 'I didn't know 'e from Adam, I don't think I'd ever
met 'e, but he was a cousin so us had to go to his funeral.'

The way in which chance and choice operate may be seen in
the Brown family. Edna Brown's father's father came from 'far
away' and apparently her father, an only child, has always
regretted that he knows so little about his paternal kin. Edna
commented: 'I don't know anything about him (i.e. her
grandfather) at all. He died when father was a baby, so I
can't go back farther. We know he had a sister, but that's all.'
Thus a whole set of kin are, as it were, lost. In the same way,
Edna knows very little about her mother's sister's daughter
Nora: 'She married a chap in the Army not long ago. I don't
know anything about him. They move around a lot, I don't
suppose I'll ever see her.' Choice may be seen at work in John
Brown's account of his brothers and sisters: 'There's a family
party at Reg's every Christmas. He's got a big house. All the
families come except Cissie and Emma. Cissie won't go to
things like that. . . . I haven't seen her for five years. . . . We
don't have much to do with them, although they live so near. . . .
Emma lives too far away, I suppose.' John had seen all his
other siblings at least once in the preceding eighteen months,
some of them very frequently.

As one might expect, chance and selection tend to become
increasingly important towards the periphery of the kin
universe. We have already seen how unusual circumstances
may bring individuals into the range of recognized kin, particularly those distantly related. As another example we may
take those of Edna Brown's kindred who are related to her

[1] Firth, op. cit., p. 44, '. . . the lack of formalized kin obligations leaves
the tie without that necessary support of periodic repetition which gives
it content'.

through her mother's parents. Speaking of her maternal grandfather's brother John and his descendants, she remarked: 'I don't really know much about them. John married a local girl. I don't know what his children are called: he has a son and daughter. His son has a business in Bristol; he's married. I don't know anything about her, but I met her once. . . . They have a son in some kind of technical job and a married daughter, Heather. I think she lives at Bristol too. I don't think she has any children. I wouldn't know her really. Frank's other daughter is married and they have three children. They must be as old as I am. I don't know anything about that family at all.' In the same way, Edna knows little about the descendants of her mother's mother's brother and sister Jim and Kate. Jim emigrated to South Africa. In sharp contrast, the third sibling Dick and his family are well known and visited from time to time. Dick and his wife live with their married daughter Jane in a town about forty miles from Ashworthy—'we call in to see them whenever we're passsing'. Dick's other children, Robert, Dora, Edie and Charlie live in different parts of the county and Edna had visited them all within the past two years. She is well informed about recent events in their families.

The importance of personal choice within the general set of kinship values can be seen very clearly in the giving of Christian names. Nowadays, 'prestige' names, culled from the cinema and the 'Birth Columns' of the newspapers are in fashion,[1] but formerly a child was often named after a favoured member of the kin group. This is evident in the genealogies collected during the field work, which also reveal the common practice of naming one son after the father and one daughter after the mother in the earlier generations.

Social relations between kin

From what has already been said, it will be obvious that there are important differences in the content and intensity of social relations between the individuals joined together in a kin network. Some of the kindred who are 'claimed' have no social relations with the person who claims them; this is particularly

[1] This has been noted in other communities: see for example, *Sociology of An English Village*, p. 80, and Firth, op. cit., p. 45.

true of kin who are not known by name. Of the nominated kin, some may have social relations of the most tenuous, formalized and sporadic kind, amounting perhaps to no more than the sending of a Christmas card once a year: others stand in a close and constant relationship, manifested in frequent meetings and exchange of services. Following Firth once more, it is possible to categorize the type of social relations by distinguishing between *effective* and *non-effective* kin,[1] and by subdividing effective kin into *intimate* kin and *peripheral* kin. Intimate kin see each other often (for the purposes of this study defined as at least once every six weeks on an average throughout the year) are 'good friends' and have a fairly well-defined set of rights and duties governing their behaviour as kin. Peripheral kin see each other at irregular and infrequent intervals, behave towards each other with more restraint than intimate kin and do not normally expect an intensive exchange of services or contacts.

These categories are, of course, likely to change in membership from time to time and they merge gradually into each other at certain points. The proportion in each category found in any one person's kin universe depends on a number of variables, among the more important being household composition, mobility of the individual members, their territorial distribution and possibly their social status range. Wide differences in proportions are therefore to be expected. Again the Browns furnish one example: in Fig. 17 effective kin are shown as intimate or peripheral.

There are 11 intimate and 49 peripheral kin out of a total of 109 persons 'on John's side'; on 'Edna's side' there are 13 intimate and 26 peripheral kin out of a total of 101 persons. They are, however, not neatly divided between John and Edna by consanguinity. In addition to the effective kin on 'his own side', John accepts 10 intimate kin on 'Edna's side' as 'relations I like to see often'. The three people whom Edna claims as intimate kin but who are excluded from John's circle are Meg, Bob's wife and Ken: 'I suppose you would call them members of the family and we see a lot of them, but they're

[1] Op. cit., p. 45, 'By effective kin is meant all kin with whom some social contact is maintained, as by correspondence, occasional visits, or attendance at family ceremonial.'

not my relatives.' In addition, John accepts only 13 of the 26 peripheral members of Edna's consanguineal kin and their affines. For her part, Edna regarded 8 of John's 11 intimate kin as 'close relations, although they're on his side' and the remaining 3 as peripheral. Of the 49 peripheral kin 'on John's side', Edna has 32: 'I don't have much to do with some of John's distant relatives.' Thus John has 21 intimate kin and 62 peripheral kin, and Edna has 21 intimate kin and 61 peripheral kin.

In one significant respect the 'two sides of the family' are important in the distribution of effective kin. John Brown has no effective kin on 'Edna's side' other than those persons who are her effective kin also: similarly Edna has no effective kin on 'John's side' who are not her husband's effective kin. The same is true of intimate and peripheral kin respectively. It is difficult to judge from the limited evidence available how far the Browns can be considered representative in this respect. They are, after all, isolated from their kindred, none of whom live in Ashworthy, and they tend to visit them with their children as a family group. A few examples of individuals having effective kin drawn from 'the other side of the family', but who are not effective kin of their spouses were recorded during the field work.

In general, the proportion of intimate kin appears to be influenced particularly by their territorial distribution and individual mobility. About two-thirds of the farm families in Ashworthy own a car or van, but well under a fifth of village households have their own means of transport. They must rely on the three buses a week which run to Longbridge, while longer journeys are much more difficult and inconvenient. As a result, for the majority of people, the number of intimate kin is largely determined by where kindred live. Those individuals who have relatively large numbers of kinfolk living in Ashworthy or adjoining parishes are likely to have more intimate kin than those whose kindred live farther away.[1] On the other hand, peripheral kin are much less influenced by distance and mobility, partly because occasional meetings are possible on

[1] Distance and mobility set broad limits, within which choice and temperament operate.

important occasions, such as a Conservative Association Rally
or a big farm sale, when special buses are arranged, and partly
because the high degree of family mobility within the Ashworthy area keeps a significant proportion of kindred within
effective range.

One might, therefore, expect farmers to have a greater
proportion of both peripheral and intimate kin than villagers.[1]
The majority of farmers possess cars and they meet other
farmers frequently at markets and sales. They are, moreover,
bound closely together by like interests arising from a common
occupation. Unfortunately, the limited evidence available can
not be used to confirm this expectation and it must be remembered that other variables influencing range of kindred
must be taken into account.

Two examples can be used to illustrate these factors. The
bachelor in household K (see Table Nineteen and p. 164 above)
has, by his own account, no intimate kin and only 8 kin who
can be described as having social contact of a significant kind.
He is a farmer but does not own a car. He has lived in Ashworthy all his life. In contrast, another farm family, household
C, has 215 recognized kin, of whom 94 are effective kin and
38 are intimate kin. This family owns a car and uses it to visit
two households of 12 intimate kin who live about nine miles
from Ashworthy. Significantly enough, it was said that: 'We
visit them because we had a farm over there for six years before
we came here. We got to know them well, so we keep it up.'

John Brown has a car and the range and number of his
effective kin are influenced by his ability to visit distant families with ease. At the same time he is free *not* to visit them: 'I
haven't seen my sister Emma for years. . . . It must be two
hundred miles (to her home) . . . I was up there last year . . .
about twenty miles away, but I didn't go to see her.' Edna
Brown, on the other hand, cannot drive and is dependent on
her husband or on public transport to visit kindred: 'I always
go with John to visit my family . . . I haven't seen John's sister
Emma for years.'

In short, then, distance between kin, the degree of difficulty

[1] Except, of course, the 'Up Country Johnnies' who are mostly far
removed from any kindred.

in travelling to visit, and a history of short-distance movement within the Ashworthy area form the background conditions against which social relations between kin must be examined. The specific content of social relations depends on other factors, particularly individual choice and interests shared or not shared. Using the Brown family again as an 'apt illustration', social relations can be examined in some detail among one group of kindred.

John and Edna Brown are tied by links of deep affection and constant visiting to their respective parents. They each feel, in common with most English people, that this is a natural state of affairs and cannot imagine it otherwise. As Edna put it: 'Nobody can be closer to you than your own mother and father.' Each keeps in touch with 'home' by letter and 'go there whenever we can'. Both their children were christened at Edna's mother's home, with John's mother present. When Reg was born, 'Edna went to her Mum and Dad and my Mum came to look after me', and when John was born 'the two Grannies came for a week each'. When Edna was ill her mother came for a week and then returned home because 'she has Dad to look after': John's mother arrived the same day and stayed until Edna had recovered.

In these and many other ways the Browns maintain the closest possible ties with their parents: as they see it, they are 'one family'. John commented: 'I see as much of Edna's Mum as I do my own.' Apart from the three parents, social relations are developed most fully with those intimate kin whom John and Edna have in common, and within this group particularly with siblings. Edna sees little of her brother and his family,[1] but keeps in close touch with them by letter: thus although she had not met him for nearly three years, he was said to be 'the closest to me next to Mum and Dad'. He is godparent to both Edna's children and although he was unable to attend their christening he 'feels a bit responsible for them growing up'. Here, at least, distance has had no effect on the intimacy of a kin relationship. John regards his brother-in-law as 'very close—because he's so close to Edna and the children'.

Of John Brown's siblings, only David and Alice can be

[1] He is a regular soldier, stationed abroad.

regarded as intimate kin. 'We're a big family,' said John, 'and in big families you're bound to be closer to some than the rest. We see a lot of David and Alice. We get on really well. We usually see the rest, except Emma, about once a year. We send them all a Christmas card and we send presents to all the children. They do the same. But I'm not *really* close to them—of course I'm *fond* of them.' From other remarks it became clear that John feels more closely tied to his siblings than other consanguineal kin: 'After all, they are my brothers and sisters.' At the same time, John numbers among his intimate kin three affines, Cyril, May and Fred, as well as Fred's daughter Mary, and David's four children. He said: 'I see much more of Cyril than Dot. . . . We often go to a football match together. I went to school with him. We are good friends.' Fred and May are brought into the range of intimacy because they are married to Alice and David and because, presumably, they 'get on well' with John himself. Edna normally accompanies John when he visits David's house and also sees 'a lot of' Alice and her daughter Mary: 'We are very close. . . . I don't see much of Dot. John goes up there to see Cyril; they are great pals.'

There is clearly a predominant element of personal choice in deciding which kin become intimate and which are peripheral, but the latter implies social relations which vary greatly in depth and emotional content. Several of John Brown's siblings may be peripheral kin, but in terms of overt relations which can be measured they are much closer to him than the great majority of other consanguineal and affinal kin. This is particularly evident in formal exchanges, such as Christmas cards and birthday presents, and at ceremonial occasions. For example, during one of the interviews, John mentioned that he and his family were attending the twenty-first birthday party of his brother Reg's daughter Jean that same evening: 'All the family will be there, except Emma and her family. I'm Jean's godfather. I've never done anything about it though—but we'll have to give her a very respectable present . . . it will be expected. . . . I suppose we are a clannish lot. We feel a duty to be together at "do's" like this.' Three days later John mentioned that his sister Cissie and her family had not attended the birthday party after all—'they *said* they had mumps' he commented. It may be that John's relationship with Cissie, about which he was reluctant to speak, is strained and distant (see above p. 166).

John's intimate kin on 'his side of the family' are confined to his mother, his siblings and their wives and children. Edna's intimate kin 'on her side' extend farther. In her view, this was the result of special circumstances: 'I saw my Aunt Joan about two weeks ago and I saw Pat and her family at the same time. We are close to them because Auntie lost her husband when Pat was six, so they came to live with us (i.e. with her parents). Pat and Bob are more like a brother and sister than cousins. Even when they left, they still came on holidays with us. I saw Bob about a month ago. They were on holiday, so we went to spend a day with them.' She is godmother to Simon, Pat's eldest boy, and attended his christening. In contrast, she had not seen her Aunt Jane for 'years and years' and knows very little about her children Lil and Nora (see above p. 166).

In general, Ashworthy folk do not normally have intimate kin on 'their own side of the family' beyond the range of parents and siblings with their wives and children. Moreover, since husband and wife share the majority of intimate kin from their respective 'sides', an individual's intimate kin on his or her spouse's side are drawn from the same small limited group. There appears to be a more or less sharp break at that distance. Brothers, sisters, nephews and nieces may be sent Christmas and birthday cards and presents as a matter of course: uncles, aunts and particularly first cousins may be sent Christmas cards, but only rarely are given presents or are remembered on their birthdays. In the same way, first cousins are not normally invited to weddings or christenings as *guests*, although they may well attend the church or chapel service. John Brown, for example, invited all his siblings and their children to his wedding—'but I didn't go farther, there are far too many of them'. Edna, however, invited some of her more distant relatives, 'because I didn't have many in the family and it would have looked funny'. Similarly, when John's father died, his father's and his own first cousins were not invited as *mourners*—'but some of them were there at the funeral'. Thus limits are set on the range of kindred who are normally invited to family 'occasions', but at the same time others beyond this limit may attend, with approval, because it is felt in some way to be appropriate.

The prominent landmarks in the family cycle are, indeed, a very striking indication of the general importance of kinship and of the distinctions which are made between kin. The local weekly newspaper, which covers a large tract of the county including Ashworthy, has a considerable proportion of its space devoted to christenings, weddings and, above all, funerals. (In some weeks, the pages devoted to funerals give the impression that an epidemic has decimated the country-side.) Even more important, each account makes an explicit distinction between 'family', 'bearers', 'mourners', 'sympathizers', and 'unable to attend', giving their kin relationship, and it is normal to find each week a paragraph or two correcting errors in detail; for example:

'In our report of the funeral service of Mrs. Elsie White of Holton last Friday we inadvertently included Mr. George Chapman among the sympathizers. Mr. Chapman, who is a nephew of Mrs. White, was one of the mourners. Sympathizers present also included Mr. and Mrs. Alf Fox (Holton) and Mr. E. N. Higgs (Oak). Wreaths were sent by Messrs. Round and Gale, Edie and Bert, John and family, Mr. & Mrs. Brown and family and A. Rowlands.'

The distinctions between categories of attendance directly reflect the organization of the dead person's kinship universe as interpreted by the next-of-kin responsible for the funeral arrangements. This is clearly seen in the funeral of Doris Graves, who died while the field work was being carried out.

The Graves funeral (Fig. 18)

Doris Graves, the wife of a villager, died suddenly in the summer of 1958. Her funeral service, which took place in the village Chapel, was attended by people who came mostly from the Ashworthy area: a few came from well outside it. Since Mrs. Graves was not a prominent member of the community and had always been a housewife, the people attending the funeral were kin, friends or neighbours.[1] A list was made of people attending the service as bearers, mourners, those invited to be present and those who came without invitation. The 99 individuals in the first three categories who were there are shown in Fig. 18, which demonstrates their kin relationship: in addition there were 43 uninvited persons. More than two-thirds of those invited were kindred, made up of 31 consanguineal and 33 affinal kin of the deceased.

The six bearers, described in the newspaper report as nephews, were—as Fig. 18 shows—two nephews, two nieces' husbands (one of whom was also Doris's first cousin's son), and two nephews of the bereaved husband Ted. Doris was childless and it is very common in the Ashworthy area for nephews to acts as bearers in the absence of sons or sons-in-law.

Of Doris's three siblings, two were mourners: they both live in Ashworthy. Her brother lives in the United States and the newspaper account records that he was unable to attend, but that he visited his family in 1957. The remaining mourners were composed of two sisters' husbands; one dead brother's widow; four nephews and a nephew's wife; one first cousin on the paternal side and his wife, and four first cousins on the maternal side with one of their spouses;[2] two first cousins' children and three first cousins' children's spouses; all these are found 'on Doris's side' of the family. Other mourners 'on Ted's side' were a brother and his wife and one other brother's wife; four first cousins, one of whom (B in Fig. 18) is married to a son of Doris's first cousin, and four first cousin's spouses; one nephew and two nephews' spouses.

[1] Consistent with the importance attached generally to funerals, a person's employer and fellow employees, representatives of various official bodies or voluntary organizations, etc., attend the service of well-known or popular individuals. Their names, with the title of the group they represent, are listed in newspaper accounts. At the funeral of a much respected local figure in Ashworthy, which occurred about three weeks after the death of Mrs. Graves, twelve organizations were represented by sixty-four individuals.

[2] He is also a first cousin's son; see A in Fig. 18. The charting of kinship is difficult in such an area as Ashworthy, because intermarriage and consequent inter-relationships give individuals several kin positions at once.

People who were invited to be present, but not as mourners, are distributed through much the same kinship range, apart from the one person (C in Fig. 18) who is Doris's first cousin's daughter's son. In addition, 38 wreaths were sent, ten from the families of mourners; a further six were from other kindred, including one from the sole survivor of Doris's parent's generation, her mother's sister (D). Those people listed as unable to attend in the newspaper report included two brothers-in-law and two sisters-in-law.

Thus 17 of the mourners were consanguineal kin and 26 were affinal kin of the dead woman: several of the latter are, of course, consanguineal kin of her husband. The range of invited kin at this funeral provides, as it were, an outline map of Doris Graves's social relations with her kindred and at the same time indicates the general strength of kinship ties. As one might expect, kin 'on Doris's side' considerably outnumber kin from 'Ted's side'. Her siblings and their spouses were expected to attend; his were not, and those who did were intimate kin, as were those of Ted's siblings' children who were mourners or bearers. All of them live in Ashworthy. In contrast to the funeral of John Brown's father (see above, p. 173), at Doris Graves's funeral there were a number of first cousins and their families. This may partly reflect a wider range of close kinship ties, but it is also in part a reflection of a more generalized kin sentiment. John Brown is one of eight children, his father had six brothers and sisters, and his mother twelve siblings; there were, therefore, a large number of 'close relatives' available to attend the funeral. Doris Graves, on the other hand, was childless and had only three siblings alive, one of them living thousands of miles away. If her 'family' was to be well represented, then more distant kin must be invited. A poorly attended funeral is widely regarded as 'not good enough' or 'not proper' in Ashworthy.

Equally significant are those kindred who were not invited; or did not attend; or did not even send wreaths or apologies. Behaviour of the latter kind is carefully noted and heavily criticized in Ashworthy. The two men marked 'E' in Fig. 18 are typical examples. They are nephews of Doris Graves, who live within a few miles of Ashworthy. The fact that their parents

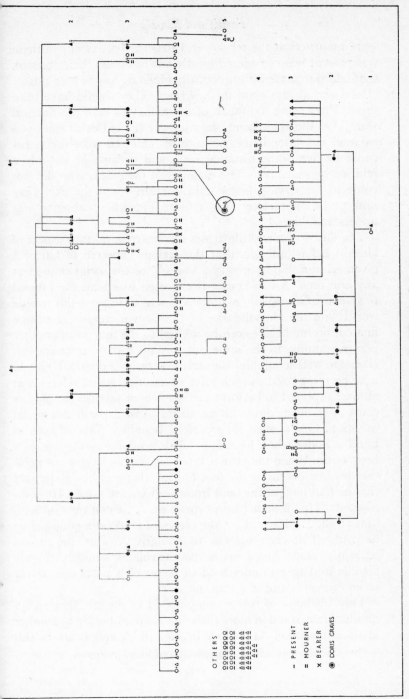

Fig. 18. The funeral of Doris Graves.

Family and Kinship

were mourners at the service and that the wife of one of them was present was considered locally not to excuse their absence, but indeed to make it unnecessarily obvious. As one man put it: 'Doris was always good to they boys. They should have been there. They think too much of the money to take the time off work.' On the other hand, the widower (F) of Doris's sister was excused non-attendance, because his children were there, because he lives some distance away and because he is 'only a relative by marriage'. The majority of the others who did not come to the service, first cousins' children and the like, were said to be 'not close', i.e. remote kin whose absence was understandable.

The Graves funeral illustrates one other important aspect of kinship behaviour, viz. that the actions expected of kin of a given relationship may vary according to the social context at any one time. A first cousin is expected to attend the funeral to give a sufficiently large gathering and to impress the outside world with the kin solidarity of the Graves family. The same first cousin might not even be invited to the funeral of another person standing in the same relationship if there were enough close kindred available. Similarly, certain individual kinfolk may be recognized as such after years of no social relations at all and expected to perform certain acts or services simply because it is their 'duty' as kin to do so in a particular social situation. One farmer, for example, bought a piece of land to build a house when he retired. The vendor was the son of a first cousin. When the farmer listed his kinfolk he did not mention his first cousin or the son, but in talking of his life he said that he had bought the land from 'a distant relative'. He commented: 'He's a man I never speak to. .... I don't get on with him at all. .... He sold me the piece (of land) at a good price: he couldn't do anything else to a relative.'[1] Thus the role of 'cousin', 'uncle' and so on is, like the role of 'stranger', highly flexible and to be understood in terms of a particular set or series of events and circumstances.

This flexibility of role is complicated by the fact that an individual may stand in more than one kin relationship to another at the same time. As we saw in Fig. 18, A and B are in this

[1] See also the very similar example quoted on p. 52 above.

178

Family and Kinship

position, which must be fairly common in rural communities characterized by intermarriage within a relatively small population.[1] Situations are therefore possible in which an individual is expected to act in one way because of one kin relationship and in quite a different manner by virtue of the other. The man A attended Doris's funeral as a mourner because he was the son of her first cousin and *not* as the husband of a first cousin's daughter. He thought of himself simply as 'a blood relative'. The woman B was not invited as a first cousin of Doris's husband (none of her sibs were mourners although all but one live in the village) but as the wife of one of Doris's first cousin's children. There are, no doubt, more spectacular instances of this conflict of roles: unfortunately none were recorded during the field work.

Taken in conjunction with the importance of chance and personal choice in kin behaviour and recognition, this variation in role(s) according to circumstances gives kinship in Ashworthy a complexity which frequently bewilders the outsider. The 'Up Country Johnnies' have found, often to their cost, that kinship may suddenly become important in a situation where it was previously unsuspected. 'How was I to know they were related, they've always ignored each other' or some such remark, was heard frequently. Stated in more general terms, social relations which arise from kin recognition are seen to be capable of great diversity and also to be closely related to other aspects of the social structure in an extremely subtle fashion, while yet maintaining common features and regularities which permit the use of the term 'a kinship system'.

Social relations in everyday life

The funerals and weddings which demonstrate important aspects of kin behaviour are relatively uncommon events in the life of a family and are therefore invested with a high emotional content. As with visits to kin living far away, they are 'occasions' to be remembered and discussed. Most social relations

[1] Cf. M. Gluckman, *Custom and Conflict in Africa* (Oxford 1955), p. 22 et. seq.

between kin are not of this kind: they are matter-of-fact, frequent, and concerned primarily with the business of everyday living. Some aspects of them have already been discussed; farmers borrow machinery from kindred and lend equipment in return; kindred co-operate in the harvest, at threshing days and sheep dipping and in certain kinds of routine farm work, for example potato-lifting. Villagers who are kindred borrow and lend amongst themselves, help at time of illness, 'baby-sit', bring back goods from Longbridge, etc. (In this respect the individual's behaviour differs little from the way he acts towards friends and neighbours.) The particular patterns of these social relations between households are, of course, a direct reflection of the geographical distribution of kindred and the grouping of intimate and peripheral kin. For example, John and Edna Brown do not have continuous everyday contacts with kin because none of them live in Ashworthy. Ted Graves, a mason by occupation, has helped many of his kindred in house repairs because they live near to him in the village, particularly those who are intimate kin.

In general then, the fact that Ashworthy is a remote country parish, dependent on farming, has a direct effect on social relations between kin. In common with other communities of the same kind, 'face-to-face' contacts predominate. Physical proximity and the need for economic co-operation provide the broad positive conditions within which personal selection operates.[1] At the same time there are sectors of the social life in which people are divided into groups of opposing or unequal interest. As we saw in the first chapter, Ashworthy is divided into Methodists and Anglicans, farmers and villagers and Liberals and Conservatives, divisions which might be expected to affect social relations between kindred. Social class or status distinctions might also be expected to have their effects. The adjustments and conflicts which arise from these differing aspects of the social life form the theme of the last chapter.

[1] Physical separation, however, does not mean the breakdown of social relations between kin: they may be difficult or inconvenient, but they occur and these difficulties may well enhance their importance and emotional content.

Ashworthy and South Borough

In this analysis of family and kinship many references have been made to Professor Firth's study of a London Borough. His method and order of treatment have been followed more or less closely, partly to enable fruitful comparisons to be made in a much neglected field of study, and partly because of the striking similarities which can be observed between the kinship systems of these two widely separated and very different localities.

In both Ashworthy and South Borough the elementary family household is dominant, but kinship links outside it are significant in determining social relations; the relationship between parent and child is fundamental; recognition of kindred is shallow in depth and relatively wide in extension within the relevant generations; quite considerable numbers of individuals are claimed as kindred; great variations occur in the range and numbers of kin who are known, claimed, and with whom purposeful social relations take place; there are sharp gradations in kinship ties; social contact and its degree of intimacy are not invariably a direct reflection of physical proximity; chance and personal choice are crucial in the recognition of kin and in the establishment and perpetuation of social relations between kin; kin recognition varies considerably from individual to individual, but women tend to have a greater knowledge than men; the kinship system is patrinominal and 'optionally bilateral';[1] the ties between siblings are closer and more developed than between remoter kin; kinship forms the basis of certain exchanges of services and of a great deal of social intercourse marked by friendliness, companionship and the interchange of information and opinions.

These major similarities are remarkable, particularly in the light of the great differences in context between Ashworthy and a block of flats in London. It is, indeed, tempting to suggest that the comparison justifies the view that the similarities represent characteristics of English kinship as a whole. There are also differences, but they can be explained largely in terms of the differing circumstances of life in the two places. Thus South

[1] See Firth, op. cit., p. 63. The bilateral principle is seen, of course, in the use of the terms 'mother's side' and 'father's side' as parts of a whole.

Borough is a matri-centred system, Ashworthy is patri-centred but with the mother-child link important because of the domestic organization of child-rearing and housekeeping. In South Borough the husband/father normally works away from his family, home and locality; in Ashworthy he works at or near home, with his family and, sometimes, kindred. Patterns of inheritance of land, goods and skills, reinforce the link between father and son. Again, in the localized Ashworthy system, intermarriage makes likely the existence of individuals with more than one kin role and position. In London this possibility is, for obvious reasons, remote. In Ashworthy face-to-face social relations in a community where 'everyone knows everyone else' give kin behaviour a different orientation from that found in South Borough, where only a small proportion of the population enjoy close social relations with each other. Differences in ease of travelling also have their effects.

Studies of other communities tend to confirm the results of the comparison. Bethnal Green[1] and Woodford,[2] like South Borough, are matri-centred: Gosforth[3] and rural communities in County Clare[4] and Montgomeryshire[5] are, like Ashworthy, patri-centred, and for largely 'the same reasons. The results from a Yorkshire village,[6] however, and from Banbury,[7]

[1] M. Young and P. Wilmott, *Family and Kinship in East London*, Institute of Community Studies (London 1957).

[2] P. Willmott and M. Young, *Family and Class in a London Suburb*, Institute of Community Studies (London 1960).

[3] *Sociology of an English Village: Gosforth*, and 'Kinship and Farming in West Cumberland' *Man*, No. 25 (1956).

[4] Arensberg, op. cit.

[5] Rees, op. cit.

[6] A Curle, 'Kinship Structure in an English Village', *Man*, No. 100 (1952).

[7] Margaret Stacey, *Tradition and Change. A Study of Banbury.* (Oxford 1960). This study confirms the South Borough/Ashworthy analysis on a number of important points. On others, however, it is markedly different and it may well be that this is a consequence of the method of study. To give one example: '. . . . the extended family is shallow and narrow: knowledge rarely extends beyond grandparents, nor does it extend far in width' (pp. 116–17). This conclusion is based on a special kinship study which 'took no account of cousins or of . . . nephews and nieces' (p. 117).

though not easily compared, suggest important differences. Further study is needed, but it does at least seem as if the general structure of English kinship is now clearly established, many decades after this was achieved for obscure tribal groups in the Australian Desert or the darker regions of Africa.

CHAPTER SEVEN

KINSHIP AND SOCIAL LIFE

IN the Ashworthy area 'everybody knows everybody else' and therefore social relations between kindred assume an importance which they may not possess in large urban centres. When a person in Ashworthy acts in a certain way towards his kindred, his actions are judged not only by his kinfolk but also by friends, neighbours and others. There is no hard and fast division between the demands of kinship and those which arise from neighbourliness, religious or political affiliation, etc., and so decisions which are made every day about particular actions and events in specific social situations are informed and influenced by considerations arising from many different sectors of the total social life. There is, of course, nothing new about this: it has long been a commonplace in sociology. Whereas, however, in a town or city the actors in any given situation may be drawn from a very large number of people, in Ashworthy they come from a relatively small group and it is therefore possible to examine the significance of kin behaviour in the whole social structure in a way that is often impossible in an urban context.

This final chapter confirms the importance of change in the countryside. It will be shown that, just as relations between kindred must be regarded in terms of a flexible, permissive system operating within a framework of population movement, so too must other aspects of the social life be seen as in a state of dynamic equilibrium.

Kinship and religion

The religious life of the parish was outlined in the first chapter of this study and it is merely necessary here to recall that roughly half the inhabitants are Anglican and half Methodist. Religious affiliation is important enough to be immediately

Kinship and Social Life

recognizable in many of the things which people do, say and believe. Religion, therefore, divides the parish into two clearly defined sets of people in a very real sense. Relations between them are generally amicable and, as we have noted earlier, an 'accommodation' has been reached. There are, however, occasions when the interests and moral values of the two groups conflict, and there is a whole corpus of incidents, real and imaginary, which can be recalled to demonstrate the inferiority or superiority of one or the other. A typical example is the account, given by an Anglican farmer, of an event which was said to have taken place in a neighbouring parish some few years before: 'This old chap was caretaker of the chapel, see, and his wife died. He'd looked after the place for years and years—and he was an old man. Well, a fortnight after the funeral, they went along and told him the house was wanted and he had to go into the Old People's Home at Longbridge. He's there now. *That's* Chapel people for you. He's given his life for that place and that's what he got as a testimonial.'

Given this religious dichotomy one might perhaps expect a correspondingly neat division into Anglican and Methodist families, but it does not occur. Their distribution by households is as follows:

TABLE TWENTY

Religious Affiliation by households 1960[1]

	Anglican	Methodist	Mixed*	Not known
Farmers	31	27	9	8
Others	44	33	14	6
Total	75	60	23	14

*i.e. one spouse Methodist, the other Anglican.

Thus 13·4 per cent of all households, composed of ninety-four people, are neither entirely Anglican nor Methodist. Moreover, many of the households, including those shown in the first two

[1] The affiliation is given as stated by informants: it is not always supported by attendance at Church or Chapel. Ashworthy has its share of 'indifferent believers', known locally as 'devil dodgers'.

columns of the table, have 'mixed' marriages in their family histories. For example, Ernest Cornish, a farmer, is Anglican and his wife Emily is a Methodist; his five children, including a married daughter, are Methodist. Living in the Cornish household are Ernest's mother, an Anglican, and two of Emily's first cousins, both Anglican. Ernest's parents and four grand-parents were Anglican, as are all his consanguineal kin still living in Ashworthy. However, his brother John, who left the parish in 1951, married a Methodist: his children are Methodist and one of them is married to a Methodist. Emily's father and paternal grandparents were Methodist; her father's brother and his wife were Methodist, but two of their three children, who live with Emily, are Anglican. Emily's mother was an Anglican born to Anglican parents who became a Methodist when she married.[1] On Sundays Ernest goes to Church while Emily and the children go to Chapel.

To take one further example; John and Albert Smith are sons of a Methodist farmer. Albert, a bachelor, is still a Metho-dist; John, who married the daughter of a prominent Metho-dist family, is now an Anglican, and so is his wife.

The existence of these 'mixed' families must be seen first in a historical context. At the beginning of the nineteenth century Ashworthy was virtually Anglican. By 1820 there were perhaps thirty Methodists in the parish; by 1841 there were about sixty to eighty, including twenty members of the Wesleyan Chapel. During the remainder of the nineteenth century the number of Bible Christian Methodists grew steadily, while the number of Wesleyans declined, so that by 1907, when the Bible Christians became part of the United Methodist Church, about half the inhabitants were Nonconformist, of whom only eight were Wesleyan. The Wesleyan Chapel closed a year later. Thus Methodism grew, first by conversion of families or individual members of families and later by the birth of children into such families. Households which were part Anglican and part Methodist have therefore been a feature of Ashworthy life for nearly a century and a half. Changes in religious affiliation have also occurred on marriage and, occasionally, for reasons

[1] For further material on the Cornish family, see above pp. 64–7 and Fig. 10.

other than the strictly 'religious' one. One former Methodist, for example, 'became an Anglican' in his mid-thirties because it was a qualification for the job he now holds; his wife and children changed churches at the same time. Another Methodist became an Anglican because, in his own words, 'I was tired of being pestered all the time'. His wife still attends the Chapel.

In this situation, where formal religious observance is only partly a guide and where conflict lies just beneath the surface, it is extremely difficult for an outside observer to gather the data necessary for a thorough-going analysis of the relationship between kinship behaviour and values on the one hand and those which derive from religious beliefs on the other. Clearly, however, this relationship has various levels or degrees of intensity or emotional content. Within the elementary family, differences in religious affiliation must be seen in the context of intimate and continuous social relations. Such differences between more remote kin, for example siblings or first cousins, are less pervasive and lasting in their influence, although they may become important in certain circumstances. Religious differences between parents and children are likewise influenced by household composition, marital status and the particular patterns of authority which exist.

The observer must rely on those overt manifestations of the relationship which he is able to record and, obviously, chance plays a large part in determining what is seen and heard. Nevertheless, certain generalizations are possible. First, it may be stated as a general rule that kinship loyalties override religious loyalties, certainly within the framework of the elementary family. The most striking illustration of this is, perhaps, to be seen by walking through the Church and Chapel graveyards. Man and wife are nearly always buried side by side in Ashworthy and often there are 'family plots' with persons from several generations and of widely differing kin relationships. Thus Chapel-goers of long standing are buried in the shadow of the Church, and Anglicans in the field near the Chapel. The concensus of opinion was summed up by the man who said: 'Families here like to be buried in the same ground. A lot buy a piece of land and when the first one's buried they dig the grave eight feet instead of six. It can be opened then for the other one (i.e. spouse). If my own wife was to die before me, naturally she would be buried in the Church, and when my turn came I would lie beside her.' He is a Methodist and his wife is an Anglican. In the same way, people attend the funerals of kindred who are members of a different denomination.

Other evidence of the subordination of the religious division to kinship sentiment is plentiful. Of seventeen persons whose kindred were recorded as including both Methodists and Anglicans, only one had intimate kin limited to his own denomination. When the others were asked if the difference in religion had any influence on their social relations with kin who were 'very close', all replied firmly in the negative and the majority clearly thought the question was foolish. When they were asked further about the effects of such widely accepted differences as the attitude towards visiting the village inn, they described means of circumventing them, for example 'running over to the Green Man at Holton' or 'Us gets Jack Taylor to leave a crate of beer when he'm passing'.[1]

In many ways the most crucial test of kinship loyalty occurs when a person decides to marry someone of a different denomination. It is a decision which conflicts with the belief and associated values held by and transmitted by parents; it may offend other kindred. Indeed, stark examples were quoted of young people being 'shown the door' or 'sent packing without even a kind word', but they were always in families from other localities. No examples could be found in Ashworthy. The quoting of instances from other communities is, of course, often employed in a wide variety of circumstances where people feel that their collective reputation is in some way at stake. They are normally accompanied by claims of superiority or of qualities which are believed to be desirable, such as tolerance, broadmindedness, friendliness, etc. It does, however, seem as if Ashworthy people are on the whole genuinely tolerant of 'mixed' marriages, while not approving of them. A typical view was: 'The parents be often disappointed of course, but they don't hold it against them. And remember it be their own

---

[1] Some Methodists who never enter the village inn, have beer delivered regularly to their homes.

child they'm considering.' On the other hand, it may also be that such marriages simply do not occur in families who have strong religious feelings and that the situation where one is contemplated is never reached. There is no way of discovering precisely how often this is so, but there are certainly a few households in Ashworthy where it is difficult to imagine it being otherwise. In such families, kinship sentiment and religious feelings are so closely knit and reinforce each other to such an extent that to distinguish between them is little more than an academic exercise.

The second generalization that can be made is that religious affiliation provides the basis for social relations of a regular and meaningful kind which act to strengthen kinship solidarity among kindred in the same religious group and to weaken it among kindred divided among the two churches. Methodists who are kindred see each other regularly at the Chapel services, at 'Sankey Evenings', at the Methodist Young People's Guild and other meetings organized by the Chapel officials. Anglicans who are kindred meet at Church services, Fêtes and Garden Parties, Sales of Work, Patronal Festivals, the Mother's Union, etc. It is true that people of both denominations attend Garden Parties and the like, which are important village occasions, but such events are relatively rare. Moreover, the greater part of the most fruitful social contact occurs during the weeks spent in organizing these activities, when close co-operation based on common aims, and a sense of achievement when everything is ready bring about strong feelings of solidarity and companionship. For example, a bachelor, in speaking of his kindred, said: 'I see a lot more of some relatives. . . . People like Annie, she's my first cousin's daughter; well I see her every week on Sundays and on Thursdays. On Thursdays we're at the Guild— it's quite a lot of work and you must get on well with them, else it wouldn't work. . . . I think of Annie as close, though she baint really.' Then there was the Anglican housewife who remarked 'Us always has a stall at the Fête. Us spends weeks and weeks on it. I always do it with my sister—us knows each other's ways.'

There are, in addition, the many activities not directly connected with the Church or Chapel, but in which participation is partly determined by religious affiliation and partly by individual interest. The Football Team, its Supporters' Club and the Darts Team are typical examples. Throughout the year, therefore, the people of Ashworthy meet regularly in groups which cut across kinship ties, serve to keep kindred apart and occasionally to bring them into opposition. Even in those associations which are specifically undenominational, such as the Village Band and the Men's Social Club, division into cliques of Anglicans or Methodists occurs regularly.

This dual effect of religious membership on kin relations is significantly strengthened by the third general characteristic, which is that individuals tend to conform to the behaviour patterns, with their associated moral values, which they have absorbed as children and young adults. Change in religious affiliation and 'mixed' marriages do not normally, therefore, bring about overt changes in the way people behave or in many of the activities in which they participate. A typical example which illustrates this is the Brookes family. Jim Brookes is an Anglican; his wife and two children are Methodist. Jim is often seen in the village pub and is noted as a skilled darts player; he is also a member of the Football Team and a member of its committee. His attendance at church is confined to 'the big days, weddings and funerals'. Jim's father and father's brother live in the village and are prominent officials of the Football Team, the Men's Social Club and the Conservative Club. Like Jim, they are 'regulars' at the pub. Jim's wife Mary attends the Chapel every Sunday. She has 'never' been in the pub and does not go to watch football matches. Her children are being brought up as 'proper Methodists' and great interest is taken in them by Mary's mother and father, who live just outside the village. Mary, her children and her parents attend the Chapel as a group and the children are sent to the Chapel Sunday-school. Mary's brother Sam, who is a bachelor, also lives in the parish. Jim said of him: 'I never see him. I don't know what he does with himself.' Jim's children, on the other hand, see 'Uncle Sam' at chapel every week.

In this household, therefore, the interests of husband and wife were to a considerable extent pre-determined by their religious affiliation and outside the home they do not often coincide.[1] They see a great deal of their respective parents, but very much less of their spouse's parents, who are not brought into a purposeful social relationship by Jim and Mary's marriage. Mary saw her children's future quite clearly: Jim was evasive and vague: 'They can please theyselves.'

The position of children of mixed marriages can be seen in the Cornish family. Ernest Cornish is Anglican; his two sons and his son-in-law are Methodists, who attend the chapel services fairly often. All three young men have been, at one time or another, members of the Football Team, and two are committee members. They are among the four or five Methodists who can be seen in the village pub, although they are not 'regulars'. During the field work they came about once a fortnight. One of Ernest's sons is 'seriously' courting an Anglican farmer's daughter and appears likely to marry her. In a community like Ashworthy, where the religious divisions are not rigid and where the ties between father and son are particularly strong (and Ernest Cornish is a farmer), the young men of the Cornish family live much the same kind of life as their father without friction or difficulty. In contrast, Ernest's three daughters conform much more closely to the locally accepted model of Methodist behaviour. Here the tie between mother and daughter is, of course, important, as well as the general separation between the lives of the two sexes, which, as we shall see later, is another important division in the social structure.

Kinship and political parties

In this section, politics are considered only in terms of membership of national political parties: 'local politics', i.e. the structure of authority in parish associations, is discussed later. In general, the political alignment of Ashworthy is simple: Methodists are Liberal, Anglicans are Conservative. There is a very small minority of professed Socialists. This division is, of course, characteristic and well-established over a great part of

---

[1] Cf. Gluckman, *Custom and Conflict in Africa*, p. 79; 'But where relatives, neighbours, friends, and workmates tend to be the same people . . . the activities of spouses become separated. This is certainly the position in long-settled rural areas.' See also below pp. 193–94.

the rural West Country, and has been manifest in national and local elections.

The Ashworthy Branch of the Liberal Association is an active body which holds frequent Social Evenings, Whist Drives, Dances and 'Brains Trusts'. There were seven meetings in July and August of 1958. The President, Chairman, Secretary, Treasurer and eleven of the twelve Committee members are Methodist. Of a further twenty-seven people described as 'prominent', 'staunch' and 'very active' Liberals, twenty-five were Methodists. At the seven summer meetings, the door-stewards, masters of ceremonies and other officials, as well as the women who supplied refreshments were, with the one exception of the Anglican Committee member, all 'chapel folk'.

The Conservative Assocation was less active during the period of field work, with only three social events. Fifteen of its sixteen officers were Anglican: the one Methodist was a Committee member. All of the fourteen other people described as 'strong' or 'true blue' Conservatives were Anglican. One further characteristic may be noted: all the 'larger' and more prosperous farmers and nearly all the independent tradesmen were Conservative.

Now it seems reasonable to suppose that most of the members of the two political associations vote for their own candidates at elections: most of the 'staunch' Liberals and 'true blue' Conservatives stated flatly that they did so.[1] There was, however, a small number of people who admitted that they did not: they explained their behaviour in such terms as 'I voted Liberal last time; I always have. I suppose I ought to be in the (Liberal) Club, but Ted (the Secretary of the Conservative Association) comes in on Christmas morning with presents for both the children and asks for my subscription. What can you do? It's best to pay and forget about it.' As these people see it, voting at elections is a matter of individual conscience, but membership of local political associations must take into account social pressures from neighbours, friends or kindred.

Since allegiance to a political party and religious affiliation are so closely linked in Ashworthy, the relationship between the former and kinship behaviour and loyalties is much the same as

[1] The remainder refused to answer.

that described in the preceding section. Kindred who are active in the affairs of the same political association are brought closer together through the common points of view and the mutual satisfaction derived from working side by side. Kindred who have differing political views are drawn into a network of social relations which runs counter to the kinship network.

'*It's a Man's World*'

It has been suggested by some sociologists that rural communities are divided into separate groups of men and women, 'largely opposed to one another'.[1] Certainly the separation can be seen in the everyday life of Ashworthy. Many men spend their leisure time in the Social Club, with the Village Band or in the pub, all essentially masculine preserves. Only three local women entered the bar of the pub during the field work. Women attend the Women's Institute or the Mother's Union. The Football Team is all male, its Supporters' Club has a Women's Committee. At gatherings of both sexes, such as farm sales and garden parties, groups of men and of women, of boys and of girls are particularly noticeable. Indeed, on the first evening of the field work, which happened to be a Church Festival, the Village Band performed in the open air to an audience which was split up neatly into small groups of the same sex. In certain circumstances this separation is held to be desirable. 'Maidens' and 'lads' are expected to keep apart and mixed groups are frowned on by parents. The children waiting for the school bus in the morning stand in clusters of the same sex about ten yards apart and sit separately in the bus during its journey to Longbridge.

This separation is appreciated by the people of Ashworthy both in specific local contexts and in a more general form. One village housewife remarked: 'We live in a man's world and we have to put up with it. I'm stuck in the house all day and my husband is out. If he's not at work, he's over at the Social Club

---

[1] Gluckman, *Custom and Conflict in Africa*, p. 79. This view is developed in R. Frankenberg, *Village on the Border* (London 1957): see, for example, p. 51 *et. seq.*: 'For outside the union of man and woman in the home, and except for a brief period of courtship and early marriage, there seem to be two villages, one of men and one of women, which rarely mingle. . . . When they do meet . . . they often come into conflict.'

playing darts or billiards. When he's not there, he's in the pub. . . . That club is a second wife to him.' Another commented: 'People round here believe a woman's place is in the home. All the village things are for the men. There's nothing really for a woman to do, except the W.I. once a month.' In contrast, a tradesman said: 'We have an active lot of women in Ashworthy, a brainy lot. They keep things humming. We couldn't do without them.'

There is, then, a man's world and a woman's world, and in a number of village families the male and female members spend relatively little time together, apart from meals. On the other hand, there are a great many activities and events in which both sexes participate. The whist drives, dances and social evenings, the meetings of the Methodist Young People's Guild and of the two political associations, and such events as Skittles Week are typical examples. Family groups are numerous, if not predominant, at garden parties, church fêtes and farm sales. In farm families particularly, but also among a number of village families, parents and children spend a great deal of time at home together and go out to market or to Longbridge as a group.

While, therefore, the separation of social life between the sexes is important, it is not all-embracing and there was very little evidence of opposition or conflict between the sexes as groups. Among farmers and craftsmen at least the family is a close-knit unit, bound by common interests: elsewhere in the parish there are many families where the men work near to their homes, returning for their midday meal or spending much of their working time in the village. Their interests may often be different from those of their wives and daughters and their networks of social relations may be predominantly masculine, but they are by no means exclusively so. In general it may be said that the differing roles and activities of men and women influence the pattern of social relations between kindred, but to a lesser extent than differences which arise from religious and political affiliation.

Class, status and kinship

The great importance of social class divisions in English life generally might easily lead to the expectation that class and status have important effects on relations between kindred. My own experience in Gosforth, with its highly developed social class system, certainly led me to anticipate a similar situation in Ashworthy.[1] The parish is, however, quite different: it is remarkably lacking in class consciousness and there are no well-defined groups of people whose behaviour sets them apart from others in social status. In every-day conversation values and judgements based on class considerations are heard very rarely indeed. 'Social climbing' is virtually unknown.

This state of affairs seems all the more remarkable in the light of the recent history of the parish. As we saw earlier in this study, a great part of Ashworthy was owned by the Bishop family until about thirty years ago. They were large land-owners by English standards and they lived in two mansions inside the parish itself. Members of the family reached the highest ranks of the Armed Forces and the Church of England. There can be no doubt that during the nineteenth century there were well-marked social classes in Ashworthy. At the top of the hierarchy were the Bishops, the Rector and three or four families of 'gentry'. Their influence over the life of the parish was considerable, resting as it did on the ownership of land and houses and on considerable wealth. Below them in the hier-archy—but at a considerable social distance from them—were the substantial yeomen, owner-occupiers, most of whose families were long-established. The ten or fifteen families in this group tended to intermarry or to marry among yeomen of similar status in near-by parishes, and they buttressed their social distinctiveness by sending their children to grammar school. Next there came the remaining owner-occupiers and more prosperous tenant farmers, followed by the poorer tenant farmers, particularly those in 'hard-working' farms,[2] and the village craftsmen. Then, the largest class of all, there were the farm labourers and other manual workers and their families in the village, and finally, at the bottom of the hierarchy, the paupers, widows and others whose poverty marked them out.

Membership of these classes probably tended to remain fixed, at least until about the middle of the nineteenth century,

[1] See *Sociology of An English Village*, Chapters V and VI.
[2] See above p. 37.

although as we have seen from the Enumeration Schedules, individual families rose within the lower ranks of the social scale by means of the agricultural ladder, while others fell sharply to the lowest class.[1] Even as early as 1851, however, evidence of a change is apparent. The uppermost class was to remain inviolate until the Bishop family disappeared in the 1930's; the other class divisions were eroded away until none remained.

Several factors can be recognized as responsible for the change, which can be more or less limited to the years between 1840 and 1920 or 1930. The first was a general change in attitudes towards social class, particularly during the early years of this century. The First World War, in particular, had great effects in weakening the foundations of the established social order. Secondly, and very much more important, there were local factors peculiar to the Ashworthy area. From the 1840's, and possibly earlier, the population of Ashworthy was subject to constant change through migration, particularly over a short distance. This was combined, as we saw in Part One of this study, with changes in land-holding and in the farm population as yeoman families died out and agricultural labourers became farmers by climbing the agricultural ladder.

Under such conditions the maintenance of social class divisions became increasingly difficult. In Ashworthy, as in present-day Gosforth, the social class system was essentially localized: its basis was that everyone knew everyone else in the parish, their class position and their ability to satisfy the criteria which determined rank in the class hierarchy. Social class was oriented and organized to fit the particular conditions of a face-to-face community. Any one social class was therefore a group of individuals recognized by everyone as belonging to a particular social level. Continuous migration brought endless changes in the ranks of all but the uppermost class; other changes took place as a result of the 'upward' and 'downward' mobility of farmers. The yeoman class dispersed and declined, to disappear completely by the 1920's. The frequent changes in land-holding meant the disappearance of a basic criterion of class position in an agricultural community—the ownership or occupation of a

[1] See above p. 122.

particular tract of land, with all the prestige that accrues from long residence. Thus each class became increasingly difficult to identify and to define in terms of individual families. So many of the people in the parish were 'strangers' while others were changing their occupational and economic status for better or worse, that the traditional system, based on close personal knowledge, withered away.

Other factors contributed to the decay of the established class divisions. The appearance of Methodism, which seems to have spread through all the classes except the gentry in an indiscriminate way, produced a new social division in the parish which cut sharply across the class hierarchy. The Anglican Church, itself hierarchical, had for centuries been a powerful force in maintaining the social order. In Ashworthy, Church people sat according to their status during services, the Bishops in their own pew at the front, behind them the yeomen and so on to the paupers at the back. With the spread of Methodism there grew up in the parish a large group of people who were not only unwilling to recognize the close Anglican-social class relationship, but who were also committed to the importance of the individual and opposed to a rigid hierarchy. Moreover, those things which gave a person high prestige as a Methodist— austerity, a clearly defined code of conduct, etc.—were quite different from the traditional means of achieving high prestige in the community.

The small upper class had not been affected by these disruptive pressures: their position was too strongly established. But whereas in Gosforth and other parts of England this class was revitalized by an invasion of *nouveau riche* industrialists wishing to become country gentlemen, in Ashworthy—a remote and relatively unattractive rural area—the gentry became more and more isolated from the rest of the community. With the decline of the country estate in the early years of this century, and especially after 1914, this small group, whose wealth lay almost entirely in the land they owned, could not survive the double assault of heavy death duties and the agricultural depression of the interwar period. In Ashworthy their end was sudden, violent and perhaps symbolic. The Bishop estate was sold in two parts; Ashworthy House, their home, was demolished and the last of the family took his own life in the year during which the second part of the estate was broken up. The second Bishop house was divided into flats: it is now owned by a Methodist lay preacher.

Finally there are the effects of changes in the occupational structure of the parish, particularly the decline in the numbers of farm labourers and of rural craftsmen. In the nineteenth century, the farmers were placed above the agricultural workers in the social scale largely because the farmers were employers and the labourers their employees. Nowadays there are few farm labourers and therefore no large group of families directly dependent on another. Relevant here is the fact that the tied cottage has virtually disappeared: well over a half of the villagers own their houses.

There are, then, no status groups in Ashworthy and the community is not divided into social classes. The local people, many of whom remember the Bishop family, speak of social class in the past tense: 'Ashworthy House was broken up and sold in bits. That's what the snobbishness of the old upper class was—he didn't want anybody to live there. That's not country life today, Jack's as good as his master.' And again, 'Wilfred Bishop was a rich man. It was wrong that one man should own all that property. That day has passed in the country—and a good thing too.'

However the absence of social class divisions does not mean that status and prestige do not have their place in the social life of Ashworthy. Some individuals and families have high prestige, others are widely regarded as socially inferior for one reason or another. Typical evaluations were:

'They have a private income and they've travelled all over the world. . . . They have definitely come down in the world.'

'She were very worried when she saw you talking to her husband. She thought he would say too much. She don't like it known that her mother and father were ordinary and that they've never had any money in the bank.'

'They want the world. To be honest with you they think they are *it*. They think they'm a cut above the rest. . . . They wouldn't have the time to go to a funeral, even a relative, but they always find time to be out baling or cutting for other people.'

'He'm a proper farmer. His place is like a garden. He'm always
ready to give advice or help a chap out. He'm a grand chap, us all
respects him.'

'I would tread my cabbages into the ground before I'd sell one
to '*e*. When he's after something, people would rather not go into it
at all. You'll get nowhere with '*e*.'

It must be stressed, however, that only a small minority of
people are widely accepted as having high or low status. To
a striking extent, Ashworthy is a place where people think of
themselves as social equals. Those people who are recognized
as being of a different social status from the majority can be
divided into sets, each with certain common characteristics and
to whom various criteria of status are applied, but these sets
are made up of individuals who do not act as a group, who may
not even have any social contact one with another. There are,
for example, four households of people who have substantial
private incomes, who speak with received pronunciation and
who have other characteristics which would place them rather
high in the social scale in many parts of rural England. They
do not constitute an upper class or even an effective status level
because they have almost negligible social relations with each
other, because only one family plays any part at all in parish
life and because to the vast majority of people they are 'outsiders'.

The criteria which are accepted as giving high or low status
are not easily described or measured because they are based
largely on personal characteristics. Friendliness, honesty, in-
dustriousness, skill at one's work, sound judgement are typical
qualities which give high prestige. Wealth may be important,
but only if it is possessed by someone whom people call 'a
worthy man'—and it must be remembered that only a handful
of persons in the parish are considered to be wealthy. One of
the most prosperous farmers is not highly regarded because he
is generally alleged to be very bad-tempered, intolerant and
unco-operative. Certainly, wealth is not used to gain prestige
by personal display. Two farmers, each of whose land, stock
and equipment may be conservatively estimated to be worth at
least £30,000, dress no differently from the average villager,
live modestly and own small cars.

Other criteria, which are important in English rural communities, such as education, 'pedigree', and long residence have little relevance in Ashworthy. Only one person has been to a university and he no longer lives in the parish. Pedigree and long residence have little meaning because of the many changes which have characterized the demographic and economic history of the last century. The two wealthy farmers mentioned in the last paragraph are descendants of farm labourers: they are aware that many other people know this, just as they themselves are familiar with the antecedents of most of their neighbours.

Considerations of social class and prestige have, therefore, very little effect on social relations betwen kindred in Ashworthy. Indeed, the situation is that the particular working out of continuity in the farm family has contributed in a fundamental way to producing conditions in which social class divisions have broken down. Kindred are social equals, who do not 'give themselves airs' and do not marry 'above' or 'beneath' themselves. In Ashworthy there is no 'above' or 'beneath'. There are, of course, some sets of kindred in which there are individual members with high and low status but such differences appear to have little effect on social relations.

There seems every likelihood that the absence of class consciousness in Ashworthy is also typical of most of the parishes which surround it. However, as noted in Chapter One (p. 7), it does not follow that the local people have no sense of class distinction. They are fully aware that social stratification is very important in English life and they have some limited experience of it from holidays and, nearer home, from meeting some of the 'Up Country Johnnies'. But it is also something which lies outside the limits of their community with its emphasis on face-to-face relationships, something which is characteristic of strangers and outsiders. 'We are not like they people up in London', said one man; 'down here nobody worries what your father was—we're all the same.'

Since class distinction is, in the local view, an attitude held only by outsiders, the few 'Up Country Johnnies' who retain their class consciousness are simply excluded from social recognition. On the other hand, kindred who have left Ashworthy and have become 'snobs' cannot be treated in the same way. They have become outsiders by accepting values which the country people do not accept, but they are still kin. There were indications that some people had kindred who had become 'stuck up', although they were naturally reluctant to talk about them. Since, however, their numbers are almost certainly very small, they do not affect significantly the generalization that class and status have little effect on social relations between kin.

Kinship and 'local politics'

As we have seen in a preliminary way, the major social divisions in Ashworthy—between Methodist and Anglican, Liberal and Conservative, etc.—are reflected in membership of village (or more strictly parish) associations. These associations form the institutionalized framework within which power is exercised by some people over others and in which decisions affecting the everyday lives of Ashworthy folk are taken. A closer look at these associations will, therefore, reveal something of the importance of kinship in local politics.

Now from what has been said of social status in the last section, it will be evident that class considerations are of no importance in the organizational structure of village associations. Unlike Gosforth, where the class hierarchy was faithfully reproduced in the constitution and membership of each association (so that, for example, Chairmen and Presidents were invariably drawn from the upper classes), in Ashworthy official positions are filled in quite a different way. They are occupied by people who enjoy carrying out the duties of office, who are willing to give up a great deal of their leisure time in return for the satisfaction they derive from organizing activities and exercising authority. Such people are the leaders in the social life of Ashworthy.

The particular qualities necessary for a leader are not all that common and, as a result, most of the offices are held by a small number of people. One man, for example, was President of the Football Club and of the Men's Club, a Trustee of the Village Hall, a School Manager, a Parish Councillor, a Church Warden and a member of the Conservative Association

Committee, and represents the parish in the local branch of the British Legion. Another was a Parish Councillor, Trustee of the Village Hall, School Manager, Secretary to the Chapel and Superintendent of its Sunday-school. One of the women in the village was Treasurer of the Women's Committee of the Football Club and of the Women's Institute, a School Manager, Secretary of the Liberal Club, a Church Sunday-school teacher and was very prominent in Church affairs. In all, about thirty men and women fill all the official places in the village associations.

The number of people from whom officials are drawn is limited by several factors. The senior officers must be people able to negotiate with outside bodies, such as the Rural District Council, and able to deal with correspondence, minutes, accounts, etc. For this reason, tradesmen and craftsmen are prominent. There are relatively few farmers because the seasonal demands of the farm limit their free time. Religious affiliation is, as we have seen, another limiting factor. More important than all these, however, is the widespread awareness of the stresses and dangers of office. As one man put it: 'If you'm on a committee or a president of something in the village, you'm walking a bloody tight-rope all the time. Whatever you do, you'm bound to offend some people.' There are many people in Ashworthy who have refused office for this reason. Somewhat paradoxically, the local tradesmen and craftsmen are the most sensitive in this respect, since they feel themselves particularly vulnerable to public opinion: 'I couldn't be on all they committees—it would cost me money. I can't offend my customers. . . . Now Ted (a farmer) there, he can stay on committees, because he don't care if he offends people. He's got nothing to lose.'[1] In such a close-knit community as Ashworthy, 'what people will say' severely restricts the number of candidates for office.

In spite of these limitations, kinship does play some part in determining who fills positions of authority in village associations. In particular, the hereditary principle is often applied. For example, five of the eighteen Trustees of the Village Hall filled places vacated by their fathers. 'They were properly

[1] Rural craftsmen in general attach a great deal of importance to the attitudes of their customers. For a full discussion of this point see *The Country Craftsman*, especially Ch. V, 'The Craftsman in Business'.

elected,' said one man, 'but no one else had a chance.' More-over, ten of the Trustees have kindred as their colleagues—although this is no more than to be expected in a community like Ashworthy, with kinship links spread in a complex network over so many households. This might suggest that kinship is of considerable importance in the every-day running of these associations and in influencing any decisions which have to be made. In general, however, kinship ties and loyalties appear to be subordinated to other considerations and only become deci-sive on isolated occasions.

Most of the decisions which have to be made are reached amicably, but from time to time—as in all communities—disputes arise which bring groups of people into opposition: 'There are factions in the village. It might seem all peace and harmony, but they are there under the surface. People get on very well together, but under the crust it's *there*—and it really blows up sometimes.' The process of making decisions, of exercising authority, is brought sharply into focus during dis-putes and shows clearly that 'the factions' cut across the kin-ship networks, and since these factions are headed by the officials of village associations the making of decisions in normal cir-cumstances is also more or less independent of kin grouping.

There, is, for example, a long-standing feud between two village associations, which from time to time erupts into open conflict. On these occasions, feelings may run high: 'I've had nothing to do with them since a meeting when one committee member said he would knock the block off another.' Character-istically, however, two of the committee members of one asso-ciation are sons of officers in the other, and a further two committeemen are brother and brother-in-law to a man holding office 'on the other side'. Other, more remote kin links may be traced between the two committees. As the people of Ashworthy see it, close kin relationship in these circumstances may be occasionally embarrassing, but it does not affect the course of the dispute: 'Around here, if you'm a Committee member and you sees something wrong, you gets up and says so, even if you'm there and you'm my father.' This may be an exaggeration, but it is certainly true that members of the same family may find themselves in opposition.

P   203

The existence of kin links is, then, often ignored, but in another sense everyone is aware that they exist. People accept the hereditary principle in elections, they expect kindred to 'gang-up' into a united group, and they subscribe to the view that: 'If you annoy one person in Ashworthy you annoy a dozen people. It gradually works round through the relatives— you might offend twenty.' Thus, even in the most violent disputes a person hesitates before offending a member of a large group of kindred, and especially if he is a tradesman anxious to keep his customers. Similarly, those people who have few kindred in the parish, or none at all, have little protection:

> 'Fred came here from Irontown and started things going. It's been an uphill struggle. There was a row about something, I forget what, and Fred stuck his neck out over it one night. The next day a farmer called to see him and told him bluntly to stop it, otherwise he would be in trouble. Fred has to be careful. He let it go. . . . They didn't bother Jack about it—nobody said a word to *him*— he's got a lot of pull. It's all his relatives to back him up.'

The essence of village politics is, perhaps, that there are no fixed rules of behaviour. Kindred may on one occasion be on opposing sides in a dispute and ignore their relationship, and on another recognize it in order to justify acting together. A detailed analysis of the use of power and the making of decisions is outside the scope of this study, but two observations may be made. Firstly, the exercise of leadership in Ashworthy appears to resemble closely that described by Dennis for a large urban area,[1] but with the addition of a small kinship element. Secondly, in Ashworthy the use of 'the stranger' or 'outsider' in the settlement of disputes as described for other communities[2] is unknown. In the many accounts given of factional struggles, not one cited a stranger as a central character, and very few outsiders indeed play a prominent part in village associations.

[1] See N. Dennis, 'Changes in Function and Leadership Renewal', *Sociological Review*, Vol. 9, No. 1 (March 1961) pp. 55–84.

[2] For example in Frankenburg, op. cit., Gluckman, *Custom and Conflict in Africa* and R. Harris, 'Some aspects of the selection of leaders in Ballybeg, Northern Ireland', *Sociological Review*, Vol. 9, No. 2 (July 1961), pp. 137–49.

Kinship and social life

There are other divisions in the social life of the parish, between farmers and villagers, between 'Ashworthy people' and 'strangers', and between 'local people' and 'Up Country Johnnies'. Since they have little effect on social relations between kin they need not be discussed at length. Taken together with the other divisions which have been described in this chapter, they reveal a complex pattern of social 'networks' which are not neatly or rigidly related to each other. There are other networks, particularly of 'friends' and of neighbours, which bring people together into fruitful social relations: these too divide the population up, but in a rather different way.

They do not split the parish into two large groups. Their membership is much more dynamic and their structure is different. For example, a man who is a Methodist is joined in a social relationship to all the other Methodists in Ashworthy, at least nominally, and also to other Methodists in other parishes. These in turn have relations with other Methodists and so the network is formed. The individuals in the network may change their residence and the particular pattern of relationships within the network is changed, but not destroyed. On the other hand, a farmer who co-operates with a group of neighbours has close and regular social and economic relations with a small, well-defined group. This group may be joined to similar groups through one or more individuals shared with them, or it may be self-contained. Death, retirement or migration may, as we have seen earlier, bring changes in membership or may even bring its existence to an end.[1] The neighbourhood 'network' is therefore not completely interconnected, changes rather frequently, and is essentially composed of 'clusters' rather than a scattered, diffused pattern. (See Fig. 15.)

The kinship network is thus one of many and the country people of Ashworthy are joined with others in social relations in several networks at any one time. They may overlap in parts and diverge in others: new connections may be created or existing ones broken. For example, two farmer brothers may

[1] See above pp. 100–106.

also be neighbours; they are, then, joined as members of three networks: but one may be Anglican and Conservative and the other Methodist and Liberal; in each case they participate in two more sets of social relations, but ones which link them to different groups of people. If one brother, say the Anglican, should move to a new farm, he may leave his neighbour group and enter another; this would take him out of one of the groups he shared with his brother and perhaps bring him into one in which there are Methodists.

In this way the individual is seen not only to fill many roles— to be a blood relative, a Methodist, a Liberal, a 'proper Ash-worthy man' and so on, but also, in virtue of these roles, to be joined in a complex of social relationships to others who may be either Methodist or Anglican, native or 'Up Country Johnny', Liberal or Conservative. Thus kinship, in which, as we have seen, the elements of choice and chance are crucial, is one of several similar systems of social relations.

The people of Ashworthy do not, of course, see their social life in these terms. The networks are abstractions, convenient devices for analysing complex data. Nevertheless, the country people are aware that their dealings with other people are not a haphazard jumble, that the way people behave in one social context may be related to a system of human relations and that different behaviour in another context may in turn be understood by reference to different, parallel, complementary or conflicting systems. This is seen clearly in the remarks of an old retired farmer, who, having lived in Ashworthy all his life, appropriately has the last word:

'People here in Ashworthy b'aint no different from other places, they'd be a queer lot else. Us knows how to do things but us don't always do 'un. My father and his brother quarrelled. . . . They never spoke for over two years. They *knew* they weren't acting like brothers. Now if you saw them of a Sunday in chapel you'd never know there was anything between them. And they weren't men who worried about what people said either. They spoke to each other proper because that was the way to do it. Family quarrels was one thing: Chapel was different. . . .

They Up Country Johnnies don't understand the country way of going about things. They are full of puzzlement. They think people are two-faced, but they don't understand. That chap Samuels stopped me one day with a long face. He said he was fed up with old Tom and Jack Miller. They were always watching 'e, he said. Then he went into a long tale about Tom and Jack in the pub in Longbridge with some other fellows. They wouldn't look at him he said. Next day they was up helping to cut dashels (thistles).

I said: "Look, Mr. Samuels, Tom and Jack is good neighbours. They takes an interest in you. They'm not spying on you!" . . . They have been real good neighbours to him. . . . They didn't talk to 'e in the pub because they was with friends, men they'd known all their life. He was just an Up Country Johnny to they then. . . . That's what I mean. They don't understand us. Look at Alf there. He'm a proper lad. He once went up to some girls and said he had half a bed to let. He likes his pint and his darts, but he'm in Church every Sunday.'

CONCLUSION

THIS survey of one small area in the West Country is an attempt to bring a new perspective to rural community studies in England and Wales, with their emphasis on stability and the traditional way of life. It need hardly be said that further sample studies need to be made to test the generality of the findings and to enlarge aspects of the analysis. The main conclusions, which are tentative, are summarized below:

(i) The economic and social life of Ashworthy is based on the land. The physical environment therefore sets broad limits on human activity, within which man has developed ways of occupying and cultivating the land and of transmitting these ways from one generation to another. The environment is harsh and farming is difficult.

(ii) The relationship between man and the land, which is central to any understanding of the social life, is manifested in the land-holding system. Land-holding has three aspects—the field system, the occupation of land and the ownership of land. When analysed geographically, the field system, which is closely related to the physical environment, is seen to be stable. The occupation and ownership of land have been characterized by a large number of complex changes during the last hundred years, so that land-holding as a whole is in a state of 'dynamic equilibrium'.

(iii) The changes in land-holding have been accompanied by changes in the farm population. Farm families have moved from one holding to another, both within Ashworthy and between it and other parishes. This movement is complex and localized within 'the Ashworthy area'. Other changes in the composition of farmers and land-owners as a group have been brought about by (a) the dying-out of existing farm families, many of them long-established; (b) the entry into farming of labourers and small-holders by means of 'the agricultural ladder'; (c) the entry into farming of men from other occupations, the 'Up Country Johnnies', particularly since 1945.

These changes can be related to land-holding and the physical environment, and particularly to the existence of cheap farms on poor, ill-drained land.

(iv) The shifting pattern of land-holding and the related changes in the farm population are also typical of other parishes in the Ashworthy area.

(v) The farms of Ashworthy are 'family farms' and the conjugal farm family is a primary social and economic unit which shares many characteristics with farming families in other parts of Britain. The farm family relies heavily on its own manpower and passes through a life cycle, during which its ability to meet the needs of the farm varies considerably. The burden on the family has increased with the change from tenant farmers to owner-occupiers.

(vi) Kinship links and neighbourliness between farmers are important as a basis for economic co-operation, and considerably reduce the burden on the individual family.

(vii) Family farming is perpetuated by the transmission of skills, property and land from one generation to another. Continuity is achieved in Ashworthy within a framework of change in land-holding and in the farm population by each farmer attempting to set up all his sons as farmers in their own right. This is consistent with the absence of a deep attachment to the family land, which is a central characteristic of stable rural societies elsewhere.

(viii) Within Ashworthy there is a conflict between the ideal of one son inheriting the home farm and other sons being established on farms of their own. This conflict is resolved in a complex way by the imperfection of the elementary farm family as a means of ensuring biological continuity, combined with a lack of attachment to the family holding and the failure to use the wider network of kindred to provide heirs when there are no sons or daughters to inherit. In any one generation there are some families which die out and others ready to replace them.

(ix) Part of the movement of individuals from farm to farm and of change in the composition of farm families is therefore a consequence of the particular means of achieving the continuity of family farming. It has been affected by a general decrease in the size of the farm family. Other elements of change arise from the operation of 'the agricultural ladder', the coming of the 'Up Country Johnnies', the break-up of estates and other changes in land-owning.

(x) Unlike many rural communities where marriage and inheritance are very closely linked, in Ashworthy marriage is not central to the transition from one generation to another. Marriage, the transfer of economic control and the inheritance of land are loosely linked parts of a protracted process of transmission, the whole of which may be seen as a complex response to both the demands of the family-land relationship and to needs which arise from Ashworthy's place in English society at large.

(xi) Frequent changes in land-holding and in the farm population influence the territorial arrangement of social and economic relations. This can be demonstrated in the structure and operation of the neighbour network, which has characteristics not found in stable rural societies. Neighbourliness is, however, also affected by other factors, notably the mechanization of farming, a long tradition of part-time casual labour and the arrival of the 'Up Country Johnnies'.

(xii) The transmission of property and skills, which is fundamental to the organization of the farm family, can also be seen as central in the family structure of many rural craftsmen, but is unimportant in some families of rural craftsmen and nearly all families of villagers. All families, however, must be examined in terms of a general decline in population.

(xiii) The population of Ashworthy rose steadily in the first half of the nineteenth century, but has declined ever since. The decline has been accompanied by a decreasing proportion of females in the total population and by changes in the age structure of the inhabitants of the parish. In particular, the proportion of young people has declined and that of people in late-middle and old age has increased. There have also been decreases in the size of household.

(xiv) These broad demographic changes must be analysed in the light of the movement of individual families, which was shown to exist from the examination of the relationship between man and the land. The analysis shows that movement from the countryside is one part of a complex demographic change, in which short-distance migration within the Ashworthy area is very important. Both long- and short-distance migration are most marked among farm labourers and villagers, less common among rural craftsmen, with farmers as the most stable occupational group. These differences, especially in long-distance migration, reflect varying emphases on the transmission of property and skills: farmers with their interests vested in the land stand in sharp contrast to the landless farm labourers.

(xv) Migration has therefore brought about a marked decline in the numbers of farm labourers and their families, exacerbated by the mechanization of farming: rural craftsmen's families have declined to a lesser extent, largely because of the continuing role of the village as a service centre: farmers' families have declined least and show a proportional increase. These differences are clearly reflected at present in the employment opportunities for young people in the three occupational groups.

(xvi) The population changes have affected family type and structure. The most important effects have been a strengthening of the dominant position of the elementary family, an increase in the number of households composed of spinsters and widows living alone, and a sharp decrease in the number of families with additional kin. Families denuded by children leaving home appear as a significant new category. There is a general decrease in family size and the composite household disappears.

(xvii) These changes affect the three occupational groups differently. Elementary families are most common on farms and least common in the village. Denuded families are found more often in the village than on farms. Once again continuity and the role of the family as an economic unit on farms, but not in the village, can be seen as fundamental. Other differences between the three groups can be seen in age at first marriage and differences in age of husband and wife. Farmers marry relatively late and tend to be several years older than their wives. Widows and spinsters living alone are, for obvious reasons, most common in the village.

(xviii) The extended family has virtually disappeared, but the extension of kinship is still of great importance in social life. This extension is seen in recognition of kin, which is shallow in depth, has relatively wide lateral range and covers relatively large numbers of people in the kin universe of the individual. Great variations exist in the number of kindred known and recognized by individuals and in the numbers of kin with whom social relations are maintained. Chance and personal choice are fundamental in determining these variations. Women tend to have greater kin knowledge than men. Kinship forms the basis for fruitful social relations, manifested particularly in the exchange of services and in social contact with an important emotional content. In all these respects kinship in Ashworthy show very close similarities to kinship in south London, suggesting that one may reasonably speak of an English kinship system.

(xix) There are, however, differences between kinship in Ashworthy and south London, which can be related to wider aspects of the social life. In Ashworthy kinship is 'patri-centred', and the link between father and son is particularly strong; this can be explained in terms of the relationship between man and the land and the close identification of family and work. In London kinship is matri-centred, and the close link between mother and daughter dominates family life. The second important difference is that in Ashworthy individuals may occupy two or more positions, each with its own role, in a kin universe; this is to be expected in a small community.

(xx) Social relations between kindred, while largely determined by chance and choice, are affected by population movement and to a lesser extent by the remoteness of the parish.

The dynamic equilibrium which characterizes so much of the social structure brings changes in the territorial disposition of kindred and in the patterns of social relations between them.

(xxi) Social relations between kin are affected by the division of Ashworthy into Methodists and Anglicans, Liberals and Conservatives, farmers and villagers, men and women, and by differences in participation in village associations. Social class divisions are unimportant, largely because the changes in land-holding and in the population have destroyed the basis of social stratification in an agricultural community.

(xxii) Individuals who are kindred are linked in a network of social relations and there are other networks linking neighbours, friends, Methodists, etc. These networks may be complementary, overlapping or cut across each other. They are not stable, altering their structure as the individuals who make them up move, disappear and reappear. In this aspect of the social life, as in others, change is evident.

APPENDIX ONE

TABLE ONE

Male Labour on Farms

Age Group	Occupiers*	Sons		Other Relatives	Non-Relatives	
		M.	S.		M.	S.
15–19	–	–	3	1	–	8
20–29	2	1	14	1	1	4
30–39	13	4	7	1	–	1
40–49	15	1	–	1	1	–
50–59	25	–	–	–	–	–
60–69	16	–	–	1	5	–
70+	4	–	–	–	–	–
Total	75	6	24	5	7	13

TABLE TWO

Female Labour on Farms

Age Group	Occupiers*	Occupiers' Wives	Daughters		Other Relatives	Non-Relatives
			M.	S.		
15–19	–	–	–	2	–	–
20–29	–	1	–	3	3	–
30–39	–	13	1	3	1	–
40–49	–	6	1	–	1	2
50–59	–	26	–	–	3	1
60–69	2	8	–	–	1	–
70+	–	1	–	–	1	1
Total	2	55	2	8	10	4

*Including joint occupiers.
M — Married: S — Single.

APPENDIX TWO

TABLE ONE

The Sex Ratio. Females to every 100 Males

	Ashworthy	Neighbouring parishes	England and Wales
1801	104·0	100·0	105·7
1811	106·8	97·0	105·4
1821	90·8	95·2	103·6
1831	93·0	97·8	104·0
1841	93·4	94·5	104·6
1851	99·5	96·3	104·2
1861	101·2	96·2	105·3
1871	100·7	98·6	105·4
1881	98·5	100·0	105·6
1891	105·0	100·3	106·4
1901	97·7	100·3	106·8
1911	90·6	100·3	106·8
1921	103·5	97·5	109·6
1931	94·1	97·2	108·8
1951	94·6	95·5	108·5

TABLE TWO

Age Structure and Marital Status 1851. Ashworthy.

Age Group	Males				Females			
	Total	Single	Married	Widowed	Total	Single	Married	Widowed
0–4	78	78	—	—	75	75	—	—
5–9	71	71	—	—	74	74	—	—
10–14	59	59	—	—	70	70	—	—
15–19	61	61	—	—	50	50	—	—
20–24	49	44	5	—	42	30	12	—
25–29	37	14	22	1	43	12	30	1
30–34	31	10	19	2	21	7	14	—
35–39	27	5	21	1	32	3	27	2
40–44	28	1	26	1	28	3	23	2
45–49	21	7	13	1	26	4	20	2
50–54	23	1	19	3	20	3	15	2
55–59	21	3	17	1	22	2	15	5
60–64	18	4	11	3	20	1	17	2
65–69	12	—	9	3	12	2	5	5
70–74	10	—	7	3	7	1	2	4
75–79	7	—	3	4	3	1	1	1
80–84	4	—	1	3	3	—	—	3
85–89	2	—	—	2	3	—	3	—

TABLE THREE

Size of Household 1851. Ashworthy.

Size	Village		Outside Village		
	Villagers	Craftsmen	Craftsmen	Others	Farmers
1	2	–	–	1	2
2	10	2	1	5	–
3	12	2	5	8	4
4	8	10	4	8	5
5	9	3	2	10	9
6	8	6	3	8	10
7	3	5	–	4	4
8	–	1	–	1	4
9	–	1	–	–	6
10	1	1	–	–	3
11	–	1	–	–	3
12	1	–	–	–	6
13	–	–	–	–	1
14	–	–	–	1	2
	54	32	15	46	59

TABLE FOUR

Size of Household 1960. Ashworthy.

Size	Farmers	Craftsmen	Farm Labourers	Others
1	2	2	–	18
2	21	7	3	24
3	17	5	1	12
4	19	4	–	11
5	10	1	1	4
6	2	1	–	2
7	2	–	–	–
8	1	–	–	–
9	1	–	–	1
	75	20	5	72

(The small number of farm labourers' households as compared with the total number of farm labourers and their families is accounted for by single farm labourers living on farms and those farm labourers' families who are part of other households.)

APPENDIX THREE

TABLE ONE

Types of Family. Ashworthy 1851.

	Village	Craftsmen	Farmers
Elementary families	57	20	30
Childless couples	8	2	2
Denuded families—father dead	7	3	–
Denuded families—mother dead	2	–	–
Bachelor living alone	–	–	4
Spinster living alone	–	1	–
Unmarried siblings	–	–	4
Widow living alone	2	–	–
Widower living alone	–	1	1
Elementary families with added kin	13	12	10
Childless couples with added kin	4	2	4
Denuded families with added kin	5	3	1
Widow with added kin	1	1	1
Widower with added kin	–	–	1
All families with added kin	23	18	17
Three-generation families	3	–	1
Other family types	4	2	–
	106	47	59

Appendix

TABLE TWO

Number of Children Per Family* 1851.

	Villagers	Craftsmen	Farmers
None	11	4	6
1	32	10	7
2	19	13	4
3	15	6	10
4	12	5	6
5	6	3	5
6	1	2	2
7	–	–	6
8	–	–	1
9	–	–	–
10	–	–	1
	96	43	48

*i.e. children living at home: the Enumeration Schedules do not allow a distinction to be drawn between 'true' childless couples and couples whose children have all left home.

TABLE THREE

Types of Family. Ashworthy 1960.

	Village	Craftsmen*	Farmers
Elementary families	23	9	35
Childless couples	9	3	12
Denuded families: children left home	15	5	7
Denuded families: father dead	3	—	4
Denuded families: mother dead	—	—	4
Bachelor living alone	2	1	2
Spinster living alone	4	1	—
Unmarried siblings	2	—	3
Widow living alone	11	—	—
Widower living alone	2	1	2
Elementary families with added kin	—	—	2
Childless couples with added kin	1	—	—
Denuded families with added kin	—	—	—
Three-generation families with added kin	—	—	1
Widow with added kin	2	—	—
Widower with added kin	—	—	1
All families with added kin	3	—	4
Three-generation families	2	—	2
	76	20	75

*Including tradesmen and shopkeepers.

TABLE FOUR

Number of Children Per Family.* 1960.

	Villagers	Craftsmen	Farmers
None	25	8	19
1	13	4	23
2	7	3	14
3	4	1	7
4	2	1	3
5	–	–	1
6	1	–	–
	52	17	67

*i.e. children living at home: for numbers of couples with children who have left home, see Table Three.

BIBLIOGRAPHY

Arensberg, C. M. *The Irish Countryman*. New York 1950.

—and S. T. Kimball. *Family and Community in Ireland*. Cambridge, Mass. 1940.

Ashby, A. W. 'The Farmer in Business' *Journ. Proc. Agri. Econ. Soc.* X No. 2. (February 1953).

→ Barnes, J. A. 'Class and Committees in a Norwegian Island Parish' *Human Relations* VIII No. 1. (February 1945) pp. 39–58.

Bourne, F. W. *The Bible Christians: Their Origin and History 1815–1900*. London 1905.

Buchanan, R. H. 'Rural Change in an Irish Townland' *Advancement of Science* No. 56. (March 1958.) pp. 291–300.

Curle, A. 'Kinship Structure in an English Village' *Man*. No. 100 (May 1952).

Dennis, N. 'Changes in Function and Leadership Renewal' *Sociological Review* Vol. 9, No. 1. (March 1961) pp. 55–84.

Firth, R. *Two Studies of Kinship in London*. L.S.E. Monographs on Social Anthropology No. 15. London 1956.

Flatrés, P. *Géographie Rurale de quatre contrées Celtiques: Irlande, Galles Cornwall et Man*. Rennes 1957.

Frankenberg, R. *Village on the Border*. London 1957.

Gluckman, M. *Custom and Conflict in Africa*. Oxford 1955.

—'Ethnographic data in British Social Anthropology', *Sociological Review* Vol. 9. No. 1. (March 1961) pp. 5–18.

Gray, H. L. *English Field Systems*. Cambridge, Mass. 1915.

Homans, G. C. *English Villagers of the Thirteenth Century*. Harvard 1942.

Bibliography

Hoskins, W. G. *The Making of the English Landscape*. London 1955.

—and H. P. R. Finberg. *Devonshire Studies*. London 1952.

Jerrold, D. *An Introduction to the History of England from the Earliest Times to 1204*. London 1949.

Kellys County Directories.

Mendras, H. *Etudes de Sociologie Rurale*. Paris 1953.

National Farm Survey. *Summary Report*. London 1946.

Orwin, C. S. and C. S. Orwin. *The Open Fields*. Oxford 1954.

Owen, T. M. 'The Communion Season and Presbyterianism in a Hebridean Community.' *Gwerin* Vol. 1. No. 2, pp. 53–66.

Redfield, R. *Peasant Society and Culture*. Chicago 1956.

Rees, A. D. *Life in a Welsh Countryside*. Cardiff 1950.

—and E. Davies (Eds.) *Welsh Rural Communities*. Cardiff 1960.

Return of Owners of Land. London 1873.

Saville, J. *Rural Depopulation in England and Wales 1851–1951*. London 1957.

Sheppard, J. 'East Yorkshire's Agricultural Labour Force in the mid-Nineteenth Century.' *Agricultural History Review* Vol. IX. Pt. 1. (1961) pp. 43–54.

Smith, R. T. *The Negro Family in British Guiana*. London 1956.

Stacey, M. *Tradition and Change : A Study of Banbury*. Oxford 1960.

Uhlig, H. 'Langstreifenfluren in Nordenengland, Wales und Schottland.' *Deutscher Geographentag Würzburg 29 July–5 August 1957*.

—'Die Landliche Kulturlandschaft der Hebriden und der West Schottischen Hochlande.' *Erdkunde* Band XIII Lfg. 1. Bonn 1959.

—'Typen Kleinbauerlicher Siedlungen auf den Hebriden' *Erdkunde*. Band XIII. Lfg. 2. Bonn 1959.

von Dietze, C. 'Peasantry.' *Encyclopaedia of the Social Sciences* Vol. XII pp. 48–52.

Willmott, P. and M. Young. *Family and Class in a London Suburb*. London 1960.

→ Williams, W. M. 'Kinship and Farming in West Cumberland.' *Man* No. 25 (February 1956).

—*The Sociology of An English Village: Gosforth*. London 1956.

—*The Country Craftsman. A Study of some Rural Crafts and the Rural Industries Organisation in England*. London 1958.

Young, M. and Willmott, P. *Family and Kinship in East London* London 1957.

INDEX

Ackland family, 42
Age structure, 118–21, 123–4, 132, 134, 210, 216
Agricultural ladder, 37, 71, 76, 78, 196, 208–9, 210
Ames, Edward, 104–6
Anglicans, 184–91, 201, 213
Arensberg, C. M., xv, xviii, 11 n., 53–56, 58, 84 n., 86 n., 182 n., 222
Arundle Farm, 42
Ashby, A. W., 90 n., 222
Ashfield, 35, 37
Ashworthy area, 39, 43, 74, 98–100, 130, 136–7, 174, 208, 211
  climate in, 3, 12, 14
  economy of, 10, 131–2
  geology of, 12
  House, 24
  and outside world, xix–xx, 6, 43
  population change in, 115–17
  in Saxon times, 4
  soils in, 3–4, 12, 14

Banbury, 182
Barnes, A. J., 57, 59, 77, 98, 222
Bawden, M. G., xxi
Bedford, 44
Bethnal Green, 182
Bible Christian Connexion, 8, 186
Birchstowe, 40, 49, 69, 70
Birth, place of, 123, 133, 144

Bishop family, 24–28, 43, 49, 125, 195–8
Blackbury, 40, 42
Blackdown, 35, 36
Blake family, 42
Bogland, 4
Bond family, 62, 74
Bourne, F. W., 8 n., 222
Boy Scouts, 5
Bracey, H. E., xvi
Bremnes, Norway, 57, 77 n.
British Legion, 5, 202
Broadpen, 40, 42, 43, 99, 100, 116
Brookes family, 190–1
Broompark, 20, 22, 24
Brown family, 157–74
Buchanan, R. H., 11 n., 56, 222

Caley family, 93–94
Census, xxi, 67, 116, 117 n., 118, 119, 121–2, 123, 125, 126–7, 130–1, 134–5, 140, 141, 144
Chateau-Gerard, xvi
Cheshire, 44 n.
Church Farm, 42
Combe Down, 40, 99, 116
Common land, 13, 14, 19, 20, 30, 36, 80
Conservative Association, 5, 9, 170, 180, 190, 191–3, 201–2, 206, 213
Continuity of family farming, 80–83, 85, 209, 211–12